Black Journalists:
The NABJ Story

Black Journalists: The NABJ Story

Wayne Dawkins

August Press
Merrillville, Indiana

BLACK JOURNALISTS: THE NABJ STORY.
Copyright © 1997 by Wayne Dawkins.
All Rights reserved. Printed in the United
States of America. No part of this book may
be used or reproduced in any manner
whatsoever without written permission
except in the case of brief quotations
embodied in critical articles or reviews.
For information, address August Press,
8590 Polo Club Drive, Merrillville, Ind. 46410.

Design by Rob King

Cataloging-in-Publication Data
Dawkins, Wayne
Black Journalists: The NABJ Story/Wayne Dawkins
–Expanded, updated August Press ed.
1. Dawkins, Wayne. 2. National Association of
Black Journalists. 3. Afro-American Journalists

070.922   96-95514
                                 CIP

ISBN   0-9635720-4-0

Expanded, updated Second Edition

10 9 8 7 6 5 4 3 2

Dedicated to the McFarquhars:

Iris Carmen (Mom),
Uncle Handel, Fred and Hector, and Aunt Mabel.

Thank you for nourishing me all through life
with reading and writing.

Contents

Preface

In August 1981, Chicago newsman Vernon Jarrett told a cryptic story. It was about outrageous acts by a former president of the National Association of Black Journalists.

I was a first-year daily newspaper reporter attending my first conference.I did not get Jarrett's satire. But his vivid storytelling made me very curious. "Don't keep all those great stories to yourself," or, to a small circle of associates, I thought to myself. Younger journalists like me needed to learn more about the association and its people.

The journalists assembled in Louisville, Ky. were an impressive lot. It was my first time in a room with so many African-American newsmen and women from so many venues and with such a breadth of talent.

From 1984-89 I had the honor of representing members from New York, New Jersey and Connecticut as their regional director. I wrote extensively about NABJ's development for my monthly J-school alumni newsletter. I had a hunch the reporting some day would be needed.

On Labor Day 1990 I began writing a history of NABJ. This is the first in-depth accounting of the association's origins and development.

The first edition published in 1993 was largely about a period I call "Old NABJ." This was an explanation of how and why black journalists desegregated the white daily media during the Civil Rights Era to the founding of NABJ by 44 journalists in December 1975. The story advanced to the September 1983 conference when the last of the original leaders passed the torch to a new generation. Many of these new leaders running the next lap were of my generation.

This expanded update chronicles the great era of transition and growth, 1984-89. Membership multiplied five times from 334 members to at least 1,800 professionals and students. During this period our "tribe became a nation," wrote a dear friend, Betty Winston Baye. In addition to the mass of people, NABJ grew in sophistication and visibility.

And we continue to ascend. Weeks before this new edition goes to press, a few thousand NABJ members are to convene in Chicago. Young people and adults just learning about us deserve to know how far we've come.

Many founders will readily acknowledge that they did not spend a lot of time documenting NABJ activities and accomplishments. It was not because of indifference or laziness. These volunteer leaders were busy struggling to keep NABJ in continuous operation. They succeeded with limited resources and against incredible odds.

About 150 people in and outside of NABJ opened their hearts in interviews and reconstructed the early years. Also, dozens of interviewees opened their attics, basements and studies to me.These places were treasure chests of association documents and memorabilia. Because NABJ did not secure a permanent national office until fall 1985 – 10 years after founding – its records were sprinkled all over America. Many still are. Others are lost or destroyed.

Do you still ask, why a history of NABJ?

It is important to know who were the people who established this association. Half of the original 44 were very active or marginally active with NABJ.

About a dozen people practiced journalism but had not had ties to the organization for years. That changed after 1993.Many came back.Other founders left journalism for public relations, government, utility companies and the clergy.At least one founder, Max Robinson, died (1988).

Every living founder except one was interviewed.

The search for most founders was a breathtaking ride. When some founders who were out of touch with NABJ were located, they were perplexed by this project.

At least a half dozen times I was asked, "who commissioned *you* to do this?" Some did not understand why I took this on independently. Others were hostile. "What you're doing borders on the insane," said a disillusioned founder from Detroit.And a founder living in Wilmington, Del. alleged I was merely preparing a "puff piece" about NABJ.That's not my intent.

I love the National Association of Black Journalists like a best friend. That means, unlike a mere acquaintance, I will praise the association when it excels, and, unflinchingly critique its blunders and excesses. It is the very least my dear sisters and brothers of this craft deserve.

WAYNE J. DAWKINS
April 1997

Chapter 1
Pre-NABJ

By 1975, about a decade had passed since the American civil rights movement peaked. Arguably, it began in 1948 with President Harry S Truman's executive order to desegregate the armed forces and provide fair employment opportunities in federal jobs. Six years later, the U.S. Supreme Court's *Brown vs. Board of Education* decision rendered segregated public education illegal.

Then from the mid-1950s to the mid-1960s Martin Luther King Jr. and an army of non-violent warriors moved millions of Americans to dismantle legal racial discrimination. Voting rights, fair housing and equal employment opportunity laws were passed in the '60s.

These major changes alone, however, would not cool the impatience and rage boiling over in black urban areas.

Riots in Watts, Newark, Detroit and other cities were unavoidable.

With laws acting as instruments that could be used to try to break up deeply entrenched patterns of racial discrimination, it became evident how deeply divided America was along racial and class lines.

What the civil rights movement and subsequent anti-discrimination laws did help facilitate was to allow black Americans to expand their career sights. With the struggle for equal opportunity, many black people with middle-class goals no longer resigned themselves to "preaching, teaching and undertaking," the only work available to well-educated blacks.

Thousands of blacks went to college to become lawyers, doctors, bankers, engineers, psychologists, social workers, accountants and business entrepreneurs.

With American apartheid -- legal segregation -- toppled, there were opportunities for blacks to compete in the workplace. Many blacks realized that they had to maximize their effectiveness.

For example, they organized themselves into dozens of national associations. Black psychologists organized in 1968; psychiatrists, 1969; social workers, 1968; accountants, 1969; optometrists, 1969; Congressional Black Caucus, 1970; public administrators, 1971, and urban bankers, 1974.

By 1975, a group that had not yet been able to organize nationally had the potential to be one of the most influential: black journalists.

These were people with the skills to influence, enlighten and move the public to action. The product they produced and disseminated was information.

The news media acted as an important player in the civil rights revolution. The pictures on the evening news of black demonstrators in the South being assaulted by police with guard dogs, nightclubs and water cannons exposed America and the rest of the world to the disgrace of legal segregation. *The New York Times* covered the civil rights movement in the South extensively. Many of *The Times'* top correspondents were white Southerners who chronicled the turmoil and change that was taking place in their native region.

The biggest First Amendment case of that time was *New York Times vs. Sullivan,* a case linked to the black struggle for full citizenship rights.

Southern officials sued the newspaper for libel because of an advertisement that was placed by civil rights activists. Lower courts in the South ruled in favor of the officials. But in 1964, the U.S. Supreme Court overturned the ruling. Public officials could not sue successfully for libel unless it proved that published material was deliberately false or was published with malice. *The Times vs. Sullivan* ruling strengthened the press. The principle still stands.

Despite crusading and exploring the wrongs of racial discrimination and segregation by many segments of society, the mainstream news media were among the largest perpetrators of segregation and racism.

This point was amplified in the exhaustive 1968 report by the U.S. Commission on Civil Disorders, appointed by President Johnson and led by Illinois Gov. Otto Kerner. It examined the symptoms and causes that touched off the explosion of riots by blacks in U.S. cities in the mid-to late-1960s. As the Kerner Commission Report concluded that America was moving toward two societies, it noted that much of the news media maintained segregated newsrooms as it was exposing segregation and discrimination in other institutions.

"-- The journalistic profession has been shockingly backwards in seeking out, hiring, training and promoting Negroes. Fewer than 5 percent of the people employed by the news business in editorial jobs in the United States today are Negroes. Fewer than 1 percent of the editors and supervisors are Negroes, and most of them work for Negro-owned publications. The lines of various news organizations to the militant blacks are, by the admission of newsmen themselves, almost non-existent. The plaint is, "We can't find qualified Negroes." But this rings hollow from an industry where, only yesterday, jobs were scarce and promotion unthinkable for a man whose skin was black. Even today, there are virtually no Negroes in positions of editorial or executive responsibility and there is only one Negro newsman with a nationally syndicated column.

"News organizations must employ enough Negroes in positions of significant responsibility to establish an effective link to Negro actions and ideas and to meet legitimate employment expectations. Tokenism -- the hiring of one Negro reporter, or even two or three -- is no longer enough. Negro reporters are essential, but so are Negro editors, writers and commentators. Newspaper and television policies are, generally speaking, not set by reporters. Editorial decisions about which stories to cover and which to use are made by editors. Yet, very few Negroes in this country are involved in making these decisions, because very few, if any, supervisory jobs are held by Negroes.

"We urge the news media to do everything possible to train and promote their Negro reporters to positions where those who are qualified can contribute to and have an effect on policy decisions.

"It is not enough, though, as many editors have pointed out to the commission, to search for Negro journalists. Journalism is not very popular as a career for aspiring young Negroes. The starting pay is comparatively low and it is a business which has, until recently, discouraged and rejected them. The recruitment of Negro reporters must extend beyond established journalists, or those who have already formed ambitions along those lines. It must become a commitment to seek out young Negro men and women, inspire them to become -- and train them as -- journalists. Training programs should be started in high schools and intensified at colleges. Summer vacation and part-time editorial jobs, coupled with offers of permanent employment, can awaken career plans.

"We believe that the news media themselves, their audiences and the country will profit from these undertakings. For if the media are to comprehend and then to project the Negro community, they must have the help of Negroes. If the media are to report with understanding, wisdom and sympathy on the problems of the cities and problems of the black man -- for the two are increasingly interwined -- they must employ, promote and listen to Negro journalists."

The black-owned and-operated press, scores of weekly newspapers, covered the society news, published the obituaries and covered the community news that white dailies ignored. Black newspapers had a crusading tradition, often in the spirit of legendary 19th century journalists like Frederick Douglass and Ida B. Wells. The bigger papers like the *Chicago Defender, Pittsburgh Courier* and the *Afro-American* in Baltimore, railed against the evils of white supremacy and discrimination. Some papers dispatched correspondents to give extensive coverage to civil rights stories like the racially motivated murder of teen-ager Emmett Till and the desegregation of Central High School in Little Rock, Ark. in the 1950s.

But as the civil rights movement surged, much of the black press declined. Television, a new medium, grabbed the attention of many young people who would have been adult readers.

A number of the top journalists in the black press jumped at the chance to break the color line at daily newspapers.

And many young, aspiring black journalists looked forward to the opportunity to work in mainstream daily journalism, opportunity that once seemed closed.

The white-owned daily press was rigidly segregated in the 19th and early 20th century. Of course there were exceptions. Thomas Morris Chester worked for the *PhiladelphiaPress* in the 19th century. He covered the surrender of Confederate General Robert E. Lee at Appomatox Court House in Virginia in 1865. By the mid-1930s, it was estimated that five black journalists worked for mainstream dailies. After World War II blacks began to trickle, very slowly, into mainstream journalism.

One of the optimistic newcomers was Paul Delaney. He was born in Montgomery, Ala. and moved to Cleveland as a teen-ager. He graduated from Ohio State University in 1958 then applied to dozens of daily newspapers.

"I always wanted to be a writer. I didn't want to take English and literature and become a permanent student or teacher," Delaney said.

He did not worry about being the lone black in the newsroom. Such an experience would not be new to him. He was the only black in his graduating class and the only black editor on the school newspaper. He had heard of *Minneapolis Tribune* newsman Carl Rowan and Ted Poston of the *New York Post* excelling at their work. Delaney assumed that he would excel too. When he received no offers from white-owned dailies, Delaney took a job at the Baltimore *Afro-American*. He didn't like it. The idealistic young journalism graduate spent time making up letters-to-the-editor. Delaney left and went home to Cleveland and drove a cab for a year.

Delaney then went to the *Atlanta Daily World* in September 1959. "I was in the South at a critical time in history," he said.

"It was the first job I was fired from for a disagreement over civil rights. I'd argue with the editor every day." The black-owned *Daily World* was very conservative and even anti-movement. Delaney stayed in Atlanta two years and worked as a probation officer.

In 1963, five years after pursuing work on a general interest daily, he was hired by the Dayton (Ohio) *Daily News*. Delaney's persistence paid off.

The papers that hired blacks in the 1960s were usually in the big northern cities.

And at that time, the daily news media established itself as one of the power centers in America.

Washington, D.C. was a sleepy news town before the Franklin D. Roosevelt years and World War II. During and after the war, it became *the* dateline for news. Newpaper coverage of government and economics became more serious and specialized.

Instead of one or two correspondents to cover issues that affected readers in their hometown, big newspapers had a half-dozen or more correspondents to cover the president, the cabinet and Congress. Broadcast journalism exploded on the scene. As newspapers and news magazines gave readers the details, radio gave listeners news instantly and dramatically. Television news was in its infancy but it expanded in leaps and bounds in the late '50s and '60s.

Like white journalists, aspiring black journalists saw these opportunities too, and were eager to be part of it.

In the late '60s and early '70s, there were many meetings and earnest efforts by black journalists to organize. But a national organization did not crystalize. Joel Dreyfuss said black journalists got together over issues such as racism and conservatism in the media. Dreyfuss worked first for the *New York Post* then *The Washington Post*.

Many black journalists, he said, were appalled by the attempt by the Nixon administration's Justice Department to harass and intimidate *New York Times* correspondent Earl Caldwell. Caldwell wrote articles in 1970 about the Black Panthers. The authorities wanted to see his notes. Caldwell refused. He was pressured to tell what he knew about the militants to a grand jury.

The Caldwell case was a threat to the few black journalists who were working at predominately white news organizations.

Their numbers were small. There were only about 100 to 150 blacks sprinkled among 1,700 daily newspapers.

Black journalists worked hard to cultivate controversial black leaders and organizations as sources; saying anything about these sources in court would undermine that reporter-source compact.

When rioting and virtual street combat erupted in black, poor communities, daily newspapers in the '60s sent blacks to cover the dangerous assignments. Many editors feared for the safety of white reporters who almost never ventured into black areas. It was assumed they would only be targets in a riot.

Some blacks sent into the fray had no journalism experience -- they were clerks, messengers and porters at the newspapers -- but a number of them performed heroically. Robert Richardson was a messenger who did eyewitness reporting of the Watts riots. He was part of a team of *Los Angeles Times* reporters that won the Pulitzer Prize for the newspaper. After the big story he was ignored by the editors. He left journalism and lapsed into alcoholism. By 1982, he was working as an alcoholism counselor.

Marian Perry was another example. She was a black woman who worked in administration for a TV station in Philadelphia.

She walked into *The Philadelphia Bulletin's* city hall bureau with a microphone in her hand and a puzzled look on

her face. "How do you create news?" she asked Claude
Lewis, a black *Bulletin* reporter.

Perry had been sent on an assignment by her TV station
with no instructions or guidance. She was not given a
chance to succeed and did not.

After the riots subsided, new crises developed. Like
Richardson in Los Angeles, many blacks who covered the
riots were denied assignments and shunned by white editors. No longer needed to dodge bullets and rocks at the urban disturbances in to gather news, they became expenda-
ble. It seemed daily newspapers had no intention or
inclination of hiring black journalists or were satisfied
practicing tokenism.

When Vivian Aplin was hired by the *Cleveland Plain
Dealer* in December 1968, she did not begin reporting until two months later. She was hired to replace a black man
who was leaving the paper to go back to college. Until the
man left, Aplin worked at the black weekly in town, the
Call & Post.

In a city that was at least 40 percent black and had just
elected a black mayor, the leading newspaper had no interest in integrating its newsroom. Applying "the rule of one,"
a token black seat would do. Aplin was the the first black
woman to work at the paper.

The black reporters who worked and got their stories
into the newspapers battled with their white editors over a
word: Objectivity.

For many blacks, their attempts to cover black Americans with more depth and breadth than just riot or crime reporting were dismissed by whites as advocacy reporting.
Their perspective was mostly ignored.

Black journalists, many of them politicized because of
constant exposure to racism and bigotry, found the journalistic doctrine of objectivity a farce.

Meanwhile, black journalists felt blistering heat in the
black communities they tried to cover. While white editors
criticized them for being "pro-black," some community activists and spokesmen dismissed them as "Uncle Toms"
and "sellouts" to the black struggle if and when they tried

to deliver ideal daily coverage: balanced reporting of events.

Jeannye Thornton, a writer / editor with *U.S. News & World Report,* began her journalism career as a reporter for *The Chicago Tribune* in 1970. Black journalists, she said, "had a cross to bear.

"We had a terrible problem justifying to other blacks (community leaders) why we were at white news organizations. Black newspapers were losing ground and black organizations you covered wanted you to do p.r. (public relations) for them." Once a leader pleaded with Thornton to report that 600 people attended a meeting. Thornton counted only 250 people in the room.

Black journalists had a lot on their minds: The pressure and frustration of how to deal in daily newsroom culture.

Ignorance was all around. A lot of white editors, unaccustomed to black people, did not know how to interact either. Working together in a newsroom was fresh territory.

For example, when Maureen Bunyan tried to break into broadcast news at WITI-TV in Milwaukee, she said the local ABC station never had an on-air black journalist. The boss told her that she didn't "look or sound black enough" (Bunyan is cream complexioned. She immigrated to the United States from Guyana in South America).

Bunyan was asked to cut her hair and change her name -- to King. She refused and looked for work elsewhere.

Black journalists developed outlets to express their opinions and get the attention of powers who controlled daily newspapers and broadcast news.

In 1967, an organization called Black Perspectives was established in New York City by 40 journalists on the East Coast. *Philadelphia Bulletin* reporter Claude Lewis told an interviewer that "the thing we want to do is to bring some true perspective to whatever is happening in the black community."

At that time, Lewis recalled that jittery white reporters often exaggerated or distorted events involving black people and often injected race into stories when race was not relevant.

Black Perspectives aimed for a black viewpoint that would make general news coverage multidimensional, instead of limited to the narrow perspective of white males.

Thomas Johnson, a reporter at *The New York Times,* and Audreen Ballard, an editor at *Redbook,* led the organization. Vernon Jordan of the National Urban League gave them office space. Johnson recalled that Black Perspectives hired a secretary to handle its paperwork.

The group had monthly meetings at psychologist Kenneth Clark's Manhattan townhouse on East 86th Street.

In 1968, United Black Journalists organized in Chicago. Francis Ward of the *Chicago Sun-Times,* Carole Simpson of WMAQ-TV (NBC) and Barbara Reynolds of *Chicago Today,* were key players. (It went dormant. In 1972 it was revived as the Chicago Association of Black Journalists).

By 1970, organizing efforts intensified on several fronts.

Black journalists in the San Francisco Bay area published *Ball & Chain Review,* a monthly journal of news analysis, journalism criticism and war stories from the newsroom front.

In June, at Lincoln University in Jefferson City, Mo., the first National Conference of Black News Media Workers was held. Rush Greenlee, a San Francisco journalist, told the *Saturday Review* "there is a hunger among black journalists to know who they are, to clarify the role they have been playing and the one they might play in the black liberation struggle."

Clarifying the role led to divisive incidents at the conference. Valerie Gray Ward, wife of Chicago newsman Francis Ward, became angry as she watched a number of black male journalists don dashikis (a loose, often brightly colored tunic, usually worn by men) and talk about the media and black liberation struggle with white wives and girlfriends at their side.

She was not a racist, but Ward was witnessing something surreal and contradictory. When she challenged the attendance of a white woman in the audience, who was the wife of a black editor at a daily newspaper, the plenary session disintegrated, recalled Claude Lewis. People defended whom they slept with. Some were moved to tears.

Francis Ward, Valerie's husband, said the incident did not break up the meeting but it had a serious impact on the future of the organization.

Thomas Johnson said the conference "was like going to church. We forgot it (the message) after we left."

In 1972, the Congressional Black Caucus held two days of hearings on racism and the media. A number of black journalists from daily papers covered it. Rep. William Clay, D-Mo., said the black community and black journalists were "grossly excluded, distorted, mishandled and exploited" by white-controlled media. Rep. Shirley Chisholm, D-N.Y., noted that at that time only 1.5 percent of all newsroom professionals were black.

Still, there was no national organization of black journalists, an institution that could meet regularly about issues of concern and even develop programs to improve journalists' conditions. The many organizing efforts were for the most part regional in scope.

Washington Post reporter Leon Dash said several national organizing efforts failed because people were unable to reconcile contentious issues. For example, should the organized journalists be a "Negro" organization?

Reporter Paul Delaney, then at *The Washington Star,* said this caused the collapse of an effort to organize a group in Washington, D.C. in the late '60s. Some of the would-be organizers were adamant that "black" be in the title of the organization.

In the late '60s the word "Negro" was fading as acceptable usage because it was linked to segregation and second-class status. The word "black" was considered a strong political statement in the '70s.

Nevertheless, a national journalist's organization did not come together in the late 1960s.

Some people got hung up on what to call themselves; that was a very small reason for the delay.

The much larger questions concerned satisfying the special demands of gathering and disseminating news.

Who should be eligible to participate in this organization? Journalism was not a licensed profession like medicine or law.

Could occasional writers or publicists be members? Could white people be members of a black organization, like the NAACP or the Urban League?

Through the first half of the 1970s, newspeople from a handful of big-city black journalist organizations continued to see each other at national news assignments. The journalists kept the idea alive to organize a national group.

On Dec. 3, 1975, a letter from Washington, D.C. was sent to scores of black journalists. It said:

"The interim Committee for a national Association of Black Journalists with the Association of Black Journalists in Philadelphia, Chicago Association of Black Journalists, San Francisco Association of Black Journalists and the Washington Association of Black Journalists cordially invite you to the founding meeting of the National Association of Black Journalists on December 12, 1975 at 11 a.m., in Washington, D.C. at the Sheraton Park Hotel. Toward this goal, we gratefully acknowledge the groundwork laid by Black Perspective, a group of journalists back in 1967.

". . . As an additional professional rationale for your attendance at the December 12th meeting, the National Institute of Black Elected Officials will be convening in Washington, D.C., December 11-13. Hopefully, your newspaper, television or radio station or magazine will subsidize your attendance. If not, we urge you to attend as an individual or a delegate from an interested group in your city. In the latter instance, the delegate's expenses could be defrayed by the group's contributions.

". . . We look forward to seeing you with the satisfaction that Black journalists finally will have been able to 'get it together' -- in time for the critical 1976 Presidential campaigns."

The committee members listed vertically on the left side of the letterhead were:

Sherman Briscoe, NNPA;
Paul Brock, DNC Radio;
Maureen Bunyan; WTOP-TV, Washington;
Gail Christian, KNBC-TV, Los Angeles;
William Dilday, WLBT-TV, Jackson, Miss.;
Sandra Dillard, *Denver Post;*
Dexter Eure, *Boston Globe;*
Marcia Gillespie, *Essence;*
Bob Hayes, *San Francisco Examiner;*
Vernon Jarrett; *Chicago Tribune;*
Mal Johnson, Cox Broadcasting;
Luix Overbea, *Christian Science Monitor;*
Ethel Payne, *Chicago Defender;*
Vince Sanders, National Black Network;
Chuck Stone, *Philadelphia Daily News;*
Ray Taliaferro, KRON-TV, San Francisco

December 1975 would be different.

On Friday, the 12th day, the National Association of Black Journalists (NABJ) was founded by 44 newsmen and newswomen in Washington, D.C.

Chapter 2
The founding

Several events occurred quickly to make the idea a reality. The journalists were in town to cover the Third National Institute for Black Elected Public Officials. It was a consortium of eight national black political, educational and legal organizations.

The coming together seemed spontaneous to some of the journalists. For others it was calculated.

A number of times during the early- to mid-'70s, about a dozen or so black journalists who worked for daily newspapers or other major white-owned media like newsweeklies or broadcasting, would run into each other while covering national black events.

They would see each other at the Urban League or NAACP conventions. At a national black political convention in Cincinnati in 1975, *Baltimore Sun* reporter DeWayne Wickham remembered meeting Ellis Cose of the *Chicago Sun-Times,* Ed Blackwell of *The Milwaukee Journal,* Vernon Jarrett of *The Chicago Tribune,* Les Payne of *Newsday* in Long Island, N.Y. and Jack White of *Time* magazine.

"We all knew we'd see each other at another meeting," said Wickham.

Mal Johnson would see many of these journalists at the same assignments too. When they talked shop, she would hear that black journalists were not getting equal opportunities.

Mal Johnson had a coveted beat; she was first a Capitol Hill then a White House correspondent for Cox Broadcasting. She understood the frustration and barriers black journalists faced. She had had her own experiences.

Mal Johnson grew up in Philadelphia. She became a schoolteacher because her mother told her so: Mal's choices were teaching, nursing or working in a funeral home.

She taught at schools in Europe and the Pacific islands while her husband served as a career Air Force officer. He died in 1965. Mal Johnson returned to Philadelphia. She got involved in civil rights activities and worked for the North City Congress, the umbrella organization for 150 non-profit groups.

One day she got a call from WKVS-TV Channel 48 in Philadelphia. The caller asked if she would like to be interviewed for a position as public affairs manager.

When she arrived for the interview, John Gilmore, the interviewer, was stunned. He did not expect a black woman to show up. He hesitated about the availability of the job, but Johnson did not let him off the hook. Despite the awkward situation, she went through with the interview.

Johnson went home, and within a half hour, Gilmore called her and offered the job. He sounded desperate and said his job was at stake. Gilmore's boss wanted to hire Mal Johnson.

A speech helped get Mal Johnson her job at Cox Broadcasting.

She said "I was giving a speech to women broadcasters in Houston. I was giving them a hard time because they turned down $150,000 from HEW (U.S. Department of Housing, Education and Welfare) to train minority women for broadcasting jobs. The president and CEO of Cox Broadcasting, J. Leonard Reinsch, was the next speaker. I didn't know.

"In order to shut me up, I was named to the board of American Women in Radio and Television." Reinsch was at the next board meeting. He was the only male there. Reinsch hired Johnson. "He became my guiding mentor," she said.

Reinsch, the radio adviser to the White House from 1945-52, taught President Truman and Eleanor Roosevelt how to project effectively.

On race relations, Johnson said, "Though I was a product of the civil rights movement, I don't have as much animosity for all whites as others do. I know there are good ones and bad ones. I refuse to have my life narrowed by hating all whites."

Meanwhile, the Federal Communications Commission ordered television and radio stations to hire blacks and other minorities for their operations.

But the word getting back to Mal Johnson was that the regulations were not strictly enforced and at many operations that did hire blacks, they did not make a serious attempt to train them for the craft.

When the black journalists would meet at the conventions of other black organizations, the first thing some of them wondered about was whether there were enough black journalists in daily journalism to support a national organization. But as the same dozen or so people kept running into each other, they kept hearing that there were other people like them coming into the business.

A month before the Congressional Black Caucus hearings in 1972, the *Dow Jones Newspaper Fund* reported that "162 Negroes received journalism degrees, a 184-percent increase from 1969."

The first step toward establishing a national organization of black journalists occurred in Philadelphia. In 1973, the Association of Black Journalists (ABJ) was established in Philadelphia. NABJ is a direct descendant of the ABJ. The new national organization would draft a constitution that borrowed liberally from the Philadelphia document.

A number of signers at the Washington, D.C. meeting who pledged their commitment to a National Association of Black Journalists were prominent Philadelphia journalists: Chuck Stone of the *Philadelphia Daily News,* Claude Lewis and Joe Davidson of *The Bulletin,* broadcaster Reginald Bryant and Acel Moore of *The Philadelphia Inquirer*.

Two years later at the Sheraton Park Hotel, about 10 journalists met in Paul Brock's room to discuss the possibility of forming a national organization.

They included Ray Taliaferro, a San Francisco talk-show host, Sandra Dillard, *Denver Post;* Vernon Jarrett; Mal Johnson of Cox Broadcasting and Chuck Stone.

Paul Brock was a former journalist. He was a reporter with a CBS affiliate radio and TV station in the Virgin Islands from 1963-65.

From 1970-73, he was news director of WHUR-Radio in Washington, D.C. The station broke ground as the first black-oriented station to offer an hour-long news broadcast. Brock had also been a vice president with Mutual Black Network, which later became Sheridan Broadcasting, a black-oriented news and information company.

In 1975, he left to become deputy director of communications for the Democratic National Committee.

Brock remained sympathetic, however, to the idea of organizing black journalists nationally.

"There were several organizations that concerned themselves with employment and with blacks in the news media in 1973, '74 and '75," explained Brock. "A few of us felt the need for a national organization. DeWayne Wickham had a group in Baltimore. Chuck Stone was involved with a group in Philadelphia. Tony Cox was involved with a group in Los Angeles. Boston had a group.

"Eddie Williams (president of the Joint Center for Political Studies) called a number of black elected officials together for a conference.

"Since we had been talking to a number of people, maybe this would be a great opportunity to cover this and come early, then have an organization meeting.

"I sent letters to 125 to 150 black journalists, which may have been everybody. I left journalism and went to the DNC. As I went to all the cities and gathered all the names of journalists, I had a personal goal to make sure all black journalists had access.

"I would get their names and ask them who were the other black journalists in their city."

The journalists met at the Sheraton Park from the late morning through the afternoon and evening. They drafted a constitution, bylaws and a mission statement.

Maurice Williams, a 23-year-old Howard University student and one of Brock's interns at the DNC, helped fetch coffee and donuts for the visiting journalists.

In a couple of years Williams became a journalist, a radio reporter for WHUR.

(Paul Brock called him the first black journalist to die in the line of duty. While on the job as a District affairs reporter, he was shot dead while stepping off an elevator by a Hanafi Moslem gunman during a 39-hour siege in March 1977. The violence erupted in a Washington, D.C. neighborhood when Hamaas Khaal tried to avenge the deaths of the seven children and family members who were murdered by a rival religious sect in 1973. Maurice Williams, the promising, enthusiastic and well-liked journalist, was in the wrong place at the wrong time.)

Leon Dash remembered that there wasn't much shouting and screaming. People spoke passionately and earnestly but almost always in a moderate tone of voice.

"We had been through a decade of discussions," said Dash. "By this meeting I was not interested in any more discussions."

There was tension and disagreements.

Joel Dreyfuss said there was fear and loathing among black journalists who worked for giant news organizations as opposed to journalists who toiled for smaller outfits in less-glamorous cities.

Jeannye Thornton said some of the people there acted as if they were organizing a Links chapter instead of an organization of journalists. (Founded in 1946, the Links promote civic, cultural and educational activities.)

Reporter Bob Greenlee of *The New Haven Register* felt vibes or sensed a pecking order. Some of the assembled did not think he was much of a journalist because of the paper he worked for.

Willie C. (Curtis) Riddle was another journalist from the hinterlands.

He was a reporter with *The Courier-Journal* in Louisville, Ky. He joined the paper in March 1972 shortly after graduating from Southern Illinois University and a brief stint as a reporter at the *Metro East Journal* in his homtown, East St. Louis. (The paper is defunct.)

He was the only black journalist on *The Courier-Journal's* city staff.

"I remember a long session and a fairly heated discussion," said Riddle.

"It was a room full of strangers. Many people didn't know each other. I didn't know most of the people. Ten people I knew. There were eight people I knew of."

Riddle gravitated toward Bob Hayes, a reporter and columnist with the *San Francisco Examiner*.

"Bob Hayes always had a question. He was always in the middle of something."

That's because Hayes was pumped up.

"I was very impressed with the people I came in contact with," he explained in August 1991.

They talked about getting blacks into the business. They seemed to be concerned about paving the way for the younger generation.

"They seemed terribly concerned.

"For the first time, I felt I had met some real reporters."

The representatives from black-oriented media questioned how relevant the organization would be to them.

Alex Poinsett once sprayed wooden pig stys at a factory for $40 a week and pursued a dream to be a journalist. One day in 1952 he went to *Johnson Publishing Co.* in his paint-smeared clothes and convinced John H.Johnson to hire him as a library clerk.

In a month, Poinsett replaced a *Jet* magazine writer who was fired for accepting $750 from gospel singer Clara Ward (Ward called Johnson and asked, "Where's my story? I gave your man the money.")

Poinsett was with *Ebony* magazine when he joined NABJ. He agreed that an organization of black journalists was needed to break the barriers to general interest journalism. But he doubted that the organization could address his special needs in the black press.

Richard Rambeau said he doubted that blacks who worked for the majority media could really reflect what was going on in the black community because they were paid by the majority. The Detroit native represented Project BAIT (Black Awareness in Television.) It was radio and TV programming for, by and about black people.

Furthermore, some of the strongest supporters of organizing black journalists *were not* journalists, or at least not journalists anymore.

Many of these people worked in public relations or as press spokesmen. What would be done with them?

Paul Delaney, a Chicago correspondent for *The New York Times,* said he was a hardliner.

"We had to be a journalists' organization of newspeople," he recalled. "What we were trying to do, it was so new to us. We thought other people would bring conflict-of-interest matters.

"I was covering black colleges for *The Times.* For college professors to become full-fledged members of a journalists organization posed potential conflicts. And there were many more professors than journalists. They would overwhelm us.

"There were people who wanted to get involved in other issues and demonstrate." Delaney was troubled by earlier attempts to organize black journalists in the late '60s that were derailed by militant rhetoric which focused more on political issues than the craft of journalism.

There were about 80 people in the room, recalled Jeannye Thornton.

Delaney explained how the crowd thinned: "We got rid of the disc jockeys and they left in a huff.

"And we said 'no' to the advertising types and 'no' to public relations people. "The public relations people and publicists could not be dismissed entirely. For the most part they were enthusiastic, energetic and hard workers. There was particular uneasiness by many journalists because of the participation of Paul Brock."

Brock explains: "Paul Delaney and I were close, but he said it should only be journalists.

"It was not an attack against me. Maureen Bunyan, Joel Dreyfuss and Max Robinson felt the same way."

"Paul Brock was tolerated," said DeWayne Wickham. "While Chuck Stone was the visionary, Paul was the mover and shaker.

"He had connections to make things happen very quickly. People were uncomfortable because he could make things happen.

"In their discomfort, people used the 'Paul's not a journalist' (anymore) excuse."

Chuck Stone called Paul Brock "the Henry Kissinger of black journalists," because Brock was able to get them together with the skill Kissinger used to organize a number of American Jewish organizations.

Brock did not become a member but he became executive director. Maureen Bunyan of WTOP-TV in Washington, D.C. said the founders fought strenuously to limit full membership to working journalists. "However, *we journalists* didn't have time to run the organization and we also didn't have access to the resources -- space, support, etc. -- to do it. Since Paul had done such legwork, it very well fit our own needs for him to be recognized in some way. And he was willing to continue the work as organizer."

The executive director did not have to be a journalist. It was an unpaid position, or as Brock pointed out, "it wasn't even an expense-reimbursement position."

Although Brock had special status among the founders, there were p.r. people with more clout whom NABJ rejected, said co-founder Vince Sanders of National Black Network. There was a woman who was a former big-time recording artist-turned-lobbyist for an oil company.

"A lot of p.r. people were asked to leave when we got down to forming," explained Sanders. "As she left, she said 'you don't know what you're doing -- I have resources I could give you."

How to include people who were not journalists was set aside in order to establish the national organization.

Philadelphia Daily News columnist Chuck Stone presided over the meeting.

"There were basically two groups at that meeting," recalled Wickham, "Chuck Stone and the rest of us.
"Chuck was by far more than a dominant influence. He was the reason the group was formed. NABJ was Chuck's vision. He made it happen. He brought us together. He had a kind of mystical influence on us. There were a lot of big-shot black journalists, but when Chuck would walk into the room, it was the Adam Clayton Powell connection. Even then, people were turning themselves in to Chuck."

(Soon after joining the *Philadelphia Daily News* in 1972, Stone became a cult figure. Killers, escaped convicts and other criminal suspects would surrender to police, using Stone as an intermediary. The people were black and Hispanic. They feared for their safety once in police custody. They would be photographed with Stone to confirm their condition and Stone would call the police, who would handcuff the suspect and transport the person to jail.)

"He certainly had an influence on me, being a year or two into the business and I gravitated toward his sphere of influence," Wickham said.
Charlotte Robinson of *The Detroit Free Press* nominated Stone for president. Instantly, nominations for president were closed.Stone said the maneuver was discomforting. He protested, but the decision stood. By a show of hands he became the first president.
Charles Sumner Stone was born in 1924 in a segregated Hospital in St. Louis. He grew up in Hartford, Conn. Stone went to elite Wesleyan University. He was the only black in his class. He was commencement speaker, and his address was on America's broken promises to blacks.
In World War II, Stone was an Army Air Corps navigator. He was a CARE worker in India and the Gaza strip.
He entered journalism accidentally. "Journalism chose me," Stone explained.
"It was fortuitous circumstances. Like the Broadway play "A Funny Thing Happened to Me on the Way to the Forum," a funny thing happened to me on the way to the

train station in 1958.

"I had returned from India and Egypt where I was working for CARE and I was in New York getting ready to work for the Foreign Policy Association as an associate director. I was living with my sister.

"I was taking our mother to the train station on 125th Street and we ran into this old friend of mine, Al Duckett. This was very fortuitous. We stopped and talked. He had been the editor of the *Hartford Chronicle* (the black newspaper in Stone's hometown.)

"He asked me what I was going to do. I told him I was going to work for the Foreign Policy Association. He said 'don't go work for those white people. Come work for me.' He was editor of the *New York Age* at the time.

"I said 'I can't write.' He said 'yes you can. I used to read your letters to the editor to *The Hartford Courant* and *Hartford Times.* You're a terrific writer. I can train you to become a reporter. Come work for me and I'll let you cover Adam Clayton Powell exclusively.'

"He knew I liked politics. I said 'let me think about it.'

"My mother was horrified. She didn't want me to work for a black, or segregated newspaper. She always wanted us to be mainstream. Second, she didn't have high regard for journalists.

"So when we got to the train station she said 'promise me you won't do that.' I said 'I promise.'

"Then I went back and got hired. That was August 1958.

"By October, I was writing a column. In February, Duckett resigns after a dispute with the publisher. The publisher jumped me over nine people and made me the editor.

"It was very fast, too fast. I didn't stay a reporter long enough to get the training and discipline to be a good reporter.

"That is not a good career path."

Stone later became editor of other black-owned newspapers, *The Afro-American* in Washington, D.C., then *The Chicago Defender.*

At *The Defender,* Stone was fired for "authorizing stories that made Mayor (Richard) Daley look bad."

He was press secretary for New York Congressman Adam Clayton Powell Jr. Stone was author of several books, including *Black Political Power in America,* and *King Strut,* a novel based on Powell's career.

And when Stone was elected the first president of this new national organization of black journalists, he was a columnist for the *Philadelphia Daily News,* a major metropolitan newspaper.

"Our formation," Stone told *Editor & Publisher,* "is mandated by the fact that we are probably among the last groups of black professionals to organize nationally. On the eve of this multiethnic society's 200th birthday, it is fitting that such an organization come into existence."

The new organization listed a dozen objectives:

• Strengthen the ties between blacks in the white media and blacks in the black media.

• Sensitize the white media to the institutional racism in its coverage and employment practices by monitoring EEO and FCC regulations and working to seek compliance where necessary.

• Award scholarships to journalism programs that especially supported minorities.

• Expand the white media's coverage and balanced reporting of the black community.

• Become an exemplary group of professionals that honors excellence and outstanding achievement among black journalists.

• Critique through a national newsletter examples of the media's reportorial deficiencies as they affect blacks.

• Encourage journalism schools to appoint black professors through the work of a liasion committee.

• Work with high schools to identify journalists.

• Act as a clearinghouse for jobs.

• Expand opportunities for black journalists by assisting in recruiting activities.

• Work to upgrade black journalists in managerial and supervisory positions.

• Maintain a national office with a paid secretary for the clearinghouse.

The other officers elected were Francis Ward, a Chicago-based *Los Angeles Times* correspondent, as vice president, *U.S. News & World Report* reporter Jeannye Thornton was elected secretary and Allison Davis of WBZ-TV Boston was elected parliamentarian.

Claudia Polley of NBC News was elected treasurer. She did not last long.

Polley was a journalist and a singer, a mezzo contralto who studied at Julliard. Some friends convinced her to go with them to France to sing classical music and do background vocals for disco recordings.

Polley resigned as NABJ treasurer and went to Europe.

Mal Johnson took over as treasurer. DeWayne Wickham replaced her as regional director of Maryland, District of Columbia, Virginia and West Virginia. Johnson would hold the treasurer's position for eight years.

The five-member executive board was rounded out with regional representatives, called regional directors, from 10 districts.

Joe Davidson said that Chuck Stone recommended that NABJ draw its regional boundaries similar to the system used by the U.S. Dept. of Health, Education and Welfare (HEW then, now Health and Human Services -- HHS.)

Someone opened up an HEW map. "Who's from Region Eight?"

Sam Ford, a young reporter from WCCO-TV in Minneapolis, responded and became that region's representative. Unlike many people who came to the meeting with a specific objective, Ford said his trip was a reward from the general manager for his work on a documentary.

Regions would be groups of contiguous states. They could be small in land but very populous like New York, New Jersey and Connecticut, NABJ Region 2, or a vast land mass with few people like nine Rocky Mountain states that made up Region 9.

A region that would figure prominently in the development of NABJ was the eight Southern states of Region 5, contiguous from North Carolina to Mississippi. These were states that had begun experiencing a reverse migration of middle-income, middle-class black families from the North.

With lightning spontaneity, NABJ became a reality on a cold, sun-streaked Friday in northwest Washington, D.C. after at least eight years of attempts to organize.

These founding members of the National Association of Black Journalists affirmed their commitment to the organization by paying dues.

A couple of hundred dollars was collected. Most of the members paid the required $10. Max Robinson of WTOP-TV in Washington paid $25.

"We were quite impressed," said Mal Johnson.

Robinson wanted to be president of the organization. He demonstrated his commitment to the new organization with his checkbook. Several failed attempts to organize black journalists had been held at his house.

Before the Dec. 12 meeting he called some colleagues soliciting support.

One of them was Paul Delaney, who had worked for *The Washington Star* before moving to *The New York Times*.

"You'd be a great figure," Delaney told Robinson, "but you haven't done a goddam thing."

Robinson did not campaign for president at the meeting and Stone ended up the sole nominee.

Several hundred dollars was not enough money to operate a new national organization, even if the participants were volunteers. Mal Johnson said NABJ's first bank statement was $300. Johnson, Paul Brock and Bernice Brown, a retired worker for a U.S. senator, worked on NABJ's first fund-raiser. It occurred Sat., Dec. 13, the day after NABJ established itself.

They invited James Baldwin to speak at a dinner at the Capitol Hilton. "We were skinning our butt," Brock recalled. "We didn't have the money to pay for his (Baldwin's) hotel room as the plane was landing.

"We had to take money out of people's pockets."

Brock remembers borrowing about $40 to $50 each from

Vince Sanders, Chuck Stone and Max Robinson.
What happened was Baldwin nearly bankrupted the
young organization. The organizers planned to cover his
travel and hotel costs. Baldwin showed up with an entour-
age: his mother, a sister and his male friend, recalled Johnson and Brock. The organizers would have to pay lodging
for three more people.

The event was well attended. The hotel had to add some
banquet tables. About 150 people filled the room. The hotel
wanted the banquet bill paid before the food was served but
Brock had not collected all the money yet. The money
would be ready after everyone paid their $15 at the door.

Brock double-talked the Capitol Hilton staff people and
went inside the banquet room. He paid the bill afterwards.
Despite the high-wire antics, NABJ walked out with the
bills paid and with funds for its treasury.

For all the trouble, Baldwin's speech was a disappoint-
ment, according to Joel Dreyfuss. Baldwin had been living
in France for some time and had just returned to America.
The journalists were hoping to hear Baldwin's pointed analysis of social conditions in America. But his time out of the
country rendered him out of touch and off the mark.

After that first fund-raiser, Brock convinced Johnson to
take advantage of her membership in the Women's Democratic National Club. She was entitled to use the dining
room and invite guests. She reserved the room on a dozen
occasions and invited black elected officials to speak to
black journalists.

U.S. Rep. Andy Young, D-Ga., was the first speaker, recalled Johnson. Speakers such as Reps. Ron Dellums, D-
Calif., John Conyers, D-Mich., and Bill Clay, D-Mo., followed. Explained Johnson, "we charged $10 to $12. About
50 to 150 people came to the luncheons." About $7,000
was raised. NABJ had more operating funds to promote itself and to organize its first national conference.

Chapter 3
Texas Southern

Only three of the 44 founding members of the National Association of Black Journalists worked for news organizations based in the Western half of the United States.

With most of the members based in the East, why was the first national conference out West? In Houston?

The reason: NABJ made history in organizing black journalists, at about the same time Texas Southern University reached a milestone. The black institution would house the first black school of communications in the West and the second in the nation (Howard University is the other.)

"I went to Texas Southern to start the School of Communications. I was the founding dean," explained Carlton Molette, who is vice president for academic affairs for Coppin State College in Baltimore.

"Chuck Stone gave me a call. 'Would you be interested in hosting the conference? I told him that I would like to talk to the journalism faculty first. I called back and told him 'yes, we'd love to.'"

The date was set: the weekend of Oct. 2, 1976.

NABJ and the Texas Southern saw a joint opportunity to gain recognition.

The school of communications had grown from about 250 majors in 1974 to 400 majors in 1976. In 1976, about 60 of the communications majors were in the journalism sequence. The journalism faculty had many newsmen and women who worked for the *Houston Informer,* the third-oldest continuously published black newspaper in America.

Meanwhile, NABJ was trying to build its base of membership and encourage students to study the craft and join them in the newsroom.

Most of the meetings and workshops were held on campus; other sessions were held at the Ramada Inn where NABJers were lodging. Vans shuttled people between the campus and hotel.

Karen Howze, then of *The San Francisco Chronicle,* recalled that she, Joe Davidson (*Philadelphia Bulletin*); Gayle Pollard (*Miami Herald*), and Jeanne Fox (*Kansas City Times*), had something in common.

All were about 25 years old. They were some of the youngest journalists participating at the conference. They sometimes felt isolated in the cities where they worked.

Gayle Pollard was determined to go to Houston.

"Jeanne Fox called me up and told me about the conferece. I decided to charge it. Nobody had any money. Most of us then were not making more than $10,000. I left Miami with $35 in my pocket.

"I had been in the business four years. I was very ambitious and I hated Miami. I wanted to learn how to be a better reporter and get a better job. I needed relief from the Miami brain drain in the black professional class."

Pollard was a native of St. Louis. She grew up in a middle-class family. She came to *The Miami Herald* in June 1972. The Miami she saw was the only big U.S. city where black residents lost ground per capita since the passage of civil rights laws.

"When I went to Miami I saw a shortage of people like me. I looked at the census figures. Such a small number of blacks made over $10,000 in 1970. Progress had passed Miami by.

"I had a terrible time renting an apartment." A landlord about to rent her a place rejected her when he discovered that Pollard was black.

She said "I looked to the conference as time to have fun and learn from people I could trust.

"I decided to share a $36-a-night room with my sister Veronica (a reporter at *The San Francisco Chronicle*) and

Jeanne was sharing with Linda Lockhart (a reporter at The *St. Louis Post-Dispatch*).

"Friday night, people were just going to dinner. Before leaving, Karen Howze knocked on the door. She told me my sister wasn't coming. She stayed."

Howze was a reporter who worked with Pollard's sister at *The Chronicle.*

Pollard remembered the camaraderie and informality of the gathering.

For Pollard, *Miami Herald* colleague Joe Oglesby, *Philadelphia Bulletin* reporter Joe Davidson, Howze and Vivian Aplin of *The Cleveland Plain Dealer,* Friday night dinner was a trip to a soul food joint to get $2.99 barbeque sandwiches.

Other NABJers fondly remember another dinner of pizza by the pool at the Ramada Inn.

"A lot of informal mentoring occurred," said Pollard. "Paul Delaney (*New York Times,* Chicago bureau) was very instructive, so was Vernon Jarrett. Both men were on a panel about surviving in the newsroom. Their audience was black journalists with less than five years' experience.

They handled questions like: what if a source calls up and asks for the telephone number for the NAACP on your day off? Do you give it to him?

When the session broke for lunch, Pollard said Delaney took her and the other young women (Fox, Howze, Lockhart) to a popular Houston restaurant and bought them steaks.

That night many of the conferees ate dinner together at a long table that stretched end-to-end. Gayle Pollard sat next to Sandra Dillard and across from Bob Reid of NBC News in Atlanta.

Reid grew up in Miami, where Pollard worked.

They had a lot to talk about.

Bob Reid was invited to be on a conference panel because he was a bureau chief. He was a mid-level manager and at that time one of the highest-ranking black journalists nationally. He was an ideal role model for people who wanted to set their sights beyond being reporters.

In 1990, Reid explained how he became a journalist. In 1966, he was an 18-year-old student at Miami/Dade Community College. He worked for the school newspaper. Adviser Barbara Garfinkle thought highly of his skills and other teachers looked out for him.

She helped Reid get a part-time job at *The Miami Herald.* On Sundays he worked in the circulation department and made sure that people who missed the Sunday paper got a replacement. He moved on to the display advertising department. Reid had to go to a room where the lead type logos were kept in bins. He had to find the right piece of type for the order of the week. He did that for a few months. Reid moved into the newsroom and became a sports copy clerk, a copy boy who also answered telephones and took down high school sports reports and racetrack results from stringers .

Reid would occasionally write "hole in ones" -- one-paragraph reports from local golf clubs -- and take care of the agate type on the sports page. He learned to work fast.

"I'd throw a piece of paper in the typewriter and type."

But accuracy was at a premium too. "A hard, hard lesson was nothing was worse than getting the winner wrong in the seventh race at Hialieah.

"It was a job to make money. I still fought with the idea to graduate and go to law school. I had not abandoned it as a master plan.

"At *The Herald* I was under intense pressure. Ed Storin typified the Type A personality, a screamer.

"I'd tell myself 'I don't want any part of this.'"

Then, baseball scores changed Reid's career plans.

While working on the sports desk, he had to report sports scores into a machine that people called for results.

What he would recite was very simple: "New York 3, Cleveland 2."

"I played it back and listened to my voice. It sounded horrible. I said to myself 'I have to do something.'

"I took a speech course at Miami University. Ralph Renick of WTVJ-TV spoke to the class. I chatted with him afterwards and asked him questions.

"Renick was the vice president for news at the CBS affiliate station. He was a broadcast pioneer. The concept of TV editorials was credited to Ralph Apperson Renick.

"He asked me if I ever thought of getting into television. He said to give him a call. I never thought why he said so."

He did call. In the meantime, Reid had moved up at *The Herald*. He was a cub reporter on the city desk. He covered the police beat two days, two nights, and worked one day as a general assignment reporter.

"A few months later (late '67) I became disenchanted at *The Herald*. I wanted to write more than one day a week. The police beat meant giving facts to a rewrite man.

"Larry Jinks said I was doing well, but he needed someone to cover the police beat. Patience was not a strong suit of mine, especially when I feel I'm not growing.

"I called Renick. Months passed. He called me. Fred Friendly read the Kerner Commission report and said TV news should do something about coverage.

"He was involved in starting a 10-week summer program for minorities at Columbia University. Renick's station WTVJ-TV was a major contributor to the CBS Evening News (there was no Southeast bureau then).

"Friendly was looking for students. Ralph Renick said he knew some. I went to WTVJ in January 1968, expecting to go into the summer program. I was a journalist by then, different from the students (i.e. teachers, a postal worker).

"When I returned to Miami I worked as a reporter/cameraman with a 16mm fixed lens camera.

"At the summer program, because I knew how to write, I concentrated on the supervisory/management role. I went back to Miami with the seed planted that I wanted to be a manager/supervisor. I began writing and producing the weekend news as a fill-in.

"Bernard Goldberg (now a CBS correspondent) arrived. I was told to teach him the job. He took my job.

"This caused me to leave Ralph Renick." Reid was told that he was doing a good job but they wanted to give someone else a chance.

At *The Miami Herald,* Reid said he was the first black

on the city desk as a cub reporter and he was the first black in Miami on TV news in 1968.

When NABJ came to Houston, Diana Fallis was a local reporter/anchor for KTRK (ABC). She said "it was my first opportunity to talk with other black people and ask if they were feeling the things I was feeling. I was anxious to exchange notes with other people." Fallis now teaches journalism at Prairie View A&M University.

Several people interviewed said that about 80 people participated in the conference. Sandra Dillard of the *Denver Post* said at least 100 people participated and about one-third of them were students.

Based on a sign-in sheet at the last plenary session on Sunday, Oct. 3, 33 journalists from 13 states and the District of Columbia attended.

The list included three future NABJ presidents: Vernon Jarrett of *The Chicago Tribune* (1977-79); Bob Reid of NBC News, Atlanta (1979-81), and DeWayne Wickham of *The Sun,* Baltimore (1987-89.)

The list did not include president Chuck Stone or executive director Paul Brock. Or, hosts from Texas Southern that included Molette, Lucius New, Reginald Owens, Sam Andrews, George McElroy and Jane Manning.

The typewritten list acknowledged that a few journalists' names were missing. Molette said Texas Southern invited Gen. Julius Becton, commander of Fort Bliss, Texas and at that time the highest-ranking African-American in the military, to be keynote speaker (Becton is now president of Prairie View A&M University, a black institution).

The first conference was held a month before the 1976 U.S. presidential elections.

The political atmosphere generated a lot of excitement among NABJers, according to Molette. Democratic presidential candidate Jimmy Carter sent representatives who were seen as high ranking in the campaign, unlike Republican President Gerald Ford, who was not perceived as taking NABJ seriously, based on the representatives he sent.

Jeanne Fox says black Republican Arthur Fletcher gave a good address, advising, "don't ignore what the Republican

Party is doing."
NABJ released this statement on Oct. 2:

"NABJ is disturbed by the media's benign neglect of issues affecting the black community in this campaign. Our professional colleagues, however, have only responded to the issues articulated by Gerald Ford and Jimmy Carter. Both candidates are assiduously bypassing black voters.

"Moreover, they are not demonstrating the same political sensitivity to blacks they have enthusiastically reserved for other ethnics.

"While NABJ commends the inclusion of a woman panelist on the presidential debate, we deplore the fact that the same sensitivity was not extended to blacks.

"NABJ is incredulous at Jimmy Carter's apparent effort to demean the professional integrity of black journalists by attempting to divide their ranks. Mr. Carter, along with Mr. Ford, was invited in late August to NABJ's first annual conference here in Houston -- at Texas Southern University's School of Communications. Both schedules did not permit acceptance, a fact which NABJ readily accepts.

"However, Mr. Carter chose to invite -- at the eleventh hour -- a small group of black journalists to meet privately with him for 45 minutes today at 1:15 in Chevy Chase, Md. Most of those invited to both meetings chose to be with NABJ.

"This morning the journalists were notified that the time was reduced to 15 minutes, a further indication of Carter's attitudes towards black journalists.

"NABJ is not one-sided. We also wish to stress that Gerald Ford has consistently exhibited a contemptuous disdain for black needs.

"But for Carter to schedule such a meeting on the same day as the first significant black journalist conference in another city is a typical divisive tactic that caused some of the cataclysms we are witnessing in South Africa.

"NABJ does not pretend to speak for all black journalists. But we do reflect the concerns of all black people who would like to believe that candidates who say they care for them, really do!"

During the NABJ conference, the infamous Earl Butz story broke. In an unguarded moment, the secretary of the U.S. Department of Agriculture said that all black men were content to have "loose shoes, tight pussy and a warm place to shit."

Chuck Stone arranged a press conference and condemned Butz's remarks. Stone and other officers saw an opportunity to get some exposure for their organization. Butz resigned shortly after making the comment. He had a history of making crude, bigoted statements, but the "loose shoes" comment was the last straw. It came too close to a presidential election and drew too much attention.

When the NABJers held their Saturday business meeting Oct. 2, the membership debate that was a big part of the founding meeting 10 months earlier in Washington resurfaced. Carlton Molette: "The organization was trying to figure out who to define as people in and out of membership. There was particular concern in major markets where there were a lot of public relations people. NABJ didn't want to be dominated or controlled (by non-journalists.)

"It also defined journalism professors as out of membership. This left a bad taste in the mouths of Texas Southern professors, including yours truly," said Molette.

Texas Southern journalism professor George McElroy was a part-time newsman at the black-owned *Houston Informer* and weekly columnist for the daily *Houston Post*.

The disqualification of journalism instructors "riled me because I couldn't get into an organization as a journalism educator and I was not considered a professional journalist because I was a weekly columnist," McElroy said.

"Three shots and I struck out.

"We busted our guts to be host, then was slapped on the last day with this 'sorry but you're not eligible.'"

McElroy had to find this bizarre because he had been working in journalism nearly 30 years, before many of the conferees were born.

In 1937, when McElroy was a high school student, he began writing a youth column for the *Houston Informer*.

"Three dollars a column put me in the spotlight and I liked it. When I got out of the service, I enrolled at Texas Southern. I've gotten my hands dirty with news since World War II.

"I was a sports stringer with the *Houston Post* covering 'colored sports.'" McElroy moved on to teaching high school journalism, then journalism at his alma mater and writing columns for the *Informer*.

Molette said when told they were not eligible to be full voting members, most of the Texas Southern delegation walked out of the meeting.

At the time it was announced, the exclusion of journalism educators was extra painful. Those being excluded worked in the black press. The slight escalated the tension and distrust between people who worked at large white-owned news media vs. people working for smaller, struggling black-owned media.

"Eligibility," in Molette's view, "focused on where one's money came from rather than what they wrote. That excluded full-time journalism professors like me who wrote a column (for the *Informer*.)."

Jeanne Fox said NABJ was trying to set itself apart from another organization, the National Black Media Coalition, which organized in 1973 and was based in Houston, where its founder, Pluria Marshall, lived.

Marshall was also a founding member of NABJ. His affiliation then was "free-lancer."

Said Fox, "I guess some of the bylaws had been written already.

"The people from Texas Southern did a lot of gruntwork -- lining up speakers and facilities. They were surprised to learn they could not be included. Marcia Gillespie, editor of *Essence* magazine, gave a talk or workshop. One of the Texas Southern people said 'we're more involved in journalism than a magazine like Essence.'

"The decision was made to keep it (NABJ) to people in journalism jobs," Fox said. "The Texas Southern people were caught up in it.

"None of us had any personal reason to exclude them.

We wanted to keep the organization focused.

"Also, the National Black Media Coalition was based in Houston and it was broad-based and very grass roots. Pluria (Marshall) lived there.

"It (NBMC) always focused more on the broadcast industry and were sort of people on the outside looking in and being vocal rather than criticizing the content.

"We (NABJ) had the same concerns, but we wanted it to be a trade organization, in a way NBMC was not."

In struggling, at the expense of hurting supporters in order to build an organization that emphasized full-time daily journalism, NABJ got caught in unavoidably sticky dilemmas. It tried to avoid being overrun by "semijournalists," personalities who wrote part-time or occasionally for newspapers but did not have journalism credentials. But the no-full-membership for part-timers rule disqualified many old hands who worked in the black press.

Meanwhile, full-time journalists who were white could be members of NABJ. Although there was no record of whites joining NABJ in the first couple of years, this issue was debated often by the members.

"It's always been curious to me that white journalists can join," said Jeanne Fox 15 years later. "Philosophically, we agreed that that couldn't happen." However, if NABJ had barred whites who wanted to join, it would be guilty of the very discrimination it was fighting.

Mal Johnson was unforgiving. "It was such a racist situation (disqualifying the black part-timers in Houston and white journalism professors who were in sympathy with NABJ's ideals and wanted to be members.) Why would they (members) feel that way and take bucks from *Gannett,* which is white (owned)?"

"Our impolitic decision," said Wickham, "caused a very, very, ugly scene."

The closing conference event, a banquet, had to be scuttled because NABJ decided not to extend full membership to college professors.

In 1979, NABJ President Vernon Jarrett invited Molette to the national conference, but he declined.

McElroy, who has taught journalism for 31 years and is

now publisher of the *Houston Informer,* has not gone back to an NABJ conference or convention but he is involved with the the Houston Association of Black Journalists, the local affiliate.

"I've been told by scores of people that everything was copacetic a long time ago," he said. "It's been procrastination (that he has not gotten involved with the national.)

Chuck Stone in a 1990 interview described the membership conflict in Houston as "normal tensions that occur between personalities."

Molette said that although he was angry at how NABJ defined membership "it was a democratic process.

"The majority won."

Chapter 4

Lord Baltimore

Parliamentarian Allison Davis affectionately described Chuck Stone as a "mad memo writer." He fired streams of correspondence to members and potential members to keep them informed about the fledgling NABJ.

The organization was young and very frail. "Chuck said 'never say die,'" recalled Davis. "And we could have died a thousand deaths."

Said Stone, "In 1976 it was quiet turmoil. We were not fully organized and didn't have a historical memory. Everything was from scratch."

He said there were only about 50 dues-paying members.

Much of the early NABJ business was conducted in Stone's living room in West Philadelphia.

Seven weeks after the 1976 Houston conference, Chuck Stone sent a memo (Nov. 22) to journalists who attended. It was a summary of the conference and future plans of NABJ.

One of the future items, recalled Allison Davis, was consideration of associate membership. This would have allowed journalism professors and public relations people to belong to NABJ. However, since they were not news gatherers, they would not be allowed to vote or hold office.

The decision that denied membership to professors and part-time journalists bruised egos and opened wounds among people working in the black and white press. After Houston, some people vowed not to have anything to do with the new organization.

Albert Fitzpatrick, an editor at the *Akron Beacon Journal,* became active in NABJ in 1976. He said the eligibility dilemma was unavoidable.

Blacks, he said, had a double burden. They formed a journalists' organization and were determined to prove to whites that it upheld high standards. Meanwhile, journalists everywhere faced an identity dilemma. They were debating standards: Was journalism a profession or a craft? This riddle raised questions such as, should professional journalists be licensed? Or, if journalism was not a craft, were reporters not entitled to overtime?

Despite a rocky first conference, NABJ was off and running. Jeanne Fox, then a reporter for the *Kansas City Times,* attended the Houston conference and wanted to be more involved.

The Chuck Stone persona drew her to the organization. Her father, a former Urban League officer and Stone, were friends.

She got her chance in 1976 to do more when regional director Sam Ford, a reporter at WCCO-TV in Minneapolis, accepted a TV news job out of the region. Fox replaced him as regional director.

Region 8 (Missouri, Minnesota, Iowa, Kansas, Nebraska) published a newsletter and black journalists in Kansas City, St. Louis, Minneapolis-St. Paul, Omaha, and Des Moines kept in touch.

Cities in that region also initiated high school journalism workshops and encouraged black school children to enter the field.

The Midwesterners were better organized than a number of their larger and more prestigious East Coast counterparts.

DeWayne Wickham of *The Baltimore Sun,* one of the NABJ founders, had helped Stone, Mal Johnson and Paul Brock with the Houston conference.

"It was not much of a planning committee," Wickham said. "Chuck would call -- It was a straight line from Chuck to Paul to Mal and a dotted line to me.

"I was sort of a go-fer.

"That spring I had taken (U.S. Rep., D-Texas) Barbara Jordan to the correspondents' dinner. I used my contacts to get her to be a keynote speaker at our conference."

The 1977 conference site would be Baltimore, Wickham's hometown. Explained Wickham, "The decision was made after the Houston conference. I offered the idea to Chuck. I just talked to him about it."

Unlike Houston, Baltimore was an Eastern city that was accessible to many members or potential members. It was only a few hours' drive or less from Washington, Philadelphia, New York or Virginia.

The Baltimore Association of Black Media Workers (ABMW), a group that Wickham and others founded in spring 1975, was the host organization. Wickham was conference chairman.

* * *

Power was the element that attracted DeWayne Wickham to journalism.

"I liked the arrogance of power," he said. "I came to believe that journalism is one of the great power centers in this country. It had the power of persuasion and influence over people."

Wickham did not have a clue of what he wanted to be when he was a teen-ager. He grew up in Cherry Hill, the largest housing project in Baltimore. He dropped out of high school, joined the U.S. Air Force and was dispatched to Vietnam in the 1960s. "Not only was I a high school dropout," he said, " I was dumb enough to enlist at the height of the war."

Wickham survived it. He returned home in 1968. He did odd jobs for two years, and then a veteran buddy of his encouraged him to enroll at Community College of Baltimore.

Wickham received good grades on his written essays. Wickham's English teacher told him he had the potential to be a writer. The University of Maryland was recruiting students. When the recruiter looked at Wickham's evaluations, he noticed the part about writing talent. "To the unsophisticated ear," explained Wickham, "'writer' meant 'journalist.'"

Wickham enrolled at the University of Maryland as a journalism major.

He read the writing of Ernest Hemmingway and the inconoclastic Baltimorian H.L. Mencken to excess, Wickham admits. These writers molded Wickham's view of the press as power center.

He had internships, first at the Baltimore *Evening Sun* and then a summer internship in 1973 at the Richmond (Va.) *Times-Dispatch.* After graduating from Maryland in spring 1974 he was hired as a Capitol Hill correspondent for *U.S. News & World Report,* a short time after Jeannye Thornton became the first black person to write for the weekly news magazine.

It was considered a conservative magazine with paternalistic ways. The pay was good. But Wickham and other writers did not receive a byline; their work was anonymous.

After six months Wickham tried to leave. USN&WR editors thought he was unhappy about the pay and gave Wickham a $100 raise. He stayed another six months before taking a job as a local reporter at *The Sun,* in Baltimore.

His new job was a demotion. But he wanted it, he said, because he would get a byline and the persuasive powers that he assumed came with it. Furthermore, he would be working for his hometown newspaper.

Of the Baltimore newspapers, *The Sun,* the morning newspaper, featured a lot of Washington and international news and was considered more prestigious than *The Evening Sun,* which concentrated on local news.

Wickham covered local news and got occasional national assignments, covering major black events like the NAACP or Urban League conventions.

He wrestled with the dilemmas and contradictions that confounded other black journalists working at white newspapers.

"There was a significant amount of pressure we felt trying to practice the craft.

"We had to do more than journalism. Anytime someone had an interest or problem that had to do with the black community, they would come to you.

"At the same time you got tightly locked into an area of coverage that you may not have wanted to do. You were perceived as the 'head nigger in charge' of the newsroom. *The Sun* made me a political reporter, but I covered black politics."

When covering major black events, Wickham said, "In the newsroom you resented it, but you (also) resented not being asked to go. You always wanted to be there. But you wanted to do other things.

"The dilemma was you held on tightly. When I went out of town (to cover a black convention) it guaranteed that I would be on (page) A-1.

"Only once in three years did I get on A-1 locally."

Wickham tried to resolve the schizoid dilemma of the black journalist through his activities in NABJ and the Association of Black Media Workers (ABMW).

"Why organize?, " he said. "It was a basic need for survival. It was hard being the only one."

By organizing journalists as a force, it was believed, there could be opportunities for a number of blacks to work at each newspaper in a number of roles, not just as the designated black obligated to cover what was deemed black news.

* * *

The conference hotel was the Lord Baltimore.

Wickham and ABMW colleagues made hotel arrangements, lined up speakers and arranged the workshops. Chuck Stone and Mal Johnson wanted to keep their hands in the planning. Wickham complained that they were meddling, recalled Jeanne Fox.

At the January 1977 NABJ board meeting in Philadelphia, Stone accused Brock of being uncooperative.

Jeanne Fox said the conflict caught her and other board members by surprise.

Stone explained: "Paul and I developed tensions. He wanted to report to the board, I wanted him to report to me. I tendered my resignation to the board, but they refused to accept it." Stone and Brock coexisted uneasily.

One of the first things Wickham learned about conference planning was its problems.

He said, "We had no credit. So everything at the hotel required significant deposits in advance."

In Houston, many activities were on the university campus. The Texas Southern journalism professors who participated got much of it underwritten. But in Baltimore, the hotel demanded significant deposits in advance. The hotel expected the bill for large meal functions in the ballroom to be paid up front.

Wickham did not remember anything being underwritten or sponsored. All costs would be drawn from conference registration fees. Those receipts would not be available until the end of the conference.

Wickham called Jim McLean and asked for help. McLean was owner of Four Seas and Seven Winds travel agency in Baltimore. Wickham had arranged for him to be the conference travel agent.

McLean agreed to pay the up-front hotel expenses if NABJ promised to repay all expenses when the conference was over.

Linda Waller, a young reporter finishing her first year at *Gannett Westchester* (County, N.Y.) *Newspapers,* remembered the Lord Baltimore as "an old ratty place." Gayle Pollard of *The Miami Herald* remembered it differently. It was a "real nice, fancy hotel."

At least people agreed that the hotel was old.

It rained for most of the weekend, Pollard said.

Waller was representative of the scores of recently hired, young black journalists who flocked to the conference.

"We got more (people) than we anticipated," recalled Jacqueline McLean, executive vice president of Four Winds and Seven Seas travel agency. She said NABJers took up every room in the Lord Baltimore. Spillover guests were sent to the old Hilton Hotel.

Conference attendance was about 300 people, which was double the previous year's turnout.

Waller's news organization sent her to the conference with two other young journalists from the Mount Kisco and

White Plains bureaus.

Gannett Rochester (N.Y.) *Newspapers* -- the *Democrat & Chronicle and Times-Union* -- paid the expenses of eight people. The group included Charles Moses, Phil Dixon and Gregory Morris.

Michael Days was with the Rochester group. Months earlier when he was an intern reporter at the Minneapolis *Star-Tribune,* the notice about the conference came to the office.

The newspaper decided to send one person. Days drew straws with Carl Griffiths and George White. Days won.

"What was so incredible," he explained, "was there were so few people in *so many* places working one or two years."

Rodney Brooks was one of them. He worked at the *Ithaca Journal* in Upstate New York. He said he asked around to find an organization of black journalists. Brooks found out about the Baltimore conference.

In Baltimore, Mike Days had a chance to meet black journalists he didn't get a chance to meet in his city -- Minneapolis TV journalists Kate Williams and Carolyn Tyler and newspaper reporter Denise Johnson of the St. Paul *Pioneer Press & Dispatch.*

Angela Dodson, a *Gannett News Service* regional reporter in Washington, received notice in the mail and decided to go.

At the conference she remembers meeting Denise Johnson of St. Paul, Garland Thompson of *The Philadelphia Inquirer* and sportswriter Ron Thomas of the *Chicago Daily News.*

Ron Thomas said he went to Baltimore not knowing much about NABJ. But he suspected that his newspaper was about to fold. He went job hunting.

He had no hotel reservation and he remembered sleeping on the floor in Francis Ward's hotel room. Thomas was right about the *Daily News'* fate. It closed in spring 1978. He went to the *San Francisco Chronicle.*

Dodson met Mervin Aubespin of *The Courier-Journal* in Louisville. He introduced her to his boss, Chris Waddle.

The encounter became an indirect path to working at *The Courier-Journal* a few years later. The editors were attracted to her knowledge of the coal industry and of the region. Dodson grew up in Western Pennsylvania and West Virginia, which is next door to Kentucky.

William W. Sutton Jr., 21, had just graduated from Hampton Institute. He was working as an intern reporter at the *Courier-Post* in Camden /Cherry Hill, N.J.

"It felt very comfortable to see so many black journalists -- reporters, a couple of editors and columnists," he said. "There didn't seem to be too many people my age. I seemed out of the ballpark."

Most of the people were about 25 and had three- to five-years' newsroom experience. Then there was another, more experienced group, the founders like Chuck Stone, Vernon Jarrett and Acel Moore. Sutton said he was in awe of their accomplishments. They had been in the field 15 years or more.

Of the twenty-something crowd Sutton said: "What was striking was there were experienced young people and I was really excited. For example, Les Payne and Gayle Pollard. I was comfortable to be among so many people. But I was not an insider. I had never been in an organization quite like that."

Actually, Les Payne was older -- late 30s -- than the bloc of journalists Sutton described. And Payne made quite an impression on younger journalists.

Payne had recently returned from South Africa, where he filed dispatches as a *Newsday* correspondent.

He wrote about the 1976 Soweto massacre, where black South African children demonstrating against Bantu education were slaughtered by Afrikaaners. Such atrocities revived the stalled anti-apartheid movement.

Payne encouraged Sutton to abandon plans to go to graduate school and continue working in newspapers. He needed journalism experience, Payne advised.

Sutton said "I came back to the *Courier-Post* and from the combination of NABJ and Bob Dubil (executive editor of the paper) I decided to nix a full scholarship (to the

University of Michigan's graduate journalism program), nix my love interest, who was going to Michigan Law School, and stay at the *Courier-Post.* I got active in the ABJ (Philadelphia.)."

Reginald Stuart, at that time a reporter with *The New York Times,* recalled the conference this way: "A lot of people were there, several hundred, at an old antiquated hotel, the Lord Baltimore. A lot of good workshops, far less flash and fanfare (compared to what conventions would become a decade later); lots of camaraderie. We didn't have any fashion show or fashion statements."

The funniest thing he remembered occurred at the Saturday night banquet. Benjamin Hooks, member of the Federal Communication Commission and executive director-designate of the NAACP, was the keynote speaker.

He spoke about the importance of black journalists in American society. Hooks, a (Baptist) minister and fiery speaker, moved the crowd.

Stuart thought it was odd that he inspired the audience by quoting Ida B. Wells and Frederick Douglass first and saved the last word to quote Winston Churchill. "I thought, 'damn, he quotes Ida Wells and Frederick Douglass and he ends with the Churchill quote.'"

The reason the speech had such a sharp transition, said Les Payne of *Newsday,* was because Vernon Jarrett rewrote it.

Hooks gave a standard speech that quoted Winston Churchill's "dark hour" address at length. Payne said he had heard this speech at least five times.

Vernon Jarrett, a *Chicago Tribune* columnist and a friend, talked Hooks out of giving that kind of speech. Jarrett did not think it would move the black journalists. According to Payne, Jarrett substituted the beginning of Hooks' speech with his (Jarrett's) standard speech that quoted Frederick Douglass and Ida Wells. He let Hooks finish with a rousing reference to Churchill.

Vernon Jarrett recalls what happened this way:

Hooks was in a room with Chuck Stone and someone named Higgins. "We were giving him (Hooks) bits and pieces of what would be germane to journalists," said Jarrett. "He was putting his speech together while he was dressing.

"He wanted to know some of the challenges to get black journalists to understand their leadership role.

"I told him to mention (William) Monroe Trotter. I've helped a lot of people with speeches.

"Ben is an excellent extemporaneous speaker." Hooks incorporated the suggestions into his speech.

Stuart wrote an article for *The New York Times* about the conference. He says it was one of the first stories to appear in a national publication about NABJ and what the organization was trying to achieve."I quoted A.M. Rosenthal (executive editor of *The Times*) and Ben Bradlee (executive editor of *The Washington Post*) on what their commitment was (to bringing more black journalists into the ranks.)

"My editor had a terrible time getting the story through all the hoops. Rosenthal wanted to see what Bradlee said (so he could match his statements with Bradlee's). I was strongly opposed to that."

The article appeared on page 15 of the business section, Section D. It had a July 31 dateline from Baltimore but it was published three days after the conference on Wednesday, August 3.

Stuart wrote that the drive to bring more blacks into newsrooms had lost steam. Editors lost interest in recruiting minorities or claimed that they could not find enough qualified ones.

A new phenomenon emerging was many editors were more eager to hire white women than blacks.

"It's pretty easy to find women because there are more qualified women available," said Kurt Luedtke, then executive editor of *The Detroit Free Press*.

Bradlee of *The Post* said "We've doubled the percentage (of black journalists) in the past 10 years. But it's still only 10 percent."

Bradlee said of 345 news professionals at his newspaper, 34 were blacks and 75 were women. In 1972 there were 18 blacks and 43 women.

Rosenthal of *The Times* was quoted as saying "We have an affirmative action plan and we take it very seriously."

The general counsel of *The New York Times* said 50 minority employees were on the professional staff of 720 at the end of 1976 compared with 26 minority members out of 637 people in 1972.

Industrywide, despite several hundred blacks entering daily journalism in about 10 years, they only represented 1 percent of 40,000 daily newsroom journalists.

In broadcasting, the Federal Communications Commission reported that out of 34,200 professionals, 7.1 percent were black.

Broadcast professionals included people beyond the newsroom, such as technicians and engineers.

More black students were majoring in journalism. According to an Ohio State University study, from 1973 to 1976, there was a 90-percent increase in the number of black men and women declaring journalism as an undergraduate or graduate school major.

There were 2,672 black journalism students in 1976, up from 1,407.

However, the increase in total journalism enrollment was only 4.1 percent, up from 2 percent. More work and agitating for change was necessary.

Reginald Stuart was young; he was 28 years old. But Michael Days, then an intern reporter, remembered him as one of the "old pros" looked up to by many younger journalists. Stuart had been in the business seven years. His career began at *The Tennessean* in Nashville, his hometown.

When very young, Stuart says he instinctively turned to journalism.

"I liked to tell people things," he explained. When he was 10 years old, he published his own weekly newspaper, a one-page sheet printed on a hectograph machine, a metal tray with a rubbery gelatin. He called it *The Neighborhood Times*.

Stuart's aunt found a printer who printed the papers for $1.25. Young Stuart peddled his paper for about three years and closed it when he became very ill. He was able to return advertising money he collected and still clear a $20 profit.

Stuart worked as a high school correspondent for the *Nashville Banner.* He went to Tennessee State University and graduated in 1968 with a degree in sociology. Stuart was interested in being a social worker. He got discouraged, however, when he found out that a cousin who was in that field in New York City was on welfare.

Furthermore, Stuart said he realized that he could not make a profound difference as a social worker. He would not feel the personal satisfaction of effecting change.

One night, Stuart walked to the *Tennessean* to seek work. The managing editor remembered him as the boy who once sold *The Neighborhood Times.*

"Fill out this application," he said.

Three days later Stuart got a call; he began working at the newspaper in June 1968.

Stuart was a rookie with a capital "R", he recalled. "I literally had to learn on the job. They could tell whether you had writing instinct or if you could take it when you got knocked down."

Years later in 1977, Stuart held forth with slightly younger journalists who sought him out and were eager to learn from a seasoned newsman.

The conferees at Baltimore enjoyed the comradery and the chance to compare notes. There were workshops on Southern Africa, media employment and advancement, covering education, criminal justice, health care, and, how to cope in the newsroom.

There was a workshop on covering the black community. The participants debated strategies on how to convince white editors and news directors to cover stories that involved black people.

In the late '70s, a lot of white news managers assumed blacks no longer were "good copy" like they were in the turbulent '60s.

Panelist Gayle Pollard described story suggestions that were dismissed by editors with "we did that in 1969."

The workshop emphasized that black reporters had a responsibility to see that their news organizations covered the
black community. This was not limited to black reporters
writing the stories. It also meant habitually suggesting story
ideas; critiquing stories about blacks in memos, or constantly reminding news managers of their duty to cover the entire community.

Acel Moore of *The Philadelphia Inquirer* was honored
with NABJ's first Ida B. Wells award. Moore won the Puli-
tizer Prize in 1977.

On Friday night, a crab feast for the NABJers was held
in the Inner Harbor. People sat at picnic tables with little
mallets and cracked crabs as they drank beer provided by
Budweiser.

Many conferees were unaware of the political struggle
among the officers. Chuck Stone wanted to be president for
another year. The NABJ constitution allowed its president
to serve a one-year term and not succeed himself. However,
the previous year in Houston, Stone convinced members to
suspend the rules to allow him and the entire board of directors to serve another year. The board needed more time
to get NABJ functioning. The members agreed.

At the Baltimore conference, Stone again asked the
board to suspend the rules and the election of officers.
Wickham objected.

Wickham asked, "Why have a constitution that pre-
scribes a term of office, but then we constantly suspend the
rules?"

Wickham and Stone got into a violent argument. Stone
berated Wickham and accused him of using the conference
to promote DeWayne Wickham.

Stone suspected that Wickham was eager to become the
next NABJ president.

"He (Wickham) was nakedly ambitious," said Stone in a
1991 interview.

"I was accused of having presidential ambitions," recalled Wickham.

"I just didn't think it was right. People were working very
hard to make it (NABJ) happen. Somewhere down the line
I wanted a shot at one of these jobs. But I couldn't if we

kept suspending the rules."

Joe Davidson, a *Philadelphia Bulletin* reporter at the time and the Region 3 director (Pennsylvania and Delaware), remembered that Stone's argument with Wickham was so intense, both men appeared ready to throw blows.

The board meeting ended and the officers split into regional caucuses. They would decide whether to hold an election or extend the term of the current board.

The Philadelphia delegation was about 40 members strong and probably the largest bloc at the conference. Many of them decided to pre-empt Stone's NABJ ambitions. Acel Moore was president of the Association of Black Journalists of Philadelphia. He told members it would be wrong to change the bylaws. It could allow NABJ to be controlled by one person or group.

Furthermore, Stone did not come to the local group before the national conference and make a case for extending his presidential term.

On principle, said Moore, the ABJ could not back Stone. The bylaws were clear.

"It was not pleasant," said Davidson. As the regional representative in Stone's home base, Davidson participated in the ouster.

"The way we worked that was not right. I told Chuck that afterwards.

"Chuck had to go. But we didn't deal with him correctly because we didn't deal on principle. It was personality-driven."

Stone charmed many people. But he also made many enemies.

Stone treated his black Philadelphia journalist colleagues duplicitously. There was the militant, pro-black Stone. Having the energy and courage to establish NABJ was evident. But his other side, a "Jeckielcal side" as Reginald Bryant described it, pandered to white news executives at the *Philadelphia Daily News,* or to the media generally. That attitude was "I'm not like those other Negroes."

Chuck Stone was rejected for two reasons, said Reginald Bryant, "Many members could not conceive of having his leadership indefinitely, and it would set a bad precedent.

"Chuck seemed to be not just angered, but he removed himself from participation."

Bulletin reporter Elmer Smith said the Philadelphia journalists met in a hotel room and decided to draft Vernon Jarrett of *The Chicago Tribune* for the president instead of favorite son Stone.

Tyree Johnson, a *Philadelphia Daily News* reporter, was in Stone's corner. "I tried not to get involved in the politics," he said. "But with Chuck being a co-worker, I was going with him."

Stone, however, did not have many supporters like Johnson. Stone was not present when the Philadelphians voted against him.

When Stone found out, Wickham's recollection was that Stone exacted two commitments from NABJ officers: That Vernon Jarrett would be president and that DeWayne Wickham would not get support for any national office.

John White of *The Washington Star* remembers that the Lord Baltimore Hotel was rife with rumors from the Saturday night banquet into Sunday morning then afternoon when the business meeting and elections took place. Having the business meeting shortly after noon when many people were checking out of the the hotel and heading home made the atmosphere more chaotic.

"It was a tense meeting," said Sarah-Ann Shaw of WBZ-TV and Region 1 director (New England). "A lot of people had left. Some were asking whether there was a quorum."

People had conflicting interpretations of the NABJ constitution and bylaws and the role of officers such as regional directors or the president.

Wickham did have presidential ambitions. Les Payne said he talked Wickham out of running. The young organization needed an elder at the top, Payne told him.

Jeanne Fox said that Wickham was hoping that people would step forward and praise him for organizing a good conference and then nominate him. Such a scenario did not materialize.

Instead, Wickham was nominated for vice president. He

was defeated.

Vernon Jarrett became president with no opposition.

He called his nomination a "pure draft" because he did not seek the presidency; a coalition of Philadelphians and other journalists from around the country asked him to serve.

Jarrett's news experience spanned 30 years. He began in the black press as a reporter for the *Associated Negro Press* and later the *Chicago Defender*.

When he was elected NABJ president Jarrett was a triple threat: A columnist for *The Chicago Tribune,* a radio personality and a TV journalist.

Jarrett was aware of the acrimony between Stone and the Philadelphians. "Chuck and I were friends for a long time," he said. They met in 1950 when Jarrett was with the *Chicago Globe,* a new black newspaper. Stone had just completed his masters degree at the University of Chicago. Jarrett said he got Stone his first writing job as a free-lancer.

"Whatever happened," at the caucuses in Baltimore, said Jarrett, "didn't affect my relationship with him. "It never reached the point of a showdown."

There were some changes among other nationally elected officers. Allison Davis of WBZ-TV, the former parliamentarian, was elected vice president. The new parliamentarian was Roger Clendening of the *St. Petersburg Times.* Linda Lockhart of the *St. Louis Post Dispatch* was the new secretary.

Some people conspired to oust Mal Johnson from the treasurer's post.

Jeanne Fox called Mal "crotchety and uncooperative."

Sarah-Ann Shaw called Mal "tart-tongued," but for good reasons.

"As treasurer she felt personally responsible," explained Shaw. "She wouldn't let anyone handle the money. She felt her integrity was at stake."

Mal Johnson made no apologies. She said that "everyone in the organization was on an ego trip.

"None of them wanted to participate as leaders and do the work.

"I had most of the burden of the organization.

"I didn't care about being appreciated. I did care about their dedication. Some of them only wanted to chase the girls."

Fox and Gayle Pollard encouraged Elaine Leaphart, a University of Michigan classmate, to run for treasurer. Leaphart worked for KQV, an all-news radio station in Pittsburgh. Leaphart won the election.

Annoyed, Mal Johnson left Baltimore before the post-conference board meeting. She took NABJ's checkbook with her.

The bills were due. Travel agent Jim McLean, who pre-paid several thousand dollars worth of hotel bills, wanted to be reimbursed.

"Where is the money?" McLean asked Wickham. Weeks passed. No check was sent to McLean.

Paul Brock raised questions about items on the bill that he thought may have been exorbitant or unnecessary.

Said Chuck Stone in 1991: "Did I clash with DeWayne? Yes, over money. Did Mal tell you about his expenses? We had some horrendous expenses that were charged to the organization that were not authorized. We got these bills -- Mal didn't mention this to you?

"We had big expenses at the hotel. Vince Sanders was good on this. He said we had a moral obligation to pay it. It damn near depleted our treasury."

Out of patience, McLean threatened to sue Wickham in order to get his money. Jim McLean was eventually paid.

Many years later Jackie McLean, Jim's wife and business partner, said with a laugh, "obviously we got it, because we still talk to DeWayne."

Monte Trammer replaced DeWayne Wickham as Region 4 director (Md., Washington, D.C., Va. and W. Va.). Trammer was a new *Baltimore Sun* reporter and ABMW member who helped host the conference.

He coordinated a couple of workshops then left the conference each day to cover his beat in Towson, Md., 12 miles from Baltimore.

Trammer didn't think of asking his editors for a couple of

days off to work on the conference. He worked 'round the clock.

Trammer's first duty as regional director was to go to the fall 1977 board meeting and get McLean's money from Mal Johnson.

Trammer also collected a $500 check that was owed to the Association of Black Media Workers. It was reimbursement for ABMW funds that were spent to host the national conference.

Mal Johnson was back in the treasurer's seat. Elaine Leaphart had to give up the position. Her husband had a military obligation to go to Europe. She went with him.

It was deja vu for Mal Johnson. Again, she was appointed to replace an elected treasurer who left for Europe. Claudia Polley did it the first time.

DeWayne Wickham, loser of a national election and wounded by the bruising confrontation with his mentor Chuck Stone, became less active in NABJ affairs. He stayed away for several years.

Chuck Stone, the man who combined personal charisma with an orderly, structured vision that created NABJ, after years of false starts by many black journalists, bailed out almost completely.

In a 1991 interview, Stone said he stopped participating for several reasons. He decided not to break his vacation to go to NABJ conferences.

Furthermore, he stopped going to *all* conferences (i.e. political ones) because they lost their relevance.

In Stone's view, it was time for the old heads of NABJ to bow out and let the young members guide it.

Stone distanced himself from NABJ with two exceptions:

• He attended the 10th anniversary convention in 1985 in Baltimore, the venue where he vacated the presidency eight years earlier.

• In 1988, he wrote a critique of journalism education and participated in an NABJ seminar called "Kerner Plus 20."

While Stone bailed out of NABJ activities, he got into a bruising fight in Philadelphia with fellow NABJ founders Reginald Bryant and Acel Moore over control of a TV show.

Bryant and Moore were co-producers of "Black Perspective on the News." It began in the early 1970s as a local show on Public Broadcasting System (PBS) affiliate WHYY-TV, Philadelphia. From 1974 to 1978 the show went national on PBS and aired in 160 cities.

The public affairs show was revolutionary for its time.

Instead of black journalists interviewing only black sources, the producers invited white newsmakers too.

Rep. Claude Pepper, D-Fla., an advocate for the elderly, was invited and questioned about Social Security so that black older folks could get a clear explanation on what they were entitled to.

The head of the Miss America pageant was put on the hot seat to explain why African-American women were barred from competing.

"Every time Acel and I went to a city for 'Black Perspective on the News,'" explained Bryant, "we met a journalist we could use on the show. Places like Minnesota and Alabama."

When a dispute between WHYY general manager James Carrion, Bryant and Moore developed, so did the blood feud between Stone, Bryant and Moore.

Bryant explained: "Our relationship with PBS was very positive. But it was clear that Carrion's disposition toward the program was antithetical.

"Mr. Carrion made a statement, that kind of program had its day. It's time for 'Greek Perspective on the News.'"

"The joke wasn't funny, but prophetic.

"We did a program -- the 140th show -- with Nazi Frank Collin and Ku Klux Klansman David Duke. *Philadelphia Daily News* reporter Kitty Caparella saw the opening. We used a clip from 'Birth of a Nation.' She wrote a story two weeks before the opening.

"A furor developed. Jewish Americans took exception that we had them (Duke and Collin). They asked to see the program before it aired.

"It wasn't for them to decide. You would have thought the general manager would have been supportive. No, it was Carrion's chance to grandstand. The g.m. said parts of the show were objectionable."

A schism grew. Some stations wouldn't take it. Sixty-five stations, less than half of the stations that normally broadcast "Black Perspective" did show it.

The no-shows included WNET-TV in New York City and stations in New Jersey and St. Louis.

Bryant received death threats. Pig's blood was splattered on his house.

The Association of Black Journalists in Philadelphia re-acted.

It pledged that the pressure applied to "Black Perspective on the News" was an attack on all its members.

"No one would step up to fill our spots," said Reginald Bryant.

"Except, Chuck Stone.

"Chuck Stone was a meglomaniac," Bryant said. "The feud was one-sided. Chuck did negative things that affected me and my writing career. Chuck demeaned Acel about winning his Pulitzer. He (Chuck) went around the news-room suggesting that he (Acel) didn't write it. Chuck's de-meanor was duplicitous.

"I respect him for his brain but I take exception to his ab-solute missing of the mark. He's more prosaic than factual."

Thus, in 1979, Stone began running the show under a new name, "Other Voices." Bryant had registered the name "Black Perspective on the News" in 1974 and it could not be used without his permission.

"Other Voices" was canceled a few months later in 1979.

In a June 17, 1991 interview, Chuck Stone explained the situation as he remembered it:

DeWayne Wickham, said Stone, "did a hell of a job (put-ting on the Baltimore conference.)

"But we had to come to grips with what do we do now?

"Do you re-elect me as president for a third term?

"The biggest opposition to me was from Philadelphia. Reggie Bryant and I had some differences of opinion over "Black Persepctive on the News" and a few other things.

"So Reggie and Joe Davidson and Acel Moore got together and put this two-year thing to me. That was the Philadelphia plan.

"That was good. I didn't care. The point is when people came to me and asked if I was going to run for re-election, I said I didn't know. I didn't want to do anything that was going to hamper the organization. I didn't think the organization could take me for a third term. Nor should it.

"I stayed away. I didn't go to the (caucus) meeting. I did it deliberately to allow the organization to make a decision independent of me. And it did."

Chapter 5
Jimmy Carter

Vernon Jarrett, the second NABJ president, sacrificed a lot of time and personal funds in order to travel around the country, promote NABJ and encourage people to join.

He got involved with the American Society of Newspaper Editors. (ASNE) Ten years had passed since the Kerner Commission report.

In Kerner's section on the media, it scolded white news organizations for being "woefully backward in hiring, training and promoting" people of color. The commission strongly recommended that news organizations integrate their shops.

ASNE had a minorities committee that was supposed to be tracking the progress of blacks entering the newspaper business. But in the mid '70s the committee became inactive because editors lost interest.

Jay T. Harris, a news executive at *Knight-Ridder,* explained: "In spring 1977 Gene (Eugene) Patterson, editor of *The St. Petersburg Times* and president of ASNE, asked Rich Smyser to look at coverage 10 years after Kerner. I was at Northwestern (Medill School of Journalism.) He asked me to do staff work for the committee.

"In September 1977 there was a two-day conference sponsored by the Ford Foundation and the *Gannett* Urban Journalism Center. Vernon Jarrett was there, and a number of NABJ leaders."

(The editorial seminar, held at the United Nations Sept. 26 and 27, had 130 participants representing the American Society of Newspaper Editors, National Conference of Editorial Writers, American Society of Magazine Editors and about 20 NABJ members.)

This linkage was significant. It was one of the first times NABJ connected with a predominately white journalism organziation to work toward desegregating daily mainstream journalism.

At the conference, initial results were presented and there was a two-day discussion. The following spring, April 1978, final results of the employment survey were released.

The report, Minority Employment in Daily Newspapers, prepared by Jay T. Harris of the Frank E. Gannett Journalism Center, Medill School of Journalism, Northwestern University, said that:

Based on responses from 59 percent of 1,760 daily newspapers, in a decade, the proportion of newspapers employing minority journalists increased from 20 percent to 32 percent.

There were about 400 minority journalists in 1968; a decade later, 1,700. However, the sharp increases only increased minority newsroom employment in the United States to 4 percent.

Black journalists were 2 percent of all newsroom employees. (and 11 percent of the general population).

Note: In 1972, ASNE conducted what was believed to be the first census of black journalists working at daily newspapers. The survey counted 250 black men and women journalists, based on the newpapers that responded.

At least 17 percent of the American population then was comprised of people who were black, Hispanic or of Asian descent.

A trouble spot was that 38 percent of the minority journalists indentified in the survey were employed by 34 U.S. newspapers.

That meant that a significant amount of the few minority journalists in the business were concentrated at only 2 percent of the daily newspapers. This was the most glaring finding of how segregated the industry was.

Most of these papers were the largest in the country, places where experienced journalists peak and finish their careers. These were not normal starting places for young or inexperienced journalists.

Daily newspapering is a farm team establishment, much like professional baseball. Many journalists mastered their craft at small- and medium-size newspapers before advancing to the big time. Broadcast journalism often applied those rules, too.

A lot of black journalists were starting in the big time where there was a higher risk of failure if they were poorly prepared or not nurtured.

Smaller newspapers were reluctant to hire minorities and many minorities did not realize the value of small- and medium-size communities.

In April 1978, the ASNE board voted unanimously to adopt a resolution on minority employment.

It included this language:

"Leaders among minority journalists have urged the industry to set a goal of minority employment by the year 2000 equivalent to the percentage of minority persons within the national population. The (ASNE Minorities) Committee believes this is a fair and attainable goal. Indeed, it will be the objective of the ASNE to achieve this goal earlier than the year 2000."

Jay Harris conducted the ASNE minority employment survey or census for the next five years (1978-83).

In early 1978 Vernon Jarrett served on the original committee of three major news organizations created to promote the integration of blacks into the total editorial process. The committee had representatives from NABJ, the National Conference of Editorial Writers and the National Broadcast Editorial Association.

In April 1978 the NABJ board held its business meeting in New York City. The officers were also guests of the United Nations for a day. They toured the facilities and went to a reception with Coretta Scott King, the widow of Martin Luther King Jr.

Representatives from African nations briefed the group. This was the NABJ board's first official plunge into international affairs.

*   *   *

At the Baltimore conference, the board of directors had agreed that it would seek a meeting with President Carter at the White House.

"Knowing Jimmy and Rosalyn Carter well, I didn't have a hard time setting it up," said Mal Johnson, who was Cox Broadcasting's White House correspondent. She and Paul Brock made the arrangements with the White House staff.

The date was set for NABJ's first and only meeting with a U.S. president: Feb. 16, 1978. They were part of a 29-member group of people from national black press groups. The others were officers from the National Newspaper Publishers Association (NNPA), the organization of publishers of black-owned newspapers, and the National Organization of Black-Owned Broadcasting, a new organization.

Twelve of the 15 NABJ officers came. Many, like Jarrett and Joe Davidson and Monte Trammer, paid their own way. Paul Brock participated.

It was a full day of tours and visits and briefings with cabinet officials. Eleanor Holmes Norton, the Equal Employment Opportunity commissioner, and Ernest Green, assistant secretary for employment and training for the Department of Labor, spoke to the group.

Patricia Roberts Harris, secretary of the Department of Housing and Urban Development (HUD), invited the group to her office. Lunch was served. According to Linda Lockhart, Mal Johnson told them that Roberts-Harris' cordiality was special because she was not known to break bread with black journalists.

There was a photo session and each visitor shook hands with President Carter as the official White House photographer took pictures.

For the 30-minute meeting with Carter, the journalists and publishers sat two rows deep around the oval table in the Cabinet room.

The night before, the NABJ officers caucused in Vernon

Jarrett's hotel room. For their rare opportunity to interview the president of the United States, they debated what would be the most relevant questions to ask.

Many questions, recalled NABJ secretary Lockhart, would be civil rights-related.

Joe Davidson recalled a stark difference between what NABJ colleagues asked and what the publishers asked the president.

"We (the NABJers) were asking journalistic questions. The publishers asked questions like 'When are you (Carter) going to visit my city,' like a chamber of commerce.

"There was a clear distinction between black journalists (who worked for white media) and the publishers. Some of us approached the meeting as an opportunity to ask hard questions. There were a lot of inconsistencies in the Carter administration. The NNPA people (seemed to be happy) to be there." Mal Johnson agreed with Davidson that the journalists were asking good public policy questions.

Then, Calvin Rolark, publisher of the Washington (D.C.) *Informer,* a black weekly, broke the flow.

"Mr. President," he asked, "why don't you buy an ad in my newspapers?"

Carter was stunned by the question.

"Well," the president said, "that's not my job."

"We're running out of time" said Press Secretary Jody Powell.

The session ended.

Roger Clendening, a *St. Petersburg Times* reporter and NABJ parliamentarian, remembered the event: "It was kind of exciting for me, getting that opportunity, having grown up in the projects in New York. I wrote one story out of the news conference and made a lot of contacts. It gave the organization quite a lot of exposure."

Allison Davis, the WBZ-TV writer/producer and NABJ vice president, remembered the menu: Coca-Cola and ham sandwiches with a bowl of potato chips.

"Two days before the meeting," she said "we had the worst snowstorm of the century." The Northeast was buried with about 20 inches.

"It was the first time that NABJ was a legitimate organization to a lot of large corporate media outlets," Davis said. "I was at Westinghouse Broadcasting (WBZ). To get a letter from the White House was a turning point in my career. The president seemingly legitimized our organization. I found it a big boost.

"President Carter didn't spend a lot of time with us. He brought in a lot of blacks dealing with minority concerns.

"The president saw us (NABJ and NNPA people) as all the same. I never got the impression that the White House understood the distinction or they wouldn't have invited us together.

"Frankly it was just a ceremony, but significant for legitimizing the organization in the eyes of white folks."

*   *   *

The third annual national conference was in Jarrett's town, Chicago, Aug. 24-27. Like the previous summer, the conferees stayed in an aging downtown hotel, the Pick-Congress on South Michigan Avenue.

Attendance grew substantially. Linda Lockhart said turnout was about double the Baltimore conference, which could have meant about 500 people.

About 300 NABJers took a tour of Johnson Publishing Co. headquarters where *Ebony* and *Jet* magazines were produced. "I never thought I would live to see this many black journalists in one room," publisher John H. Johnson said happily. However, he noted soberly that "we still have a long, long way to go," before equity is achieved in the communications industry. Some encouraging news that month was the promotion of Robert McGruder of the *Cleveland Plain Dealer* to city editor. He became only the 12th black person nationally holding a position as a newsroom supervisor or executive at a daily newspaper.

Federal Judge Leon Higginbotham addressed the conferees. He was author of *In the Matter of Color: Race and the American Legal Process*.

Andrew Young, U.S. Representative to the United

Nations, addressed the NABJers. The previous month he caused a flap when he said that there were perhaps "hundreds of political prisoners" in U.S. prisons when asked about oppression in the Soviet Union.

Young apparently was thinking of the Rev. Ben Chavis and nine other defendants in North Carolina called the Wilmington 10, when he made his "political prisioners" remark.

Conservatives and hawks wanted Young fired.

In his *Chicago Tribune* column "Young faces black journalists," Jarrett wrote: "While these black journalists are not antagonistic toward Young as so many of their white peers appear to be, they did not hesitate to question him sharply about his long praise of the Carter administration."

Some of the questions were:

"Why did you not vote for sanctions against South Africa in the U.N.?

"Why dosen't President Carter do something about the Wilmington 10 if he's interested in human rights around the world?

"Mr. Ambassador, would you comment on U.S. policy toward Zaire and (President) Mobutu."

"Most of the standing-room-only audience," said Jarrett "were highly sympathetic and held a very high regard for Ambassador Young. He received a long and loud standing ovation before he spoke, and despite what several people considered his lengthy defense of the Carter administration, he was cheered as he left the ballroom.

"The point to remember however, is that these journalists did not permit their respect for him to curb their insistence on accountability."

Another major speaker at the conference was John Reinhardt. He was then director of the U.S. Information Agency, former assistant secretary of state for public affairs and former ambassador to Nigeria.

Ovie Carter of *The Chicago Tribune,* a 1975 Pulitzer Prize winner for international reporting, was honored.

Jeanne Fox called the Chicago conference Jarrett's triumph. He sparred with antagonistic whites who ques-

tioned why black journalists were meeting and organizing.
"Is it a black separatist outfit? Is our (NABJ's) purpose to
'give whitey a hard time' they asked.

"Probably the best answer to our critics," replied Jarrett
"is that we do not define racial integration to mean the ex-
tinction of blacks either biologically, culturally or spiritual-
ly. We are a people with a heritage that should not be blot-
ted out. There is nothing racist or separatist about that."

* * *

John White of Baltimore affectionately called Vernon
Jarrett an "amateur historian." Throughout his career, Jarrett urged black journalists to document current events and
become the scholars who can inform and enlighten large
numbers of people.

What Jarrett and NABJ officers did accomplish in two
years was:

• A meeting with President Carter;

• A visit with U.N. officials, making NABJ's interest in
international affairs known;

• Starting its first joint project with leaders of white-
controlled journalism organizations, and,

• Putting on a successful annual conference that attracted
more people to NABJ.

Chapter 6
K.C. Blues

Jeanne Fox recalls Acel Moore encouraging her to run for national office at the Baltimore conference in 1977.

She declined. Fox preferred to concentrate on being regional director in the Midwest. St. Louis, and Kansas City, where Fox worked then, separated by 200 miles, were especially active.

Jeanne Fox was born in St. Louis but she lived in Washington, D.C., Minneapolis, and Madrid, Spain, where she went to high school. Her father worked for the Urban League and the U.S. State Department. He helped recruit blacks for the foreign service.

Fox went to the University of Michigan, not sure of what she wanted to do for a career. She worked for the school newspaper and the black student magazine, and as an editorial assistant for the American Automobile Association (AAA). "I enjoyed the comradeship and the work," she said. "I decided to pursue it."

Fox became a reporter at the *Kansas City Times.* In early 1976, she learned about the founding NABJ meeting in Washington. Her family was living in the District of Columbia. "I was really interested and wanted to be involved. I contacted Chuck Stone." She joined and offered her services. Fox's first involvement was attending the 1976 Houston conference.

TV journalist Sam Ford of WCCO-News in Minneapolis was then Midwest regional director. Ford left for a job in New York and Fox succeeded him.

The board picked Kansas City to be the 1979 conference

site on Aug. 9. It was to follow the Chicago conference in 1978, based on the organizational strength of the region.

Fox arranged for the hotel and put together the program. Minutes show that Bobby (Bob) Reid was conference co-chairman.

Members in Region 8 had a lot of energy. At NABJ's founding meeting in December 1975, a charge from the members to its regional directors was to stage regional conferences.

Region 8's rep, Sam Ford, was the only one who took it literally.

After talking to Jeanne Fox, Ford and about 10 Twin Cities-area journalists got together for a meeting with other Midwest-area journalists at the Meulbach Hotel in Kansas City in December 1976.

Meanwhile in St. Louis, journalists Gerald Boyd, George Curry, Linda Lockhart and Sheila Rule, all of the *St. Louis Post-Dispatch,* organized a chapter and ran a high school journalism workshop.

Kansas City had its local organization, the Kansas City Association of Black Journalists.

According to at least a half-dozen people, the Kansas City Association of Black Journalists was established in the early- to mid '70s. It went dormant and was revived in 1977 because of Fox.

Gerald Jordan, a reporter at the *Kansas City Star,* was a member.

"It grew as news people came to town," he explained. "It was a way to make sure they'd be taken in the fold and not flounder.

"A rallying point was to put the *Star* on notice that some things have to go. Things (we challenged) that would be laughable now, like why no black baby was ever the New Year's baby (on the front page) or why crime suspects were indentified by race.

"A bad point was membership. The rule then was, 'there is no rule.'

"Journalism is an unlicensed field anyway. When meetings took on the trappings of a viable organization, calls came from p.r. people and newsletter people. There began to be a chasm -- professional disagreement more than generational disagreement.

"Jeanne (Fox) was the most enduring. She cemented the region. She traveled to Minneapolis in the winter for a regional." She and Derrick Jackson traveled to cities to talk about organizing."

Such activity and initiative in Region 8 made it seem ideal to pull off a Kansas City conference.

But it wasn't in the cards.

Fox remembered difficulties. "It was really hard working with Vernon (Jarrett.) He had real commitment -- but he was hard to reach." His *Chicago Tribune* job and television and radio jobs kept him very busy, according to Fox. NABJ business often had Jarrett traveling around the country promoting the organization.

In early June, Fox applied to the Editing Program for Minority Journalists. It was an intensive eight-week copy editing program in Berkeley, Calif., run by the Institute for Journalism Education. IJE built an excellent reputation for training about a dozen minority journalists each year and sending them into the daily newspaper ranks.

Nancy Hicks of IJE notified Fox that a spot was still open. Fox accepted and left Kansas City June 6.

Meanwhile, Bob Reid changed jobs and moved to another part of the country.

"I left things in Vernon's hands," Fox said.

Vernon Jarrett recalled that "there was a lot of confusion with the hotel and unpreparedness by the locals."

Kansas City conference plans began to unravel.

"A lot of it was my fault because I wasn't there," Fox said. "We needed someone to make sure panelists were there (confirmed), that registration material got to people. Vernon called two to three weeks before the convention in August."

That meant that Jarrett canceled it on or about July 27.

Registrations trickled in. According to several people, only a dozen members pre-registered.

Early NABJ conferences were notorious for low preregistration, followed by a crush of people who would register on site.

But this time the low numbers made officers especially anxious.

This convinced the board to change the location. It was switched to the Mayflower Hotel in Washington, D.C. and Sept. 23-26 were the new dates.

Explained Allison Davis, "For the number of people we had, it was crucial for the organization to try and see that our numbers increased. The feeling was that we would get larger numbers in Washington. Many people lived near the D.C. area. It would be easier for people to get their companies to sponsor a trip if the company could get something (a story) out of it.

"During the Carter years more stories were easier to come by because he had many blacks in his administration -- and there were more opportunities for black journalists. The feeling was 'let's try it in D.C. Let's get companies to sponsor events and continue to grow.'

"We didn't have convention planners. Mal (Johnson) had the time and the energy to put it together."

Gerald Jordan worked for the *Kansas City Star* for most of the 1970s then went to Harvard for a fellowship and from there to *The Boston Globe.*

He returned to the *Star* in 1979 and witnessed Fox and other members of KCABJ preparing to host the national conference.

He recalled that "Capital Cities, owners of the K.C. papers, had a spoken commitment to minority representation. It wanted high visibility and offered assistance.

"By the summer, registration was slow coming in. Six weeks before the conference it was pay or lose the hotel. We (NABJ) decided to latch on to the Congressional Black Caucus legislative weekend (in October.)

"There was the feeling that the Easterners dumped on Kansas City. It was pronounced. If Easterners said they didn't want to travel, they didn't. Cap Cities was pissed off with some things.

"It cost more than money. It cost ill will. I stayed away

a few years."

Lewis Diuguid was a newsman at the *Kansas City Times* and a member of KCABJ. He would attend the meetings, help out in the student journalism workshops and drive here and there to get things for organization functions.

KCABJ, he said "ran on the force of a few people. We didn't have a structure to exist despite the members. If a personality left the group, the show was over."

The organization was supposed to have a federal identification number for tax purposes and to conduct transactions, but it didn't. KCABJ was using the Social Security number of an ex-member.

"I don't think we could have done that (host a national conference) in 1979," said Diuguid in 1991.

The official estimated conference attendance was 270 people, close to the number of people who went to Chicago the previous year (according to the NABJ estimate.)

The numbers were disappointing. The conference was brought to Washington to continue growth. It didn't.

Karen Howze of *The San Francisco Chronicle* called the get-the-black-journalists-to-Washington reasoning false logic, or a case of trying to be something they were not.

Going to Washington was good for the Vernon Jarretts and Mal Johnsons who were used to covering major black events. But much of the membership had grunts like Howze who were young and "covered kids and zoos," as she put it. "I was not a reporter who could justify going to Washington (to get a story.) My editor would say 'who cares?'

"They (NABJ leadership) wanted stature.

"I wanted fellowship."

Furthermore, it is believed Eastern bias killed the Kansas City conference, not money. It was cheaper to fly and lodge in Kansas City. In Washington, according to Howze, the Mayflower Hotel charged $185 a night.

To save money, many of the conference-goers slept four to five people to a room, Howze said.

The conference was, as planned, at about the time of the Congressional Black Caucus weekend.

It was 14 months before the 1980 presidential election.

The Carter administration was under fire. Inflation eroded consumers' budgets and buying power. It looked like incumbent Carter might not get a clear shot to run for re-election in 1980.

U.S. Sen. Charles Percy, R-Ill., addressed the NABJ conference and in remarks afterwards said "the last thing any sensible Republican would want" was U.S. Sen. Ted Kennedy, D-Mass., on the presidential ticket.

People laughed when someone asked Percy if his back-handed tribute (or draft Kennedy endorsement) was a GOP plot to split the Democrats.

*   *   *

Jeanne Fox completed the summer editing program at Berkeley and headed for the Washington conference.

She decided to run for NABJ president.

"Many people seemed out of the picture," she explained. "I thought I could do a lot better. We had a really good region -- Kansas City, St. Louis, the Twin Cities, Omaha, Wichita and Des Moines -- and we had a newsletter.

"We had people like Denise Johnson, Walter Middlebrook, Linda Lockhart, Gerald Boyd, Sheila Rule, Ray Metoyer and Don Williamson.

"While I didn't have Vernon's stature, I could translate what I did in the region to a national organization. The national office was a big issue."

Fox was in for a big surprise. "When I got to the conference," she said, " (Bob) Reid was running."

Said Merv Aubespin, "The key thing was it was going to be a tight race between Reid and Jeanne Fox. A lot of people were pleased he was going to run. I was originally going to support Jeanne because she was an old friend.

"Reid had a reasonable position, a high-profile position. He was in the Columbia summer program (Reid finished the program in 1968. He also worked there), and made a lot of friends on the print side. Bob was a pretty vibrant person at the time. He was a bit more charismatic (than Jeanne)."

Reid became the first broadcast president. He was with

NBC News in Atlanta. Fox backed out, said Aubespin, with the promise she would be a viable (presidential) candidate in the next election in 1981.

Said Fox, "People told me, 'Reid is a bureau chief. He can travel. Will you really have the time?' It would have been difficult. People in Kansas City (her newspaper) didn't provide support other than conference registration." Fox paid her quarterly board meeting expenses, airfare and hotel, out of her pocket.

"I talked to Bob and decided to run for vice president," said Fox.

Fox withdrew her candidacy for president. Reid was elected president by acclamation. So were unopposed nominees Karen Howze (secretary) and Roger Clendening (parliamentarian.)

In the contested races, Fox became vice president, defeating Ben Johnson, and Mal Johnson was re-elected treasurer, defeating Ann B. Walker.

Reid said a combination of things made him run for president.

"I became friends with Vernon Jarrett. I was active; I went to all the conventions. But I was not active on the board.

"Someone (Milton Jordan of *The Charlotte Observer*) left the board in my region (Region 5, eight Southern states.) Jarrett asked if I'd finish up. It got me in the inner workings of the organization.

"I was the only (black) bureau chief for any network. I might have been the highest-ranking (media person) of any black in the country. I think Vernon thought that it was important for the organization. I think he encouraged me.

"I think the real decision came when I became disenchanted with NABJ. There were tough times. The organization was soley into conventions.

"I thought that I had to challenge myself. I couldn't criticize until I did everything I could to make a difference.

"This translated into running the organization.

"I guess I won because I was running against a woman. I guess at that stage (a woman candidate was a barrier that

was never crossed.)
"I hit at the right time and circumstances. Jeanne virtually withdrew -- and ran for vice president."

* * *

Jeanne Fox said "Things got off to a fairly good start until Bob got married and moved to Los Angeles.
"He wasted a year. It took a year before Bob became focused on NABJ."
Said Reid in a 1991 interview, "when I became president, I physically made the move to Los Angeles (from Atlanta.) It was difficult on two levels. In Atlanta, I was pretty much in one place. In L.A., I was a field producer and my job was strictly to travel anywhere in the Western Hemisphere. I was on the road more than at home.
"It was impossible to get a (NABJ) board meeting on the West Coast.
"There was no money in the budget to help people do anything. Companies had to volunteer (to pay travel and hotel expenses). I paid for most of my travel to meetings on the East Coast. I must have spent thousands flying back and forth." It was very clear that the 3,000-mile, 3-hour time difference for most officers hampered communication. To make matters worse, board meeting attendance was poor.
Officers from the Western part of the country were often absent. Sandra Dillard of Denver, the Region 9 director, was regional director by default, according to Reid. In Reid's home base, Region 10, he appointed Marilynn Bailey of *The Oakland Tribune* to replace Sharon McGriff.
"It was a geographical hardship," said Karen Howze. "Nobody (board members) had money, nobody was sponsored. We couldn't get a quorum. We never met on the West Coast because it was just me and Bob.
"I didn't even tell people on my job where I was going. If you raised where you going, you'd get, 'Wow, what are they (blacks) doing now?'"
To save money, Region 3 director Tyree Johnson hosted the winter 1980 board meeting in his house in West Phila-

delphia. Mal Johnson was not happy about meeting at Tyree's house, recalled Bob Reid.

Six people attended. The officers did not have a quorum to take official action. Tyree Johnson said the executive board members decided they could attend to some NABJ business.

"I was told I couldn't vote," said Tyree. "Regional directors were excluded. I couldn't vote in my own house."

"We put Tyree in an awkward position," said Howze. "We're in the man's house. Didn't anyone explain this (the right to exclude regional reps from a vote) to him? That was difficult, trying to develop business savvy."

Bob Reid said that he had to rely on folks in the East to get the 1980 conference planning done.

Being in Los Angeles made it impossible to take care of the details in Washington.

"I started to rely more on the core group (executive board and a couple of regional directors) who could get there or consult by phone," Reid explained. "My attitude: 'Screw this, I'm going to do what I have to do and get the board to go along.' I had to be autocratic (sometimes) rather than govern. The board was helpful in making it work.

"I don't want to sound too egotistical."

*　　*　　*

Jeanne Fox said that "by then, me, Monte Trammer and Ben Johnson were in Detroit (at *The Free Press*). We worked on a committee to establish a national office. We asked the Investigative Reporters and Editors (IRE) and others how they did it (IRE set up its office at the University of Missouri.)

"It seemed to make sense to go to a university. It seemed to be the cheapest and the easiest way to do it and it would benefit students.

"And, Christine and Jay Harris were working at Northwestern" (with The Consortium.)

Vernon Jarrett asked Christine (and Jay) Harris to make arrangements for the 1979 Washington, D.C. conference.

He also asked them whether Northwestern would want to host the the national office.

Jarrett did not consult the NABJ board about these discussions. This caused an ugly scene later at the conference.

In a letter to NABJ, Christine Harris invited the organization to consider Northwestern as headquarters. She and the school of journalism helped contact NABJ members about the change in venue when the 1979 conference was moved from Kansas City to Washington. Christine Harris emphasized that the assistance was not to be taken as a move to influence NABJ.

Also, the University of Missouri School of Journalism strongly encouraged NABJ to consider its site in Columbia, Mo., as a headquarters. Investigative Reporters and Editors was based there.

In a Sept. 19 letter to Vernon Jarrett, dean Roy M. Fisher cited the J-school's commitment to attracting minority journalists.

In 1969, he said, the school established a high school-level minority recruiting program and the Dow Jones Newspaper Fund rated it as one of the country's best. The school helped the St. Louis ABJ establish its school-year journalism workshop. And Fisher said that Missouri had a minority broadcast workshop.

At the 1979 conference NABJ members had two viable proposals for a national office. But a number of people who remembered the early days were wary.

They recalled the bitterness and misunderstandings that occurred at the first conference at Texas Southern University. Then, NABJ told journalism professors that they could not be members. This set up a sour, or at best, uneasy relationship with academicians.

There was a lengthy discussion of the pros and cons of affiliating with a university. It included the problems that arose from working with Texas Southern on the 1976 Houston conference.

Sarah-Ann Shaw, Region 1 director, moved that NABJ not affiliate with any school of journalism or any other organization and that NABJ remain an independent body.

The motion was approved 7-3.

Unanimously, the board supported Mal Johnson's motion to send letters to Northwestern and Missouri thanking the schools for its offers, but, declining.

* * *

Fox, Ben Johnson and Trammer continued to look into the campus headquarters idea. They turned their attention to black colleges. Jay Harris' suggestion, said Fox, was to focus on Florida A&M University.

Howard University was a possibility too. Both predominately black universities had large journalism programs. But Howard, said Fox, seemed disorganized based on what some black journalists observed at the annual communications conference. That was a shame because Howard was in Washington, D.C. NABJ's bylaws called for placing the permanent national office in the Washington, D.C. area.

Said Fox, "Jay managed for a way to channel money to Florida A&M for staff support and an executive director.

"They had typewriters, postage machines, the means to publish a newsletter. It seemed like the best way to get something going."

But the proposal stalled. Lack of a quorum at several board meetings prevented action being taken on the campus headquarters issue.

Some officers were not about to encourage the idea. "You can't have it at a university. It's not how it's done," Mal Johnson mumbled to herself at one of the meetings, recalled Fox. The issue stalled for a year.

Chapter 7
L'Enfant

The 1980 conference was held for a second consecutive year in Washington. This time the venue was the L'Enfant Plaza Hotel.

New forces collided. It was a new decade. And an exciting, even unusual U.S. presidential campaign was in full gear. Incumbent Democrat Jimmy Carter was embattled. His polices were blamed for an inflationary and double-digit nterest-rate economy.

Meanwhile, 52 U.S. hostages were held in Iran and the No. 1 superpower seemed incapable of doing anything about it.

Ronald Reagan, a B-movie actor, ran a strong Republican candidacy, especially attracting white Southern Democrats who perceived Carter and the Democratic Party as too liberal and sympathetic to minorities and special interest groups. Rep. John Anderson, R-Ill., ran as an independent candidate. He promoted implementation of a steep gasoline tax in order to raise revenue and pay for making the nation less dependent on Mideast oil.

Within NABJ a number of regular members were impatient with their own organization. Membership growth was stagnant and conference attendance was weak. President Reid spent the first year of his two-year term in Los Angeles where his new job was based. He'd come East for board meetings but the meetings were poorly attended.

With treasurer Mal Johnson based in Washington, Reid counted on her to handle most of the conference details.

Johnson was an effective taskmaster. But the fact that Reid was three time zones and 3,000 miles away meant there could be missed communication -- and mistakes.

Furthermore, many people did not like working with Johnson. They were put off by her gruffness. Members of the local Washington Association of Black Journalists (WABJ) could have done more to help, said Reid in a 1991 interview, but didn't. "It was pretty disasterous," said Reid. "Attendance was poor, under 200 people. Previous conferences averaged 200 to 400 people and there was steady growth each year. This time, it did not increase and it was less than the previous year."

The conference, held from Sept. 28 to Oct. 1, was disorganized.

For example, a scheduled 2 1/2 hour business meeting lasted seven hours, recalled Greg Morrison, a broadcast journalist who worked in Mobile, Ala. Members met from 3 p.m. to 6:30 p.m., went to the banquet and reconvened from 10 p.m. to well past 2 p.m.

"The party we paid for was going on in the other room," said Morrison. "We were pissed off but no one wanted to leave."

NABJ members were hashing out organization rules.

But many people also postured and jockeyed for power. The way to do it was to give pedantic speeches and try to convince most of the crowd that they cared the most about NABJ and would be the next leader of the organization. Leaving the room suggested a lack of commitment.

Some long-time members grumbled that the old-guard board members had run things too long.

Roger Witherspoon of *The Atlanta Constitution* says he and Acel Moore were part of a movement to push the old guard (Reid and Paul Brock) out.

The Washington crowd, said Witherspoon, "was interested in flash and dash.

"President Carter was snubbed. This infuriated some people."

Witherspoon's friend Greg Morrison had the same recollection.

But Reid remembers it differently. "I know we invited all the candidates," he said. "I'm certain we invited all the contenders. Those (Kennedy and Anderson) are the only ones who committed and came."

Incumbent Democrat Carter did not have a clear shot at re-election. Sen. Ted Kennedy of Massachusetts challenged him. The senator's campaign, however, derailed at a stormy Democratic National Convention in New York City.

Two months later, Sen. Kennedy addressed the NABJ conference.

"I made a mistake," explained Vernon Jarrett, " and introduced him as 'the president of the United States.'

"People laughed. It sounded so partisan.

"He (Kennedy) remembered that for a long time."

After Kennedy gave his speech, no questions were accepted from the audience.

For a room full of journalists, this was odd.

"When we asked about this, Mal told us 'We're running the show,'" said Witherspoon.

When John Anderson spoke, about 200 NABJ members reacted cooly to the Illinois congressman's 30 minute address, interrupting him with applause once.

Anderson poignantly said what many blacks felt about Carter: many of them will only vote for him out of fear of a Reagan presidency.

And *The New York Times* quoted Anderson saying this: "Reagan and the Republican platform offer nothing to black Americans but cutbacks and rhetoric," Anderson told the audience. He also said that President Carter was 'deliberately manipulating the fears of black Americans to distract from his own incompetence.'"

* * *

Unlike NABJ regulars who were unhappy with the rate of progress in their organization, a number of people who did come to the conference were young new faces who found NABJ relevant.

Alexis Yancey, a producer with WFAA-TV, Dallas, had not heard of NABJ until she learned about it from co-worker Ken Smith, who was Region 7 director (Texas, La., Okla.) "I was amazed that I was in this room full of journalists such as Les Payne and Charlayne Hunter-Gault," she said. "I could talk to them. They faced the same kind of problems I faced.

"It was such a comforting and thrilling experience that I was not alone.

"A lot of black journalists were doing great things."

Myron Lowery, reporter and anchor for WMC-TV (NBC) in Memphis, Tenn., said that the $75-a-day room at the L'Enfant Plaza was at least two- to three-times more than he ever paid for a hotel room.

He said "I was impressed by the group. (It was) my first exposure. I was impressed to see so many black journalists who were doing things. It seemed pro-active. (And) it was a chance for me to meet other NBC correspondents."

"Everyone said it (the conference) was lousy, it was disorganized and nothing was done right," recalled Sam Ford, then a CBS News correspondent. "But that was what was good about it.

"It was so spontaneous. People talked to each other.

"There was a guy who went to an international conference. At a workshop he asked us what would be the next growth industry? Not oil, but telemarketing. And he was right!"

Although candidate Ronald Reagan did not participate, Bill Brock, a member of the GOP leadership, attended and spoke about the virtues of the Republican Party.

* * *

On Sunday, Sept. 28, an article entitled "Jimmy's World" appeared on the front page of *The Washington Post.*

It was written by Janet Cooke, a 25-year-old black reporter.

Cooke wrote that she witnessed the mother's boyfriend inject heroin into Jimmy, an 8-year-old black boy living in the city slums.

"The needle slides into the boy's soft skin like a straw pushed into the center of a freshly baked cake," Cooke wrote. The boy's "World" -- inner city Washington's drug culture -- physically and mentally abused Jimmy.

The article emoted sorrow and anger.

How could such a young boy be exploited so cruelly?

"Jimmy's World" was based on a tip from a Howard University doctor. The doctor said that children, younger than age 10, were using a new, more potent kind of heroin.

The controversial article also sparked a newsroom battle.

Vivian Aplin-Brownlee, Cooke's former editor at the *Post's District Weekly* section, expressed concerns about the article and the author's credibility.

"I raised questions about Janet Cooke all the time," explained Aplin-Brownlee in a 1990 interview.

Janet Cooke was the unlikeliest of reporters to have the street smarts to go into a tough neighborhood and get such a hot story.

District Weekly reporters usually were green. They needed plenty of editing and supervision.

Aplin-Brownlee joined *The Washington Post* in 1979. "I went there as an editor on the Metro staff, but I opted to be editor of the *District Weekly*," she said. "I had a heavy editing job, I had to work with young reporters.

"She (Cooke) was strange to them (poor, working-class black Washingtonians), explained Aplin-Brownlee.

"She had acrylic nails and (hair) extentions. She affected (fancied) Diana Ross.

"When she'd talk to them, she'd have to have someone interpret.

"Sharon Farmer (a *Post* free-lance photographer) would interpret.

"People would ask her (Farmer) 'what kind of nigger (Cooke) is this?'" Aplin-Brownlee said.

A black reporter who had trouble communicating with black people was unlikely to get sources to tell a story like "Jimmy's World."

Nevertheless, Cooke prepared her article under supervision of metro editor Milton Coleman.

"It was fascinating to see what was swirling around us," said conferee Gayle Pollard, who at that time was with *The Boston Globe*. "Courtland Milloy's (a black *Post* reporter) perception was it was jealousy that Coleman had her (Aplin-Brownlee's) reporter."

To dismiss Aplin-Brownlee's doubts as a turf battle with another black editor was too simple. She was a solid journalist and a critical judge of young talent.

Aplin-Brownlee grew up in Steubenville, Ohio, a town on the Pennsylvania-West Virginia border.

"I always wanted to be a writer," she said. Aplin-Brownlee graduated from Kent State University with a degree in Communications. She worked for *The Cleveland PlainDealer* from January 1969 to 1978 and worked about a year for the *San Diego Union*. She became active with NABJ in 1976 and served as Region 6 director (Midwest) when she was in Cleveland.

"In January 1980, Janet Cooke began working for me," said Aplin-Brownlee. "But when the story appeared, she was transferred out of my authority. Bob Woodward (the reporter of Watergate fame became an editor) felt that with that story she became too famous.

"I could not have anyone with the luxury of working on one story. Cooke worked on it in the summer and was closeted with Milton.

"The first time I saw the story was the morning it appeared."

Mayor Marion Barry ordered the District of Columbia police to find the boy. When they could not, the mayor called the story a hoax.

"I've been told that the story was part myth and part reality," he said. "We don't believe that the mother of a pusher would allow a reporter to see them shoot up.

Based on her story, Cooke witnessed a felony. But she stood by her story and her editors backed her.

The story won a Pulitzer Prize for feature writing in April 1981. In the Pulitzer deliberations, the already controverial story sparked a new one. The board of directors lifted the story from another judging category and placed it in the feature slot. This upset many Pulitzer jurors.

It all came apart when people got ready to publicize her feat. Someone discovered inaccuracies and exaggerations in Cooke's resume. She claimed that she graduated from elite Vassar College. Cooke only completed a year.

She also said she studied overseas at the Sorbonne (University of Paris.)

Cooke said she hyped her resume in order to be thought of as qualified to work for *The Post*.

Then Cooke admitted that the story was a lie.

"Jimmy" did not exist; he was a composite of children who may have been abused with drugs.

This revelation infuriated veteran black journalists.

When "Jimmy's World" appeared, black journalists did not condemn Cooke or *The Post* for writing about such depravity in the black community. Assuming that the story was true, such ugliness needed to be exposed so it could be erradicated. But in learning that the story was false, Cooke betrayed black journalists who fought a daily battle for credibility in white-dominated newsrooms.

"Being black and good-looking was not enough," wrote *The New York Times'* C. Gerald Fraser in a critique of the Cooke scandal. "She had to be a multilingual graduate of one of the Seven Sister colleges as well. In short, the ultimate super-negress. By creating this self, Cooke was playing up to white fantasies about blacks just as she did when she wrote "Jimmy's World.'"

Cynically, Cooke played up to many white's assumptions that depravity was a way of life in black communities.

The other betrayal was that Cooke hyped her credentials. In order for a black person to be qualified to work in the major white media, her schooling had to be more elite than white people's.

Cooke's deceit sent ripples through newsrooms. White editors did not slam on the brakes and stop hiring black journalists. However, a number of editors questioned closely the credentials of applicants.

Cooke never returned to daily journalism. The Wilmington, Del., *News-Journal,* a *Gannett* newspaper, tried to re-
habilitate Cooke by hiring her. But when the word got
around that newsroom, the idea was killed.

"We don't run a halfway house for liars," said a journalist
who obviously was outraged.

*   *   *

In retrospect, Bob Reid said that the 1980 conference
"was not something I was proud of."

There were too many mishaps. Attendance was very
poor. There was to be a luncheon for syndicated columnist
and TV commentator Carl Rowan. He was being honored
with the Lifetime Achievement Award.

But Rowan did not show up. It was not known whether
he forgot the date or was not notified by NABJ.

Either way, said Reid "It was a bitter pill."

Maybe the mixup was for the best. At the banquet Reid
said that people talked throughout the keynoter's speech.

"I was embarrassed by the demeanor of the members,"
he said. "This is not what we're about.

"It wasn't the most awful convention we had. But it re-
flected on me. That convention triggered a commitment.

"I decided that I had to take matters into my own hands. I
took stock of myself. I had to do better in spite of the system."

The "system" was an NABJ in the limited role of a convention organization.

Said Al Fitzpatrick, an editor at the Akron, Ohio *Beacon-
Journal,* "NABJ was a good organization with good inten-
tions. But it was going through the process or growing and
internal strife.

"While it was growing in numbers, it was not growing in
stature.

"We were operating with presidents who had to use their
offices as the national office. We were not operating with
sound business footing.

"It was amazing that some things were accomplished.

"While NABJ was growing, it did not grow as fast as it could have."

With the board's approval Reid established a number of programs and services during the final 12 months of his two-year term.

The Washington conference ended with many journalists fascinated with the "Jimmy's World" story by Janet Cooke.

America's misery level was sky high because of inflation and interest rates. American hostages were still in Iran.

And the country was on the edge of a revolution. Ronald Reagan was elected president in November. He initiated a decade of right-wing politics from the White House.

Black journalists -- particularly the columnists -- debated whether Reagan's right-wing philosophy would cripple black America. Or, whether he was *good* for black Americans, in the sense that Reagan would inspire blacks to organize and agitate like their lives depended on it.

Chapter 8
Louisville

NABJ was not progressing as quickly as many members wanted.

But at the 1980 conference that many people considered a bust, an unlikely initiative energized it.

Mervin Aubespin of *The Courier-Journal* in Louisville, Ky., and the Region 5 director, made a formal proposal that the City of Louisville and the Louisville Association of Black Communicators host the 1981 conference.

This was unprecedented.

"We broke the monotony," said Aubespin, of the NABJ board always selecting the annual conference site.

With the exception of the bittersweet 1976 inaugural conference in Houston, there had never been a conference in the South.

Furthermore, conferences were always in big cities, not moderately large ones like Louisville. The Kansas City conference was killed in part for that very reason.

Aubespin was aware of the obstacles and had a plan to woo the board. To make the presentation he brought a representative from the City of Louisville and the city visitors and tourist bureau.

"We rehearsed our presentation," explained Aubespin. "We had it so tight the board was most comfortable.

"We (NABJ) had gone to Washington at the last minute in 1979. This was a bit of relief."

At the board meeting Aubespin and Anne Long of the visitors and tourist bureau flipped through a chart that exlained projected costs. Other charts with 200- and 300-mile maps compared mileage between cities.

Louisville was sold as a convenient city to reach by air from numerous points. Louisville was clearly a Southern city, but it was in a border state closely linked to the Midwest. Cincinnati, Indianapolis, Chicago and Detroit were a short flight or reasonable automobile drive away.

The presenters gave board members miniature Louisville Slugger baseball bats, cigarette lighters, jackets and tiny bottles of bourbon.

The city representatives bought wine for all of the tables at the banquet. With the bottles came cards that read "compliments of the City of Louisville and LABC."

Aubespin promised that a strong local organization would make the conference arrangements.

About 25 people from LABC were at the Washington conference, recalls Aubespin. He said his newspaper promised to give him all the time he needed to put on the conference. Also, there was the promise of media companies' willingness to underwrite events.

Bob Reid said "getting the convention to Louisville was not without some daring." Aubespin said the toughest skeptic -- Mal Johnson -- bought the proposal.

She organized the last two conferences, one of them a conference that was pulled from another city at the 11th hour. Letting other people take care of organizing the annual conference would be a relief for the board.

They approved the proposal on the first vote, said Aubespin. He was named conference chairman.

Bob Reid said he worked with the board to establish a number of lasting programs. This would make NABJ more than a convention organization that served its members for one week in the summer.

Said Aubespin, "He (Reid) wasn't necessarily the person who came up with all of the ideas, but a lot of things transpired."

In spring 1981, Reid published volume one, number one of *NABJ News*. For the first 4 1/2 years NABJ did not have a newsletter. The lack of such an instrument was a

conspicuous omission for a group of journalists.
In his signed "Message from the president," Reid said:

"As I've traveled across the country on behalf of NABJ
I've been asked two equally frustrating questions with a
disturbing regularity:
"1. Whites generally ask: 'Why is it necessary in this day
and age to have an organization for black journalists?'
"2. Blacks often want to know: 'What can NABJ or other
such organizations do for us?'
"The first question represents an attitude among even the
most enlightened whites that the problems of race discrimination in employment has been solved. After all, there are a
few very visible blacks on television at both the network
and local level and editors and columnists at some of the
major newspapers.
"The question some black journalists ask reveals a similar attitude, although one that often arises from a more personal feeling of professional success and well-being. Both
attitudes have developed out of profound misconceptions
of the depth and nature of the problems confronting the average black journalist in this country and the tenuous nature
of the progress we've made collectively and individually."

The eight-page *NABJ News* led with a story headlined:
"Janet Cooke's editor says incident will do little harm to
blacks." It was an account of *Washington Post* District of
Columbia editor Milton Coleman addressing the Region 8
conference about "Jimmy's World," a story written by
Cooke. The story stirred controversy last September. It
won a Pulitzer Prize in April. That month, Cooke admitted
the story was hoax.
Coleman, quoted in the *NABJ News,* said:

"Obviously this is going to have some effect. But the
news media aren't going away tomorrow and neither are
black folks.
"One of the problems black people have had in the past
is that they looked at the news media and said either you

control it or you ignore it . . . the problem is you can't control it because it's not our media. And you can't ignore it because it's too powerful. So you'd best just get in there and slug it out and try to change it."

Coleman added that "systematic breakdown" was responsible for Cooke's story getting by *Post* editors. Editors, he said, "operate on the assumption that the reporter is telling the truth."

Janet Cooke's bogus story made many blacks working in general interest journalism angry or anxious.

Would the incident give white editors a convenient excuse to avoid hiring more African-Americans?

The Wall Street Journal suggested double-checking the resumes of black applicants.

U.S. News & World Report printed a stern lecture by author and Pulitzer prize-winner James Michener. He said:

"When blind Samson pulled down the central pillars of the temple at Gaza, the entire structure fell. When Janet Cooke turned in a fake story, she knocked down the central pillar of her profession -- integrity -- and the reverberations went far.

". . . The damage Miss Cooke has done to black and women reporters is incalcuable, and she should have anticipated this when she wrote her fake story and allowed it to be nominated for a Pulitzer.

". . . Recent requirements that a company must have a balanced staff should not be interpreted as meaning that it must have an incompetent one or one ignorant of the great traditions."

Al Fitzpatrick, who had already held numerous editing posts and had served as a Pulitzer juror, was not as concerned. In 1990 he said he was only surprised that two things happened: The Pulitzer board put "Jimmy's World" in a different category, and, it received the prize.

"We were not totally shocked," said Fitzpatrick in 1990. "There was no bowing of heads or begging forgiveness, or saying we (blacks) would not recover.

"We did not condone it but white editors bought the story. The public is not aware of all the politics that transpires in a newsroom.

"If Janet Cooke had several black editors maybe this thing might not have happened.

"I'm sure Milton Coleman didn't edit every story Janet Cooke had written."

The NABJ News' front page also carried a one-column story headlined "Negotiations under way for national office." There was a one-column story below headlined "Awards deadline June 15th."

Said Reid: "We had to make sense of our awards."

NABJ honored outstanding journalists at its annual conferences but there was no clear system on how the awards were designated or named.

The board came up with two awards: Lifetime Achievement, which honored a career, and Journalist of the Year, which recognized an outstanding year of work.

The board also initiated a competitive awards program. It recognized the outstanding work of journalists covering the black condition. Awards were given for the best work in print, photojournalism, television and radio.

During the last half of Reid's term, NABJ established a scholarship program for college students pursuing journalism careers. The organization awarded $1,000 to the winner. Keith Thomas, a 22-year-old from Wakulla Springs, Fla., and a recent graduate of Florida A&M University, was the first winner. The scholarship helped pay his expenses at Northwestern where he pursued a masters in journalism.

In a 1991 interview, Thomas said, "I felt like I was in awe of a lot of people, Les Payne for example.

"I'm from this little town that's always mispronounced and here I am with all these people. They never treated me like I was less. It was one of the high points of my career."

Thomas became a reporter at *The Miami Herald* and later the Atlanta *Journal & Constitution.*

Reid's adminstration established rules for local black journalists' organizations to become NABJ affiliate chapters.

The Louisville Association of Black Communicators, 55-members strong, became the first.

In addition the NABJ board had at least a couple of officers who knew that area. Region 6 (Midwest states) director Ben Johnson grew up in Louisville and had worked at the *Louisville Defender,* the black weekly. He later worked for *TheCourier-Journal.*

Parliamentarian Monte Trammer grew up in Indianapolis, a 2 1/2-hour drive away on I-64.

Trammer was at *The Detroit Free Press* after stops in Indianapolis and Baltimore.

In addition to being known for baseball bats and bourbon, the city was known for Kentucky Fried Chicken, the Kentucky Derby and for being Muhammad Ali's hometown.

Its major newspaper, *TheCourier-Journal,* was arguably the best newspaper in the South. It often graced industry top 10 lists for journalistic quality and enterprise, ranking it with major metropolitan heavyweights like *The New York Times, Los Angeles Times, The Wall Street Journal, Chicago Tribune* and *Washington Post.*

TheCourier-Journal was the state newspaper. The Bingham family, the owners, also published a large afternoon paper, *The Louisville Times,* and owned WHAS-TV, a CBS affiliate.

"Challenging a Changing Nation" was the NABJ conference theme.

By late August, U.S. citizens had an eight-month taste of Reaganism and "New Federalism," or, less big government and deregulation.

The nation was in the grips of a severe recession. Many working-class white families were caught off guard. Many were rudely tossed from their jobs and out on the street.

For blacks, the recession was really a depression. Adult unemployment hovered around 20 percent. The factory and manual labor jobs were being replaced by white collar and high-tech jobs that required more education.

These were some of the challenges Americans faced in the first full year of a new decade.

But for NABJ members, the immediate challenge was getting to Louisville, Ky.

One of the first challenges to President Reagan's new policies was a strike by air traffic controllers, unionized workers who endorsed Reagan for president, then struck for better wages.

The traffic controllers assumed they had a strong hand even though legally they were not allowed to strike.

They were essential to keeping flights moving quickly and safely.

Reagan fired the strikers. Managers picked up the extra work. The shortage of controllers made flying long distances to any city, in this case Louisville, adventurous.

It took Gayle Pollard a full day to get to Louisville from San Francisco, where she was teaching at a summer journalism program.

Bob Maynard, editor of *The Tribune,* Oakland, Calif. had his flight diverted to a Midwestern city and was late getting to the conference.

He was to be honored as "Journalist of the Year."

Nevertheless, many people attended.

Financial records and Angela Dodson's article in *Editor & Publisher* said about 250 people participated. That was still a good or even relatively better turnout than the two Washington conferences.

"Eighty-one took us to another level," said Pollard. "It was the first convention I remembered that wasn't clubby. We didn't know most of the people."

One of the newcomers was Alice Bonner of *The Washington Post.* She returned to her newspaper in July 1980 after completing a Nieman fellowship, and, motherhood.

She did not have much of a chance to participate in the 1980 national conference in Washington, D.C. That fall, however, Bonner did begin attending meetings of the Washington Association of Black Journalists (WABJ). Bonner said she got involved because she was turned off by the slow pace of the local organization.

"Isaiah Poole (Region 4 director and a *Black Enterprise* magazine correspondent) did a lot of work," said Bonner, "but D.C. is a very transient town. We pulled in Leon Wynter, Bobbi (LaBarbara) Bowman and Tom Morgan from *The* (Washington) *Post.* Our thrust was to get to Louisville in 1981 and make a difference."

Alice Bonner chose journalism as a schoolgirl. In 1965 she was among a handful of black kids who desegregated schools in Dinwiddie County, Va. She went to the predominately white high school under federal mandate.

Bonner had what she called a "superior" English teacher and an "extraordinary" Social Studies teacher.

"They got me excited in learning," said Bonner. "A guidance counselor gave career preference tests. My career choice was working with words. I settled on journalism from the 10th grade on.

"It was discouraging at first. The books about journalism only had white guys with cigars and fedoras. It was just a question of getting there.

"I was steered to a black college (Howard University) which had journalism classes. It was thrilling to go and ask questions about people's lives. This had social significance.

"I did survey interviewing for the United Planning Organization in Washington, D.C. It was practice for class and it could not be published.

"It affirmed the (my) need to be a newspaper reporter.

"We went to New York tenements and asked tenants about their lives in fall 1967. By spring 1968 the places where they lived burned down.

"There was a lot of turmoil at that time.

"I applied repeatedly to D.C.'s three dailies (*The Star*, the *Daily News* and *The Post* .)

"The summer after my junior year, *The Washington Post* hired me as a full-time night copy aid."

Soon, Bonner became a reporter.

Holding the conference in the South, especially a Southern city at the edge of the Midwestern United States, attracted members who were becoming the base of NABJ.

One of the great underreported stories of the 1970s was

the reverse migration of blacks from the North to the South. The press missed the story, said an executive editor from a major Northern newspaper, because no official called a press conference.

Tens of thousands of black Americans returned to the places their grandparents fled. Unlike poorly educated, un- and underemployed people who were trapped in big Northern cities, the new migrants were often stable families looking for home ownership, good education for the children and employment opportunities.

This was a good pool from which to draw journalists, just like other professions and crafts.

New York, Chicago, Los Angeles and Washington, D.C. are big fishponds. But even for black journalists who grew up in these cities, it was wiser to seek work in the smaller cities and towns and work their way back to the big city, if they were so inclined.

There was a constant push to desegregate and integrate all daily media operations. Black people lived all over America, not only in big cities. Complete coverage of their lives was needed.

Broadcast journalist Greg Morrison looked forward to coming to the annual conferences.

"Many people overlook that NABJ is more than a professional organization but an extended family," he said many years later. "It kept me sane in Mobile (at that time he was with WALA-TV.) It was a lifeline for a lot of black journalists who thought they were out there by themselves."

As Morrison was checking in at Galt House, the hotel, someone bellowed "My man!"

It was Dennis Bell, a reporter with *Newsday*. Like long-lost friends, they embraced.

Such a scene was not unusual as scores of black journalists were reunited for several days.

The scene must have seemed peculiar, even startling, for conferees from the Knights of Columbus, who were checking out of Galt House. Many of them were leaving the hotel wearing their conventioneer hats.

The Friday morning of the convention NABJ members began the day with a social event: a riverboat cruise along the Ohio River aboard The Belle of Louisville. People strolled along the three decks of the boat. They enjoyed the breeze and sparkling sunshine. They took time to check out nametags, introduce themselves and enjoy the brunch.

It was an NABJ election year and the end of Bob Reid's two-year term. For the first time there was a real contest for president. Conferees had a choice.

The race featured a pair of opposites. Ben Johnson of The *Detroit Free Press* and Region 5 director (Michigan, Ohio, Indiana, Illinois, Wisconsin) was running against Les Payne of *Newsday* and Region 2 director (New York, New Jersey and Connecticut).

Johnson, a gregarious man with a football lineman-like frame and an easy smile, campaigned aggressively.

He was like a professional politician, or, a parody of one.

"I was the first to campaign," Johnson said in 1991. "I started the sloganeering and campaign materials.

"He (his opponent Payne) had to run out and spend money for stick-ons (nametags)."

Johnson's wife Mary Bullard campaigned with him with their infant daughter in a stroller.

On the boat ride Ben Johnson passed out large campaign buttons, firm handshakes, and a pitch to elect him.

"I was criticized considerably for that because I decided to run at a time when the leadership of the organization was selected kind of in a back room," Johnson said. "People would say, 'you run for president, you run for vice president. No, I don't want to. OK, you run for secretary.'

"Francis Ward came to me that morning and put his arm around me. Roger Witherspoon did the same thing.

"Francis said, 'brother, what are you doing man? Don't you know you're going to get creamed?

'You can't go up against Les Payne. He's so well-respected in the business.'

"I said, 'Hey, I want my shot.'" Johnson was 31 years old.

Johnson's first taste of journalism was in the military. He was a Marine Corps military journalist from 1968-70. After the military, he worked several summers at the *Louisville Defender*.

When NABJ was founded Johnson was a student at Lincoln University in Missouri. He joined NABJ in 1977 and went to the first big conference in Baltimore. At that time Johnson was a reporter at *The Courier-Journal* in Louisville, Ky., his hometown. He moved on to the Gary (Ind.) *Post-Tribune*.

In 1981 he was at *The Detroit Free Press*.

Compared to the gregarious Ben Johnson, Les Payne's style was muted.

There wasn't noticeable campaigning for Payne on the riverboat trip, at least not as overt as Johnson's.

Payne said Marilynn Bailey of *The Oakland Tribune* organized his supporters.

The campaign slogan was "Les is more."

Payne grew up in Tuscaloosa, Ala. He said he had a cousin who used to read to him. "I learned to read at age 3. I was familiarized with what was good writing.

"My grandfather was a janitor at the county library."

When Payne was 12 the family moved to Hartford, Conn.

"In Hartford I grew up with three papers, *The Hartford Courant, Hartford Times* and *PittsburghCourier* (national edition); my stepfather would bring it," he explained. "The only journalist I knew was Bill Matney (a reporter for NBC. Payne said he did not realize that Matney was an African-American because he was very light-complexioned).

"I chose journalism. I wanted to be a writer. I started in the 10th grade.

"In my junior year of college I was thinking of how I could make my living writing. The University of Connecticut did not have a journalism major.

"I graduated with an English degree.

"The problems I faced in 1964 were what black journalism aspirants faced.

"Journalism was never a career accessible to us.

"I was interested in daily journalism. Out of college I had

no hope of getting a job in Hartford. I delivered *The Courant.* But I didn't apply.
"I went into the Army. It paid $27 to $30 a month.
"That was open to us" (blacks).
Payne became a 2nd lieutenant and an air defense artillery officer at the Nike military battery. It was a three-year commitment.
"I wanted to go to the Columbia Graduate School of Journalism," said Payne. "But leaves were frozen because of the '65 military buildup.
"I was sent to Vietnam as a journalist (information officer). There was a shortage of these officers.
"I was sent to defense information school (before Vietnam) for nine weeks in Indiana."
He communicated with troops through *The Observer* weekly newspapers and *Stars and Stripes.* Payne wrote pamphlets about 10 rest and relaxation (r & r) sites in Asia.
Payne was on Gen. William Westmoreland's staff. He wrote speeches for the general.
Payne said, "I worked with 500 civilian journalists in Vietnam at one time. I met Tom Johnson (*New York Times*), Wallace Terry and Jesse Lewis of *The Washington Post.*
"He (Lewis) was doing stories on black soldiers.
"I realized the power and influence of the press. In *The Washington Post,* Westmoreland gave credit to black NCOs (non-commissioned officers) but none were on his staff. LBJ (President Lyndon Johnson) chewed him out.
"Also, there was a story about Confederate flags that got an officer bounced.
"I saw it (journalism) as a lever, not a career, allowing me to effect change or wield influence for black people."
Payne advanced to captain in Vietnam. It was January 1968.
"I returned to Fort Bliss (El Paso, Texas)," he explained.
"I planned on going to Columbia.
Bill Nack, then a 1st Lt. (at the time of Payne's 1991 interview, Nack was with *Sports Illustrated*) was someone Payne characterized as "a brilliant writer and good friend."
Nack went to *Newsday.*
Payne never heard of the Long Island newspaper. *News-*

day was looking for black reporters. Bill Moyers, the editor, set up a program to hire six black reporters.

"Nack recommended me in a classically written three-page letter," recalled Payne.

"'But Bill,' I told him, 'I'm going to Columbia.'

"He told me, 'You can come here.'

"I flew up, in uniform, and took the test," said Payne. "I was hired on the spot." After his discharge from the Army Payne went to *Newsday.*

When he ran for NABJ president, he had worked at the newspaper for a dozen years as a suburban reporter, national and foreign correspondent, national editor and columnist. Payne was part of a team of reporters who produced "The Heroin Trail," which won a Pulitzer Prize in 1974.

He reported from South Africa in 1976.

* * *

In the executive board meeting just before the conference opened, NABJ officers agreed to two important changes.

A second vice president post was created.

There were complaints by some TV journalists that they were treated like second-class citizens.

"There was no real animosity between broadcast and print journalists," explained Norma Wade of *The Dallas Morning News,* "but there was real competition.

"There was a feeling that the broadcast people were real glamorous. Print people felt a little intimidated.

"Emotions were strong and people were protective of their own interests.

"This went on for five or six years," going back to NABJ's founding.

Bob Reid's election in 1979 as NABJ 's first broadcast president set the stage for a second vice president.

The other change was to allow the immediate past president of NABJ to serve a two-year term as a voting member.

The intent was to allow a smoother transition from the departing president to the incoming president. The new president could consult with the past president on continuing projects and board precedents.

This could avoid duplication of work.

This addition was critical because journalists are such transient beings. It was easy for NABJ projects to derail because people moved around.

"Before that," explained Reid, "NABJ had no memory. This would provide transition."

Instead of electing 15 officers, the members were faced with electing 16 officers and an immediate past president.

The business meeting was when NABJ candidates were nominated.

The new vice president/broadcast post immediately caused controversy.

Member Reginald Stuart of *The New York Times* said it was not clear how to elect the two vice presidents.

He nominated Denise Johnson, a newswoman at the *St. Paul Pioneer Press*. She hosted a weekly public affairs TV program. Denise Johnson was a native Minnesotan who began working at the *Pioneer Press* in 1974 when she was 20 years old. She joined NABJ in 1977.

In 1979 Johnson became Region 8 director.

"I nominated Denise with the promise that Merv (Aubespin) would second it.

"I said 'Denise is a hybrid, she's broadcast and print.'

"Everybody (members) jumped up.

"Meanwhile, Merv left the room and I had no one to second the nomination. I was ridiculed for trying an end run.

"Denise said, 'I withdraw.'"

The other candidate was Myron Lowery, a reporter and weekend anchor for WMC-TV (NBC) in Memphis, Tenn. Lowery had been a journalist for 10 years. He grew up in Columbus, Ohio and moved to Memphis to attend Le-Moyne-Owen College. He earned a master's degree in education from New York University and taught in the New York City school system.

Hollis Price, president of LeMoyne-Owen, called Lowery in 1971. He asked him if he was interested in changing careers.

WMC hired Price as an urban affairs coordinator to make recommendations on desegregating and diversifying its staff.

Price made his pitch. Lowery jumped at the opportunity.

In 1973, two years after becoming a journalist, Lowery helped organize the Memphis Association of Black Communicators.

The presidential candidates were nominated and they gave their speeches.

Ben Johnson: "I think this organization needs someone to help organize it, and when I got up to make my speech I said I wanted to help this organization and the things I'm going to do are very simple.

"I want to get us together but some of the things I want to do are real easy.

"I want to makesure you get your membership card on time, that there's a newsletter and you get that mailed to you and you know what this organization is all about.

"Les got up, " said Johnson, "and blew me away."

Les Payne's eyes luminate from his face, fixing intensely on a subject, or, target. He speaks in clipped authoritative sentences. Payne was born a Southerner but his speech pattern seems mostly a product of his New England upbringing and lessons he learned in the military.

"Brothers and sisters," Payne told the members, "if you want to get your membership card on time, if you want to be able to reach your president when you want to, fine. Vote for this brother here (Johnson) because I'm not going to worry about that stuff.

"That's for a secretary or somebody else to do.

"What I want to do is to have us develop greater issues, get involved in determining who would be the decision-makers, who would set the agenda for diversity in the industry."

Members had clear choices: a candidate from Middle America who wanted NABJ to become strong by providing basic services to members in order to empower themselves vs. a prestigious editor fro New York who had a vision of the organization making near-revolutionary changes in American journalism.

While Johnson's aggressive campaigning turned off numerous conferees, Les Payne had a weak spot.

Despite the high concentration of black journalists and numerous cities in the region, NABJ Region 2 was not much of a region.

It was strong on individuals but weak on organization.

Fifteen months after NABJ was founded the New York Association of Black Journalists elected officers in March 1977. In 1979 there was a leadership fallout.

Les Payne and Vince Sanders, the outgoing two-term regional director, clashed.

NYABJ and Region 2 were inactive from 1979 to 1981.

Audrey Edwards, an editor with *Essence* magazine, was well aware of Region 2 and NYABJ's condition where she checked into Galt House.

Edwards went to the Region 2 caucus. Ten people were meeing in Les Payne's suite, she recalled.

"When I walked in, everyone jumped up and congratulated me. 'You're our new regional director,' they told me.

"It was bogus to elect me regional director like that.

"I said 'Look, the only way I'll do this is if you help me and put together a region and a New York chapter.'"

Edwards meant a NYABJ chapter that met regularly.

As for Region 2, it had to reach beyond the city to New Jersey and Connecticut. Payne and the other New Yorkers agreed to that commitment.

* * *

The membership meeting adjourned in the late afternoon and reconvened at 11 p.m. after the awards banquet for unfinished business.

This was: Should NABJ establish a permanent national office?

The answer was obviously "yes."

Lack of a permanent base and a full-time administrator stunted NABJ's ability to attract more members, serve them well, and, challenge and critique the major media consistently.

Nevertheless, NABJ members prolonged the malaise.

Florida A&M University submitted a proposal a year

ago. It was eager to house the national office. A&M officials had one condition: It wanted NABJ officers to have at
least one of its quarterly board meetings in Tallahassee.

Treasurer Mal Johnson balked at the suggestion of have-
ing the headquarters somewhere other than Washington,
D.C.

A lengthy debate ensued pitting NABJ members who
were against having the headquarters outside the Washington, D.C. area against members who objected to leaving the
decision in the hands of the board.

Jeanne Fox was on the board committee that looked at
the national office proposals. She thought the A&M proposal would be good for NABJ.

"We (committee members) wanted the board to hash it
out before it went to the general membership.

"It was the first time that the new board members heard
about it."

An hour before the A&M debate, the members elected a
new board. Some of the new officers were not familiar with
the national office dilemma, which had been an issue for
two years.

Said Fox, "Mal (Johnson) raised enough questions to
have it tabled. I remember Mal effectively torpedoing it.

"At the board meeting before the conference opened,
Mal mumbled to herself, 'Can't have it (national office) at a
university. That's not how it's done.'"

Elmer Smith said "We mishandled it in a way that colleges would feel we treated the national office proposal
cavalierly." Smith was Region 3 director (Pennsylvania,
Del.) and a *Philadelphia Bulletin* reporter. "We had an
emergency meeting at 11 p.m. and nothing happened.

"A Florida A&M representative was present.

"I was very embarrassed by it."

                          *   *   *

At the Saturday night banquet, the organization had its
first awards program that recognized outstanding work in
several categories: print, broadcast and photojournalism.

A series called "The Blacks: Progress or Promises?," by the staff of *The Philadelphia Bulletin,* was top winner among six newspapers in the print category.

Claude Lewis, an associate editor at *The Bulletin,* accepted the award for the newspaper.

The award turned out to be a deathbed tribute. Philadelphia's largest evening newspaper was going to die in five months.

Of four TV news finalists, the top award went to reporter Barbara Rodgers of KPIX-TV, San Francisco, for "Prisoners of the Palace," a story about a housing project.

"Crime by Color, Black on Black," by Al Allen of WJLB-FM, Detroit, was the top radio winner.

The photojournalism winner was Durell Hall Jr. of the *Louisville Times* for "A City in Sorrow," a 10-photograph layout about the Atlanta Child murders.

Robert C. Maynard and Max Robinson shared the Frederick Douglass Award honoring Journalists of the Year.

The audience was bursting with pride from the triumphs of two black princes of daily journalism.

In 1979 Maynard, a former *Washington Post* and York (Pa.) *Gazette & Daily Record* newsman, jumped at a chance to become editor of *The Tribune* in Oakland, Calif.

The Tribune was a long-time bastion of conservatism. It was being abandoned by white readers fleeing to the suburbs, and, black readers who regarded the paper as openly hostile.

With the help of new owner *Gannett Co.,* Maynard injected energy into the sagging newspaper. *The Tribune* took a multicultural approach to covering the racially diverse city and East Bay area. It ended a circulation freefall.

Since 1978, Max Robinson was co-anchor of ABC-TV "World News Tonight" with Peter Jennings and Frank Reynolds. Robinson moved fearlessly through TV news from Richmond, Va. to Memphis, Tenn. then to Washington, D.C. He rarely held his tongue about improving the condition of black folk. Robinson was a passionate co-founder of NABJ. His journalist sisters and brothers held him in especially high esteem.

After both men were honored, there were remarks by Kentucky Gov. John Y. Brown.

The governor gave a rambling, disjointed speech on the "New Federalism" that had much of the audience staring at each other, searching for clues on *what* Brown could be talking about. Brown's wife, Phyllis George, stared impatiently at her husband from the dais, hoping he'd finish.

Outgoing president Bob Reid announced the NABJ election results.

At the afternoon business meeting, conferees cast ballots for their choices for NABJ office.

From the bottom up, Reid gave the tally of the loser first, then winner, in contested races:

• For parliamentarian, Ralph Wright of *The Atlanta Constitution* lost to Karen Howze of *Gannett Rochester Newspapers.*
• For secretary, Jeanne Fox of *The Detroit Free Press* lost to Angela Dodson of *TheCourier-Journal.*
• Mal Johnson of Cox Broadcasting was re-elected treasurer, unanimously.
• For the new board office, vice president / broadcast, Charlene Williams of WTOP-Radio, Washington, D.C., lost to Myron Lowery of WMC-TV, Memphis, Tenn.
• For vice president / print, Mervin Aubespin of *The Courier-Journal,* the convention chairman, was elected unanimously.

Les Payne was on the dais talking to Aubespin's successor as Region 5 director, Doug Lyons of the *U.S. News & World Report* Atlanta bureau.

"Les was telling me about what he was going to do as president," said Lyons.

"Reid read the results: 'For president, Les Payne . . . 'Bob (Reid) inadvertently reversed the order.

'Oh shit! I lost,'" said Payne. His face froze momentarily, then dropped for a moment, recalled Lyons.

Then, Payne recovered.

Reid corrected himself.

Les Payne won, lopsidedly.

He pulled 116 votes, Elmer Smith recalls.

"I got 20 votes," said opponent Ben Johnson a decade later. "I was devastated and hurt that I lost."

Elmer Smith was annoyed. It was curious to him that the only election that Reid botched was the presidency.

Reid had nominated Payne for president in the afternoon. The outgoing president did not hide his distaste for Ben Johnson's antics.

Smith suspected that Reid deliberately reversed the order to "rub Ben's nose in it (the rout.)

"It (the lopsided tally) stilled the place for a second," said Smith, "then there was laughter."

Initially, Elmer Smith was turned off by Johnson's shameless campaigning.

When Smith arrived in Louisville and got on the hotel elevator, Ben Johnson and his daughter were on it.

They were festooned with campaign buttons.

Nevertheless, said Smith, Ben Johnson represented a segment of NABJ that was underrepresented: Highly credentialled black journalists in their 30s who were pragmatists instead of the more nationalist and older NABJ founders.

Johnson represented new blood and new ideas and that was good.

And unlike previous NABJ members who sulked away after an embarrassment, Johnson rebounded from the crushing defeat and remained active with the organization.

He became president of the Detroit Chapter of NABJ and chairman of the Outstanding Achievement Awards program for 1982.

In Louisville, the outgoing board voted 6-4 to hold the 1982 conference in Detroit.

It voted 9-2 to go to New Orleans in 1983.

* * *

Lerone Bennett Jr., senior editor of *Ebony* magazine and author of several books including *Before the Mayflower, a History of Black People in America,* was NABJ's 1981

Lifetime Achievement Award winner.

Bennett was weakened by a virus and high fever. But the 52-year-old journalist-historian gathered every ounce of strength to appear before the luncheon crowd at Galt House. He gave a rousing speech, a forecast of the 1980s and suggestions to improve the black condition.

He said:

"A few years ago when I started out in journalism, we could have held this convention in a telephone booth. It seems to me that your first task in this world is to make sure that there are ten, a hundred Robert Maynards in this business . . . to ensure that Robert Maynard, the Max Robinsons, are not lonely.

"When I was a boy in Mississippi, my grandmother used to say, 'son, you can't beat a horse with no horse.' By that she meant that you can't beat a fact with no fact; that you can't beat organized power with no organized power.

"I'm glad to see that black journalists have organized as black journalists because you can't beat organized hypocrisy without organized truth-telling. You can't beat organized white media without organized black media.

" . . . We have got to deal with the coalescence of the same forces that doomed the first Reconstruction and turned America back toward slavery in 1881 -- underscore that date!

". . . In 1881, as in 1981, there was a neo-conservative, pro-fascist revolt against taxes in this country. They were saying things in 1881 that they are saying in 1981: that taxes are being used to support black schoolchildren and lazy black welfare recipients.

"In 1881, as in 1981, there was a concerted and organized attempt to isolate and pick off black elected officials one-by-one, charging them with fraud and mismangement. In 1881 as in 1981, they were picking Janet Cookes out of hats and using them to browbeat black professionals and black intellectuals.

". . . Now is the time, if ever there was a time, for us to mobilize all of our resources and bring them to bear for de facto equality. Now is the time for those brothers and sisters who got lost in the pro-Reagan days, to come back home and help us run this race.

". . . White media in America can't solve the problem of race because white media are part of the problem. They are part of that problem because they reflect the values and aspirations of only one segment of the population. In that sense Marshall McLuhan was right: the medium is the message in America and the message of the medium is that white is always and everywhere right.

"It is sheer folly for a government situated in a black city like Washington, D.C., to make foreign policy based on the premise that this is a white country. Even in cities that are predominately black and brown, like Chicago, or Washington, the media still tend to organize around the idea that this is a white man's world, without even giving it a second thought.

"Black journalists have the responsibility of raising the real and dangerous question of when will the white press start to deal with the problem of educating white people about the political, economic and social realities of the 20th century."

The conference made a great impression on many newcomers, like Betty Winston Baye. She entered daily journalism late, at age 34. She was a reporter for nearly a year at *The Daily Argus,* a *Gannett* newspaper in Mount Vernon, N.Y., a New York City suburb.

Baye grew up in New York City's Lower East Side and later East Harlem. Her father, a laborer with a seventh-grade education, read the New York City newspapers voraciously. Mr. Winston would bring home the *Daily News,* the *Journal-American* or *The Herald Tribune* and read and explain the stories to her attentive oldest daughter.

Instead of college, Betty Winston went to work immediately after high school. She was an administrative assistant with Opportunities Industrialization Centers, and active in the Student Non-Violent Coordinating Committee (SNCC).

For a time, she was an actress with a Harlem theater company.

There was a time when Betty Winston thought college was for "bourgeois niggers," unlike her. But her attitude changed and she chose to matriculate and study journalism. She earned a bachelor's degree from Hunter College and a master's from Columbia University Graduate School of Journalism. During her college years she married and added the name Baye.

The Louisville conference, she said, "was heaven.

"I'll never forget seeing Max Robinson and Lerone Bennett in person. That for me was everything. Then, I decided that I wanted to be a leader in that group. I went to every workshop. I came back from NABJ exhausted."

For others, the Louisville conference recharged a lot of human batteries and it inspired a number of new people.

Furthermore, the conference made money as promised, about $20,000.

*   *   *

The new board met Sept. 27, 1981 in Washington, D.C. and Dec. 5-6 in Dallas. It rejected an offer from *Sepia,* a black magazine, to establish a joint $2,500 scholarship to be awarded annually to a black college newspaper.

The board was turned off after hearing that *Sepia* operated at a loss but *Bronze Thrills* and other less-reputable teen magazines published by that company were profitable. "Among other reasons," explained a story in the Spring 1982 *NABJ Journal,* "the board decided that it should enter such arrangements only with publications that promoted excellence in journalism."

The look of NABJ's newsletter changed. It carried a new masthead, designed by Merv Aubespin. Aubespin was a news artist before he became a reporter. The letters N, A, B, and J were set in bold Roman type and JOURNAL followed in contrasting outline bold sans serif.

Later, the official logo added an upright pen on the left and a hanging microphone on the right.

At the March 6-7 meeting in Detroit, the board agreed to co-sponsor the $10,000 Ida B. Wells Award with the National Conference of Editorial Writers and the National Broadcast Editorial Association.

The agreement picked up the work started by Vernon Jarrett when he was NABJ president from 1977-79.

The award would recognize a publisher, editor or broadcast owner who exhibited leadership in providing job opportunities for minorities in American journalism.

The award was a bust of Ida B. Wells, the fearless 19th-century black newspaperwoman, and two scholarships totalling $10,000 which would be awarded in the winner's name to a college.

In other business there were discussions about establishing the national office. Wilberforce in Ohio, a historically black college, was added as a possible site, joining Florida A&M, Howard University and Hampton Institute.

The addition obstructed instead of smoothed the attempt to settle into a national office. Les Payne was not overly enthusiastic about the national office anyway.

"The national office at a campus was a good idea," he said in 1991. "I favored it personally.

"Florida A&M was too remote. Hampton and Howard were acceptable.

"But I didn't think we were at the point that it (the office) was at the top of our priority list. I talked to Hampton about an office and archives for Martin Luther King's papers. Someone checked out Howard.

"Some people favored it (the national office) strongly.

Basically it was a good idea, but one we couldn't make work."

Chapter 9
Book Cadillac

"Extending Our Reach," was the theme of the 1982 national conference Aug. 19 to 22 in Detroit.

The conference book had a cover illustration of a black man holding a fountain pen over Africa. Another hand pointed a microphone toward the continental United States.

"The American public," wrote Les Payne in the book, "is not being fully informed enough about Tchula, Mississippi, Jackson, Harlem, Grenada, South Africa or Watts.

"The media is not sufficiently reporting about the Reagan administration's assault on blacks and the poor in colleges, high schools, the military, on the assembly lines, the maternity wards, and those standing idly on the boulevards, in the alleys, and on the tiers of the republic's Atticas and San Quentins.

"These issues and many others, both domestic and international, we plan to grapple with here in our workshops, plenary sessions, film festivals and during those social occasions listed throughout the four-day program.

"In Extending Our Reach,' we seek first to strengthen ties among ourselves and then to extend open arms to our brothers and sisters at home and abroad.

"We have assembled this year, not to make news, but rather to find ways to make news better."

The conference opened without its chairman, Monte Trammer. His mother died two days before. Trammer left to make arrangements and be with family.

The Book Cadillac Hotel was an old building that blended in with the aging skyscrapers downtown.

Many people complained that the hotel was old, crumbling and ratty (literally, for some people.)

The hotel was being renovated.

It opened prematurely for NABJ.

Some guest had exposed electrical wires in their rooms, obvious fire hazards. Others however, found their rooms clean and even somewhat charming.

Said Monte Trammer: "We got more people than we expected and more people earlier than we expected. We were caught a little off guard.

Why? "People were learning about us. NABJ was becoming something special. With Detroit, it was clear to the (news) industry that NABJ was important and could not be ignored.

"Now looking back, it was easy to get companies to sponsor events. The two Detroit papers had a rivalry. The car companies too put ads in the (souvenir) book. Take those factors and Detroit being big it was easier to get the word out nationally.

"When *Knight-Ridder* decides to play a major role, that's 35 papers. *Gannett,* that's 80-some (newspapers.)

"We also planned much earlier than before. Ben (Johnson), Cassandra Spratling (a *Free Press* reporter) and I drove to Louisville in 1981 and asked for the convention in 1983. We got to Louisville and found a presentation from New Orleans.

"Les (Payne), wisely, felt that New Orleans was not journalistic enough and needed more time. Les asked if we would take the convention in '82.

"Ben and I had started planning already.

"We worked faster."

At a workshop called "Integrating the Newroom -- Toward the Year 2000," top news executives assessed how the media were progressing toward reaching racial parity in newsrooms by the end of the century.

As Larry Jinks, a *Knight-Ridder* vice president spoke,

Gayle Pollard, Thomas Morgan, Morris Thompson and Earnestine Young, sat in the back of the room and giggled occasionally. Jinks' words triggered bittersweet memories.

They all once worked for *Knight-Ridder* and Jinks at *The Miami Herald,* the corporate home of *K-R.* Detroit was the reunion of *Herald* alumni. For most of them, The *Herald* was their first job in the business. Now all of them were at other papers, Pollard at *The Boston Globe;* Morgan, *The Washington Post;* Thompson, *Newsday,* and Young, the *Philadelphia Daily News.*

They remembered editors telling them that they would not amount to much.

But, they were still in the business, and, advancing.

At the Friday luncheon, Jay Harris, described as "the keeper of the numbers," spoke. About 2,700 minorities -- at least half of them black -- worked at daily newspapers. In 1982, 300 more people than in 1981. Overall, minorities made up 5.5 percent of the newsroom workforce. They remained concentrated at the biggest papers.

Two-thirds of American dailies, most of them 50,000 circulation or less, did not employ a minority journalist.

Harris had a long relationship with the luncheon sponsor, *Gannett Co.* His first reporting job at the company's paper in Wilmington, Del., the *News-Journal.* Harris later became a journalism professor at the Gannett Urban Journalism Center at Northwestern. Now he was back in the newsroom at *Gannett News Service* in Washington, D.C.

Gannett's top news executive were on the dais. They were making a major presentation.

The executives briefed the audience about the upcoming launch of USA TODAY.

It was a new newspaper and a national one.

This went against the gloomy climate of papers folding in Washington, D.C. (*Star*), Philadelphia (*Bulletin*), and Cleveland (*Press.*)

USA TODAY was to be upbeat and colorful. Its color photography was to match the slickest magazines. The weather map was color coded -- blues and purples for frigid days, reds and oranges on hot days, greens and yellows on mild days.

And pluralistically, USA TODAY promised to be more colorful than other American dailies.

The news was supposed to really reflect America's wide racial and cultural diversity.

The paper's executives told NABJ members that it was proving this commitment by assembling a mix of black, white, brown and yellow men and women throughout the reporting and editing ranks.

USA TODAY hired Monte Trammer of *The Detroit Free Press* to be deputy managing editor of its *Money* (business news) section. Karen Howze, an assistant managing editor at *Gannett Rochester Newspapers,* became USA TODAY's systems editor.

Other black journalists were also in highly visible positions.

But after hearing the pitch from executives, there was healthy skepticism by many NABJ members about the newspaper.

Trammer, who would later become publisher of a small *Gannett* paper, said in 1991 that "The industry did not believe USA TODAY had a right to exist. It was not the newspaper they envisioned. (But) the higher up the job ladder, the less criticism you encountered.

"Reporters were extremely skeptical. It was not highbrow or had long stories like *The New York Times*. Editors accepted it (USA TODAY) as marketing. Reporters were most of NABJ's members and they championed the concerns of entry-level journalists.

"USA TODAY was anathema."

Furthermore, *Gannett* had a bad reputation with some of the black journalists who worked at two of its newspapers -- the *Democrat & Chronicle* and *Times-Union* -- in Rochester, N.Y., the corporate base.

The tone of the questions was, why should we believe this new paper will have great opportunities for blacks?

John Quinn and *Gannett* executives listened and answered the accusatory questions.

Karen Howze took the microphone.

She said "Look, you know me. I can't promise they will

do what they say. There's some of us who will keep them to their promises.

"You ought to try this. . . . I'll be the first to tell you to leave this."

Howze in a 1991 interview, said "(John) Curley (the editor of USA TODAY) was flabbergasted. The color left his face." She explained that unlike some of the executives, Curley never had any dealings with NABJ.

"I told them (NABJ members) 'Either you risk (and try) this or miss an opportunity.'"

For most of her life Howze believed in working within entrenched systems to improve them.

She was a native of Detroit. She went to Catholic schools because her parents were not satisfied with the public schools. At age 13, Howze began studying to be a nun. She said she did it because "blacks were treated like crap in the Catholic church," and she thought she could help improve conditions.

At Madonna College in Livonia, Mich., Howze was a math major with a journalism minor. She had a change of heart when she was 20. She left the convent. Howze transferred to the University of Southern California and switched her major to journalism.

"I always liked writing," she explained.

"I told myself, 'If you're not going to do this religion thing, here's a way to serve your people.'"

Two days after graduation in 1972 she began work as a reporter at the *San Francisco Chronicle.* Howze became a union representative three years later when she was only 25. She also entered Hastings Law School, but continued to work. After law school, Howze worked as an instructor, in 1978, at IJE's Summer Program for Minority Journalists.

She later went to *Newsday* to work on the copy desk.

Howze joined *Gannett* in 1979 because she was offered a management position: assistant managing editor at the *Times-Union,* Rochester's evening paper. She was one of the few, if any, black women ranked so high in daily newspaper management. Her tenure was stormy.

She said she was fired from her editors job in 1980.

"John Quinn stopped me from leaving.

"I told Quinn I'm fired. He said 'No you're not. I worked too hard to get you. Come work for me.'"

She joined USA TODAY's startup team in February 1981.

At the luncheon in Detroit, after Howze told a couple of hundred NABJ members to give the *Gannett* people a try, she turned to Curley.

"I told a lot of people I respect to trust you," she said. "I'm not sure I did the right thng."

That night, conferees enjoyed a three-hour cruise of the Detroit River and Lake St. Clair on a steamer called Boblo.

There was plenty of food, drink and dancing. When the D.J. played "Jump to it," a 1982 hit song by Detroit's Areatha Franklin, dozens of conferees stomped the dance floor exuberantly, rocking the boat.

A fashion show followed. It was memorable for Lena Sherrod, a New York free-lance writer. "When these little white boys (men) came on, (black) women were applauding wildly," she said. "I thought it was very strange.

"I guess it was the incongruity of them being among all the black models and people were being gracious."

NABJ's first summer interns were recognized at a Saturday afternoon luncheon. Five college students were selected to work 10 weeks at *The National Leader, Newsday,* WNEV-TV in Boston, and KOA-TV in Denver.

In all $29,000 was raised to pay for the internships. *Newsday* put up $6,350. Jacaranda, a media consultant group working with the Nigerian Television Authority, contributed $7,000. NABJ contributed money from its treasury. And Philip Morris Inc. and Miller Brewing Co. gave $7,000 for the first "William Monroe Trotter" Internship, named after the fiery early 20th-century journalist and civil rights activist.

On the luncheon tables were Philip Morris and Miller products. Plastic buckets contained bottles of beer.

Sample packs of cigarettes were on the tables too.

"It was heavyhanded," said Les Payne.

He was aware that many members did not like the organization accepting money from alcohol and cigarette manufacturers. But Payne believed that the sponsorship wouldn't "forever soil" NABJ as a number of people feared.

On Saturday night the Nigerian Ambassador to the United States, E.Y. Eke, was keynote speaker.

He urged NABJ members to establish exchange programs with Nigerian journalists.

"You can and should serve as the agent for the arrival of the black man and the black world in their rightful place," he told NABJ members.

Eke's address kept in the spirit of the conference theme, drawing attention to issues in Africa and black communities in America.

Gil Noble, host of the Sunday news magazine show "Like It Is" on WABC-TV in New York, was the 1982 Journalist of the Year. Noble's program featured segments showing the destructive effects of heroin and other drug abuse. Profiles of Malcolm X and Adam Clayton Powell Jr., figures who often were depicted shrilly elsewhere in the daily media, were treated respectfully on "Like It Is."

Segments on news events in Africa and the Caribbean were a draw to the New York area's diverse African-American community.

Ethel Payne of *Sengstacke Newspapers* (*Chicago Defender,* et al) was recognized for Lifetime Achievement.

She was hired by *Sengstacke* after writing an article on discrimination in the military. She went on to work as a war correspondent and Washington correspondent.

Ethel Payne reported from 30 countries.

She often kidded black journalists when, with sincere awe, they called her a "pioneer." She said it made her sound like it was time to put on a bonnet and hitch her wagon buckboard.

Ethel Payne died on May 28, 1991. She was 79.

* * *

The Detroit conference succeeded in giving members the annual recharge they needed to fight racism on their jobs and to stave off stress.

It was an off-election year for NABJ so personality clashes abated.

An estimated 325 members attended, a 50-percent surge in attendance compared to the successful Louisville, Ky. conference.

NABJ name recognition grew stronger and more new faces joined the regulars.

Chapter 10
New Orleans

The 1983 New Orleans conference was most memorable for its mishaps.

New Orleans' streets sweltered in the early September heat. Streets in the center of town and in the French Quarter were a mess, broken and escavated. The city was preparing to host the 1984 World's Fair.

For the visitors who found these less-than-ideal conditions only a minor inconvenience, the cosmopolitan Southern city was a pleasant distraction.

"The setting was so powerful," said Gayle Pollard. "The attractions, the black tradition, the (French) Quarter, Cafe DeMour.

"Even panelists would skip (workshops) and go to the Quarter.

"They got back late from Chez Helene, Dookey Chase and Antoine's. There was a constant comparison of where you ate. It was fun, fun, fun."

The meeting rooms in the Fairmont Hotel were cavernous, making general sessions and workshops look less well attended.

The air conditioning required to adequately cool the rooms turned them into iceboxes. Even events during the social hours had degrees of discomfort. For example, on another side of town, NABJ members went to a nighttime reception where they were served steaming bowls of gumbo, red beans and rice and bourbon-flavored bread pudding.

They sat down in an amphitheater to catch the entertainment, actor William Marshall, performing a one-man show as Frederick Douglass.

Marshall gave a fine performance. But you could not tell by looking around at the audience. The thick night air and humidity and rich cuisine had many people nodding out in their seats.

NABJ did not have a strong local presence in the city. The organization read this correctly. New Orleans wanted the conference in 1982 but was talked out of it and convinced to put it off for a year to get better prepared.

Still, the New Orleans hosts had only a few strong workers. They talked a good game but did not have the organizational muscle to pull off a smooth-running conference.

In New Orleans NABJ held a general session called "A Black Candidacy . . . Are We Ready?" to assess whether Jesse Jackson was going to make a run for President of the United States in 1984.

For months, Jackson, director of Operation PUSH (People United to Serve Humanity), talked about running for president. Jackson's idea generated a lot of debate and excitement in black communities.

It also created great excitement among black journalists. If Jackson decided to play in the national political arena, black journalists, too, should be elevated to cover presidential politics.

Only twice in 196 years were African-Americans candidates for the office. U.S. Rep. Shirley Chisholm, D-N.Y., ran in 1972. In 1968 the Rev. Channing E. Phillips was nominated as a favorite-son candidate of the District of Columbia at the Democratic National Convention.

Georgia state Sen. Julian Bond, M. Carl Holman of the National Urban Coalition and Eddie Williams of the Joint Center for Political Studies, a Washington, D.C.-based black think tank, were the panelists.

They debated the strategies: With blacks only about 12 percent of the eligible voting population, could Jackson draw significant numbers of white voters? Or should he? Could Jackson attract enough blacks and other disenfranchished people of color to be a kingmaker? Make the Democratic and Republican parties truly responsive to social issues such as employment, housing and civil rights?

How could Jackson overcome being dismissed as a fringe candidate? Followers and much of the media called Jackson a leader, but he was never elected to anything in the political arena.

Why should anyone believe he was qualified to be president?

A number of NABJ members were visibly irritated that Jesse Jackson was not in New Orleans to tell them why he seriously considered running.

Loose talk circulated that Jackson promised to attend the conference but backed out at the last minute.

This didn't wash. Jackson was not listed in the program book. Besides, as NABJ was assessing whether America was ready for a Jackson candidacy, it was fair to ask if NABJ was ready to host Jackson.

That answer was no.

Jackson had to think of forums that would get his message out most powerfully. With only about 400 members, NABJ was not big enough.

While Jackson was thinking hard about running, decision time faced NABJ. It was time for members to elect *their* president. The battle was between favorite sons from NABJ's largest constituencies, the Northeast and the South.

Acel Moore, associate editor of *The Philadelphia Inquirer* and Mervin Aubespin, NABJ's vice-president/print and a reporter for *TheCourier-Journal* in Louisville, Ky., competed for the presidency.

Bob Reid of CBS News, NABJ president from 1979-81, entered the race very late as a long-shot candidate.

Moore was much like the outgoing president, Les Payne of *Newsday* in Long Island, N.Y.

Both men were editors, former reporters, Pulitzer Prize winners and NABJ founders.

Both men shared the NABJ Journalist of the Year award in 1979.

Journalism chose Acel Moore.

He grew up in South Philadelphia. Moore lived in the neighborhood with Ted Curson, Jimmy, Percy and Al Heath and Charles Earland, all young musicians on their way to becoming jazz greats. Moore played the clarinet at age 7. He later played in a band with Charles Earland.

Academically, Acel Moore was an average student. Besides music, he liked to read and sketch. He finished high school and entered the Army. Moore was stationed in South Carolina, Texas, Washington State, then Alaska. His final military stop was Washington, D.C. There, Moore took some college-level courses.

After his discharge, to make enough money to finish college, Moore took a job as a copy boy at *The Philadelphia Inquirer.* His college plans changed.

He apprenticed for six years and became a reporter. In a building with 5,000 employees, he became familiar with every department of the newspaper besides the newsroom.

Moore understood the importance of trying to employ more blacks in all parts of the plant. In 1967-68 Moore was one of three black professionals in a newsroom of 350 journalists.

He had a feel for the streets and for the city's black community. Moore got involved with media groups that lobbied for more black participation in the news. There was Black Communicators (1967-68), a forerunner of the Association of Black Journalists (ABJ) of Philadelphia.

In 1977, Moore became president of ABJ.

In 1978, he helped organize the NABJ Chicago convention.

This was significant because Moore's critics claimed that he was not active in NABJ affairs.

At *The Inquirer,* Moore rose from reporter to columnist and associate editor. Moore missed the 1981 Louisville conference because of his Nieman fellowship at Harvard University.

"It was the only one (conference) I ever missed," said Moore. "I didn't meet Merv. I didn't have a sense of the sentiment for Merv."

The New Orleans convention was a homecoming of sorts for Mervin Aubespin. He was from Opelousas, La. Aubespin graduated from Tuskegee Institute in 1958 and did some post-graduate work at Indiana State University in 1960.

In 1965, *The Courier-Journal* in Lousiville, Ky. hired Aubespin. He was the paper's first black artist. When riots erupted in Louisville's black community, the newspaper had no black reporters. Aubespin was drafted to cover the rage in the streets. In 1972, he spent a summer at Columbia University for a crash course on news reporting.

Aubespin knew about the attempt to establish NABJ in 1975 but he was too scared to participate.

Aubespin was deathly afraid of flying. In 1977, he drove to the Baltimore conference with a colleague.

Aubespin was excited by NABJ's value as a "battery charging session" for embattled black journalists.

Compared to NABJ's leaders, Aubespin was an undistinguished journalist. In NABJ's early years, the right pedigree -- major news organization or title -- defined who would be a leader in NABJ.

Aubespin was from a highly regarded regional newspaper, but it was not a big-city paper. He was a mere local reporter. Aubespin was ambitious and he made up for his lack of credentials by being clever and savvy.

Aubespin became a founder then president of NABJ's first affiliate, the Louisville Association of Black Communicators. In 1979 he became Region 5 director, then the first vice president/print with the national board.*

His avuncular personality was part country preacher, part ward politician. People remembered how pleasant the Louisville conference was and identified it with Aubespin, who was conference chairman.

In 1981 he was one of the officers who pushed for awarding the 1983 convention to New Orleans instead of Detroit. Most officers agreed that although Detroit wanted to host their conference in '83, they would be host city in 1982 because they were better prepared than New Orleans.

Aubespin had another reason for favoring this order: It

would give him, the Southerner, an edge if he decided to run for president.

As NABJ's fourth president, Payne lifted the organization intellectually. But as leader he was more a divisive force than a consensus builder.

At the New Orleans election he changed rules on the spot, ignoring election rules that were approved by the board.

He yielded many tough calls to Reginald Stuart, a *New York Times* national correspondent. NABJ's parliamentarian was Karen Howze. She was elected for the 1981-83 term, but in 1982 she resigned to devote her total energies to being an editor for the new national newspaper USA TODAY. Howze said she submitted a written resignation but it was disregarded by the NABJ board. The board did not appoint a replacement member.

This was a mistake. The organization faced an election without its expert on rules of debate. Like a pickup basketball player, Stuart was asked to fill in for the board member because he was seen as a member who would be impartial during this highly partisan election.

In trying to be even-handed, Stuart angered colleagues and annoyed hotel staff. Shortly after agreeing to help with the election he recognized a serious flaw:

There were no ballots.

Stuart made an unusual request. He asked the Fairmont Hotel management for dozens of index card-size telephone memo pads to use as makeshift ballots.

Then, Stuart ruled that the elections for the first and second vice presidents would be separate.

He said the NABJ constitution was not clear whether the first vice president was the candidate with the most votes or whether the two vice presidents should represent different constituents, print journalists and broadcast journalists.

Stuart was burned by this issue during the 1981 election in Louisville when he nominated *St. Paul Pioneer Press* reporter Denise Johnson for broadcast vice president. He reasoned that she qualified because she was "a hybrid." Johnson did a weekly news and public affairs show. Broadcast members roundly booed the nomination and Merv Aubes-pin, the man Stuart counted on to second his nomination, was out of the room.

Denise Johnson ended a floor fight by withdrawing her candidacy.

Two years later, Denise Johnson would again be the subject of an election controversy.

Of four candidates running for vice president, *Essence* magazine executive editor Audrey Edwards appeared to win a vice president post (the others were Johnson, Alexis Yancey and Warren Bell.)

Les Payne ruled that members would not be allowed to cast two votes for vice president : one for the print vice president , one for the broadcast vice president. They would get one vote only.

Conceivably, two candidates in the same category could get the highest totals.

The members were faced with two representatives but were stripped of the chance to vote for one of them.

The vice president/broadcast was a new board position. Myron Lowery of Memphis was elected to the newly created position in 1981. He did not seek re-election in New Orleans nor did he attend. Lowery was suing his TV station for racial discrimination. He also left journalism to run for the Memphis city council.

Audrey Edwards was stung by Payne's Machiavelian acts.

She suspected that the presidential candidate Payne backed, Acel Moore, was not a shoo-in after all. Moore failed to show up at the Region 2 caucus -- Payne's home base -- to make his pitch for office.

Edwards, the Region 2 director, supported Aubespin, who was at the caucus with longshot candidate Bob Reid.

Edwards encouraged Aubespin to run because he displayed leadership ability as an NABJ vice president.

Payne, however, did not think Aubespin had the stature to represent the organization. He was merely a reporter for a regional newspaper.

The election irregularities in New Orleans did not surprise Edwards.

"Because I knew what he had done two years ago, it didn't surprise me.

"It was so blatant, an unabashedly dictatorial move.

"He wanted to see one of his people get in. Denise (Johnson) worked with him on the scholarship program. But I did represent the (Payne's) region."

Edwards recalled her "bogus election" as regional director in 1981 when Les Payne vacated that spot to run for president.

Shortly after paying her membership dues, making her eligible to vote, she went to the regional caucus being held in Payne's suite. When Edwards entered she was congratulated enthusiastically by about 10 people: "You're our new regional director!"

Edwards called her election a fraud. She was not present to be nominated, and for that matter, eligible. And, there wasn't much of a region. The New York City chapter was inactive and there were no organizing efforts in New Jersey, Connecticut or Upstate New York. The election was conducted again and Edwards was elected officially.

She promised to hold the office if the New York chapter was revived.

In New Orleans, with the new election rule change, Edwards had to compete against Denise Johnson.

Edwards lost.

The scheduled 2 1/2-hour business meeting that Saturday took five torturous hours. Payne yielded often to the freelance parliamentarian Stuart. Stuart decided he would let all members have their say. The election, he said in a 1990 interview, was too important to abridge debate.

At this meeting members were to hear nominating speeches from the candidates for president, two vice presidents -- one for print and one for broadcast -- treasurer, secretary and parliamentarian, then elect these officers.

What ensued was NABJ members challenging each other over bylaws and resolutions. It degenerated into grandstanding and nitpicking.

Randy Daniels, the CBS correspondent, introduced a Jesse Jackson resolution that would have NABJ demand that the probable presidential candidate be included in major candidate debates. The resolution was rejected.

To many members, it seemed too political a stand for the organization of journalists.

As the meeting grew tedious and irritating, decorum was shattered. A woman from *The Washington Post* strutted demonstrably into the tension-filled room with a tray of cocktails for her friends. That sent verbal sparks flying.

"It was the worst conference I went to in terms of squabbling," said Charlene Williams of WTOP-Radio in Washington, D.C.

"I went into the corridor with two sisters and we sat and talked. I hoped everything would be OK."

Inside, someone stood up and chastised everyone for allowing the meeting to run so long that it would delay the awards banquet and the keynote speech by author Maya Angelou.

The woman who caused the stir with the tray of cocktails and other people got their refreshments from a reception table downstairs. As the meeting was going on, Albert Fitzpatrick, longtime NABJ member and *Knight-Ridder* news executive, was standing in a reception area filled with hors d'oeuvres and beverages.

He was the greeter and other *Knight-Ridder* executives were with him. The NABJ members were late and Fitzpatrick, the host, was standing and fuming.

Said Fitzpatrick, "The business meeting began at 1 p.m. They were trying to have the membership legislate the direction of the organization. It dragged into the reception time. Members started to go into the reception area and get snacks and drinks. I was not happy about this of course.

"We were selling *Knight-Ridder* but we were also selling industry."

The executives wanted to smooze and reinforce to aspiring journalists that this was a good field to enter, and for experienced ones, a good field to stay in.

"The meeting was so long," said Fitzpatrick, "it virtually destroyed our reception."

But upstairs was a room full of journalists trying to elect

their leaders and nearly every one wanted to have the last word, but no one seemed willing to relent. One person's proposal would get knocked down by another. It was more a competition than a session to build consensus.

During his five-minute candidate speech, Acel Moore talked about his early days at *The Philadelphia Inquirer* in the '60s when he would not tolerate white journalists calling him "booooy," a habitual term for summoning copy boys but also a way of devaluing black males.

Moore used the anecdote to vow that NABJ under his leadership would challenge the media powers and demand respect and increased representation in the industry.

Moore was associate editor of *The Inquirer.* Some members were wary of NABJ coming under the heavy influence of corporate power if they elected someone who was in upper management. Would the organization that existed to challenge the established media become co-opted by it?

Moore stumbled through some of his speech but it was sincere.

Merv Aubespin was next.

Monte Trammer of USA TODAY managed Aubespin's campaign. "I was lying in my room when I got a call to come quick. We were going to have to make a nomination speech and it was a chance to grab the crowd.

"Suddenly, it was showtime.

"It perturbed Les (Payne) that in my (nominating) address, I said the convention was not being run well. Les took it wrongly as a criticism of him and his administration.

"I used that as a wedge. We should elect a person (Merv Aubespin) who knows intimately the day-to-day concerns of the organization, not someone (Acel Moore) who comes to conventions."

Once nominated, Aubespin gave his candidate speech. The short, rotund man with caramel skin and a short, graying Afro spoke with the passion of a Baptist preacher who starts his sermon solemnly and works the crowd into a frenzy of call-and-response amen chants.

Aubespin promised to make NABJ a family and heal an organization smarting from a divisive election campaign.

NABJ's lofty journalistic goals were noble, but his vision

was for an organization that provided services, like a permanent mailing address and a telephone number people could call (NABJ did not have this) and a membership card that could fit in members' wallets.

Once, when Les Payne was challenged about NABJ's ability to issue membership cards in a timely fashion, he fired back "when you get it, what can you do with it?"

Processing membership cards had come to be beneath Payne who was accustomed to having access to African heads of state and comfortable with firing pointed questions at prominent news and policymakers. NABJ was led by a star for two years. It needed a foot soldier who would strenghten the foundation of the organization.

During Aubespin's speech, a member of the New York Association of Black Journalists was outwardly troubled by the bombast. He dismissed Aubespin as a "pork chop preacher" who was not worthy of leading NABJ.

But many people, especially Southerners, were attracted to Aubespin's populist style and his calls to members to "roll up their sleeves and check their egos at the door."

Aubespin edged favorite Acel Moore. According to Edwards, Merv won by about 25 votes, 125 to 100.

Bob Reid, said Edwards, got eight votes.

Records of the official count were unavailable.

In 1992, a former NABJ officer's recollection was that Aubespin won by 11 votes.

If this person's recollection is accurate, the election was so close, it could have gone to Aubespin or Moore.

That is because at least a dozen members, disgusted with the delays at the business meeting and election, stormed out and did not vote.

Said this former officer, votes just walked out of the door.

*   *   *

As important as the presidency were the changes on the national board. Thomas Morgan, a young editor with *The Washington Post,* was a diligent campaigner for Moore's presidential run. At the last minute, Morgan became a candidate for treasurer.

It occurred when he became indignant because of the way he was treated at the registration desk by long-time treasurer Mal Johnson of Cox Broadcasting.

Mal Johnson was a curmudgeon who guarded NABJ's meager funds like a hen, often to the point of insulting members who became upset if their registration payment was misplaced or membership was not recorded.

Johnson, one of the 44 founding members of NABJ, was a fixture as treasurer. She replaced the original treasurer when that officer resigned and went to Europe.

Then, another journalist was elected to the treasurer's post, but a job change compelled that person to relinquish the NABJ board position.

Mal Johnson regained the treasurer's job by default.

There was an election challenge in 1979.

Johnson put up with many indignities by male chauvinists in NABJ.

Being a custodian of other people's money was a thankless job. She gruffly reminded many people of the burden she carried.

But such behavior was unsatisfactory to Tom Morgan and others.

"The members deserve to be treated with dignity," Morgan told a cheering crowd during his candidate speech.

He won the post handily. Morgan immediately initiated changes. He explained in a 1991 interview: "Mal (Johnson) was instrumental in keeping the organization together. She was calling most of the shots.

"Mal was very resentful when she lost and refused to give up any records. Later, she gave a boxload of records to Merv.

"She never used an accountant to set up the books.

"I started with what was left in the bank: less than $50,000 profit from several years of conventions.

"There were no investments, no endowments. NABJ had not (yet) begun to seek corporate support.

"NABJ was surviving off money we paid for conventions. We gave one scholarship a year so we weren't spending a lot of money.

"We were in a position that if we had one bad year with a convention we'd be wiped out.

"After the first year of trying to do the books I knew that as we grew we'd need professional help so it (the books) could be audited. To go after corporate support, it had to be presentable.

"I went to Watson & Rice. I had them set up a bookeeping system. Two, I hired a black financial consultant to do more than keep money in bank accounts. He advised us on how to diversify.

"Merv and I wrote the funding proposals. To my knowledge that was not done before. The first national office was at *TheCourier-Journal.*

"We hired a part-time secretary, put in a phone line and an answering machine. We looked around for a few permanent sites."

Morgan said that NABJ's tax-exempt status was on the verge of being revoked because certain papers were not filed. Les Payne disputes this. He said he took care of it in the early 1980s.

Tax exemption was firmly established and a black-owned accounting firm was hired. Part of NABJ funds were invested in mutual funds and money market accounts. A financial strategy was taking shape to handle rapidly growing membership and the need to offer ambitious programs.

Mal Johnson meanwhile was crushed by the decisive defeat. Her departure from the board meant that for the first time, it had no founders.

Other significant additions to the NABJ board were the "Dallas Mafia," as one member called Paula Walker, Alexis Yancey and Ruth Allen Ollison. They all worked in broadcast news in Dallas.

The threesome were the driving forces behind what was probably the strongest local black journalist's organization at that time, the Dallas-Fort Worth Association of Black Communicators (DWFABC.)

The chapter raised large sums of scholarship money in Texas and even sponsored an NABJ scholarship. It also initiated many community outreach programs.

DFWABC was formed in 1980. Walker was president for the first three years. When Walker tried to get information on affiliating, she said NABJ secretary Angela Dodson was not forthcoming.

Before the New Orleans conference, NABJ had only two affiliates: Louisville and Detroit. A big reason that those chapters got established was that they had recently hosted national conferences.

Nevertheless, Paula Walker was dissatisfied with Dodson's response.

Dodson's explanation: In July, two months before the New Orleans conference, DFWABC sought a change in NABJ election rules and wanted a constitutional amendment. The NABJ board instructed DFWABC to raise the issue on the floor of the business meeting in New Orleans.

Angela Dodson sent a letter explaining all of this to DFWABC. The letter got lost in Texas. Dodson took time off from work before the conference. When DFWABC leaders tried to call her at *The Courier-Journal* they were unsuccessful.

The Texas folks felt slighted. Paula Walker and company came to New Orleans with chips on their shoulders. They were going to run for NABJ offices and effect change. Walker challenged Dodson for secretary and won.

Walker, a Harlem native, Allen-Ollison, who came from a tiny East Texas town and Milwaukean Yancey, brought energy and new ideas to the board.

*   *   *

President Aubespin set up NABJ's first office in two rooms donated by his newspaper, *The Courier-Journal.*

Having a place where members could call for information and service, even if it was only to leave a message on an answering machine, was a revolutionary leap of progress.

During the Payne administration, there had been talk of establishing the national office at a black college that had a journalism program, like Hampton University or Florida A&M University. But stalled negotiations and inertia among members left the proposal stuck in the mud.

Aubespin was given the time and resources from white senior editors to spend half his workdays representing NABJ. This meant conducting business from the office and traveling to business meetings to speak on behalf of the organization. Aubespin claimed to have flown at least 100,000 miles during his two-year term. He considered this quite a sacrifice; he was deathly afraid of flying.

Aubespin had to get the new board on his side. Half of the new officers did not vote for him, or, campaigned against him.

He came up with a slogan. Taking cues from Willie Stargell, the former Pittsburgh Pirate slugger and the pop group Sister Sledge, he called the board of directors "the family." He used his skill as a consensus-builder to stroke and encourage people into taking on projects and committee assignments with fervent enthusiasm.

This was a sharp break with the way NABJ executive boards operated. A board member of the previous administration figuratively said there often was "blood on the floor" after quarterly meetings.

Merv Aubespin's cabinet was not collection of rubber-stamping yes-men (and women.) He had a group of people with strong personalities, and a lot of energy. Many of the officers were younger; they were journalists with about 10 years of experience who followed the wave of black journalists who were hired after the '60s riots or the old hands of the black press.

There were heated board debates about how to move the growing organization forward.

Aubespin was proud that sharp differences eventually reached consensus, much like "African consensus," a democratic tradition of ancient Africa.

In his first year he boasted that the 17-member board had a string of dozens of unanimous votes.

*   *   *

Nineteen eighty-three closed the book on an eight-year era, the "old NABJ."

For the first time, there were no founding members on the board. Paul Brock, the first executive director, was no longer in the picture.

NABJ was indebted to Brock. At the same time he was an albatross, impeding the organization's ability to grow.

Mervin Aubespin would irrevocably change NABJ. He openly courted white news executives to become a major part of NABJ.

Their involvement would mean more jobs for black journalists. This is because Aubespin maximized his close relationship with *Courier-Journal* news executives. They could coax their peers to hire more blacks. David Hawpe, Paul Janesch and company could vouch for all the talent that assembled at NABJ conferences.

Many NABJ members justifiably were worrried, even deeply disturbed by Aubespin's strategy. Had NABJ sold its soul to the people it should be confronting every moment? Like some labor unions, had NABJ's leaders been co-opted by management?

Not necessarily.

Christine Harris explains. "NABJ has become institutionalized. It has a large base of support and membership. That's an incredible thing.

"I would like to see more black editors and general managers. That calls for a different kind of networking.

"I don't see where that is a terrible thing.

"That's where we as individuals have to mature so we use the system to our advantage and not be used."

Chapter 11
Atlanta

It is no accident that NABJ began growing in numbers quickly when the association established an easy place for people to find it.

Mervin Aubespin was elected NABJ president in the first closely contested election. Aubespin's employer, *The Courier-Journal* in Louisville, Ky., gave him office space on a half-floor in the *Courier-Journal* building on West Broadway. The new president got a phone number for NABJ. He hired a part-time secretary to field calls and perform clerical duties. Aubespin tackled *the* campaign promise he made: Cater to membership needs.

For the first 10 years NABJ did not have a permanent national office. From 1975 to 1983 it was wherever the president, a volunteer, worked, be that Philadelphia (Chuck Stone), Chicago (Vernon Jarrett), Los Angeles (Bob Reid) or Long Island (Les Payne).

Long-time treasurer Mal Johnson said NABJ did have a national office: her office at the Cox Broadcasting Washington bureau. It is true the association had a post office box in Washington. There was no phone number however, and no administrative staff to answer calls.

Newcomers attempting to join NABJ had to find the answer to what was a well-kept secret.

Attention and care grew members. Eleven months later at the annual convention in Atlanta, participation tripled compared with the 1983 gathering in New Orleans. One thousand people participated in the Atlanta convention. Seven hundred fifty of them were black journalists.

But it took more than an office and phone number to build a membership base. Board members, particularly regional directors, worked their territory. They lobbied black journalists to join, or, if they had been inactive, rejoin.

Secondly, the Atlanta convention and its organizers made a positive impression on the visitors. Convention registration was busy, but almost painless. The registration area in the Colony Square Hotel was like a cocktail reception. When it was time to work, the hotel meeting rooms in Atlanta were comfortable, unlike the frigid, oversized rooms the previous year in New Orleans that hindered conferees. The larger-than-anticipated crowds in Atlanta had a dramatic psychological effect. Workshop and general session rooms always seemed packed, some of them with standing-room only crowds spilling out of them. This created an aura of urgency and excitement.

Nineteen eighty three marked the end of "Old NABJ." There was no trace of founding members on the executive board.

And 1984 emphatically announced the coming out of the modern organization.

"The eighty-four convention was the pivotal convention," said Sam Fulwood III. "It interfaced white folks and their money with NABJ and its mission. Prior to that, NABJ conventions were small, low-budget and (unofficially but not intentionally) closed to whites."

Fulwood said he had a "shadowy" impression of NABJ when he joined in 1981. He was a three-year veteran newsman at *The Charlotte Observer*. The small group in Louisville in 1981 was warm and embracing like an extended family. Several years later, Atlanta was much bigger, more sophisticated professionally, even corporate.

"My God," gasped Fulwood. In Atlanta a huge ice sculpture was in the middle of a bustling cocktail reception sponsored by *The New York Times*. "They (industry heavies) must be taking us seriously."

NABJ's convention had also become a significant news gathering event. There was daily coverage by

Associated Press, United Press International, *The New York Times* and the *Atlanta Constitution* and *Journal.*

The fireworks began at the opening session. Milton Coleman of *The Washington Post* broke a six-month silence and faced 700 journalists to talk about his role in the "Hymietown" incident.

Several weeks after a background interview with 1984 presidential candidate the Rev. Jesse Jackson, Coleman disclosed that in a moment of exasperation Jackson had called American Jews "Hymies" and New York City "Hymietown."

Coleman's contribution was an 18-word sentence in the 48th paragraph of a 2,400-word article about Jackson and Jewish-American voters written by another *Post* reporter. A week later a *Post* editorial critical of Jackson amplified the "Hymietown" remark.

What followed:

• Jackson denied making the statement. He later admitted making it and apologized.

• Coleman was sharply criticized by Jackson supporters and Nation of Islam leader Louis Farrakhan.

• The incident drew unsubstantiated claims that black reporters assigned to cover Jackson were going easy on the first major black presidential candidate.

Coleman, a 15-year journalist, the last eight at *The Post,* said he had no regrets. "To this day I remain convinced that I did the right thing," he told the audience. "I don't come here seeking sympathy. Black people do not ask *not* to be told the downside of our heroes." Coleman said his long silence was painful, but deliberate. "I restrained from talking to prevent myself from being in the improper role of debating with presidential candidates." (By this time Jackson had ended his campaign, and Walter Mondale was selected Democratic nominee at the party's national convention.)

Although his conversation with Jackson was supposed to be "on background," meaning the words could be used but not the source, Coleman said he broke the rule because "I sought a higher standard." Jackson's "Hymie" remarks, said Coleman, suggested that as president he could say such offensive words in unguarded moments.

Many people in the audience did not believe Coleman sought higher standards. Instead, they believed he violated journalistic ethics.

His harshest critics that afternoon were peers Randy Daniels and Les Payne, then the immediate past president.

"The bottom line," said former CBS newsman Daniels, "is, and I think most people in the room would agree, if you hear a background quote, regardless of how offensive it is, if that statement is made off the record or on background, certain rules apply that you are duty bound to conform to."

Standing in a sea of seated members, Payne told Coleman he was confusing young journalists by performing "a long autopsy" on the incident. You should have written the story yourself, said Payne. since the information was so sensitive.

A broadcast journalist from Texas asked Coleman if he had not compromised himself by getting into a "black talk" background session with Jackson. "Did Jackson gather other reporters around for some 'white talk?'" she asked sarcastically. Jackson had prefaced his statement by telling Coleman, "let's talk 'black talk,'" signaling background.

In Atlanta, a young man in the crowd stood up and scornfully called Coleman a "Judas."

Without blinking, Coleman shot back, "One thing's certain, I'm no Judas, and Jesse (Jackson) ain't Jesus Christ." The room exploded with convulsive laughter. The quick exchange of verbal blows broke the tension.

Many people remained angry with Coleman. Others, however, appreciated his decision to stand before them, take a beating and tell his story.

Much of the American public learned that a National Association of Black Journalists existed because of Atlanta Mayor Andrew Young. He was invited to speak at the Friday luncheon. Young, one of Martin Luther King Jr.'s lieutenants during the civil rights revolution, was now an established politician. He was a loyal supporter of Democratic presidential candidate Mondale.

He was also frustrated because he was having trouble getting through to Mondale's top campaign aides. The mayor unleashed his frustration at NABJ's event. As cameras rolled, Young called Mondale's inner circle "a bunch of smart-ass white boys who think they know it all." His words were broadcast into American homes on national evening newscasts. What Young said stung leaders in the Mondale camp. Meanwhile, the outburst drew numerous amens from leading Georgia Democrats, black and white. Commenting on the remark, the Democratic Party, said Jesse Jackson, "must learn to accommodate new thoughts, new ideas, and that is a strategy for victory."

At the awards luncheon, speaker Lem Tucker, CBS correspondent and veteran newsman for 19 years, gave NABJ members indigestion. He spoke to the program theme of striving for excellence. Midway in the speech Tucker changed course. Tucker said he "avoided" joining organizations like NABJ for years. Tucker accused many black journalists of using organizations or lawsuits to hide their shortcomings as journalists.

"I hope I pissed you off," Tucker said at the end of his address. His mission succeeded. Applause was muted. An iciness drifted across the banquet room.

Tucker's attempt at shock treatment did not sit well with most members. He was not a member, and he bragged about it. Tucker, the guest, gratuitously insulted the hosts. And, at the event meant to salute award winners and excellence to boot. The infamous speech established an unofficial policy: Black journalists who addressed the conventions did not have to speak with the same voice, but they should *at least* be members.

Crowds spilled out of dozens of Atlanta workshop rooms. But none so much as the session called "Coping in the Newsroom," also known as the "Stress" workshop. Two hundred people crammed into a room made for half that audience. There were no chairs. A number of members sat on a ledge that ringed the room: others sat on the floor.

Most of the participants were young journalists with a few years or less of daily newsroom experience. Many said they were the only "one" (black) at their newspaper or TV station in the South or Midwest.

"War Stories from the Front," could have been a more appropriate name for the session. Twenty-three-year-olds testified about blatant and subtle racial slights in the newsroom. They said white editors and subordinates constantly second-guessed their journalistic competence or told them that stories they wanted to do about the black community were unimportant.

A young man from the *Orlando Sentinel* was in a quandary about what to do after work. Would hanging out with the handful of black reporters there marginalize him? Would an attempt to reach out and socialize with white journalists make him an "Uncle Tom" in the eyes of his black brothers and sisters?

Several people described the inferno inside them whenever a white colleague asked uneasily, "What's this, a black caucus?" or "Are you plotting to overthrow the paper?" whenever two or more black newspeople congregated at a desk or water cooler to discuss a news topic, their current assignment or anything.

The "coping" session was cathartic. People from Orlando, Fla.; Memphis; Washington, D.C.; Richmond, Va.; Windsor, Conn. and New York City told strikingly identical horror stories. A young woman from a small Midwest newspaper talked about racial insults she suffered almost daily. Her voice quivered. The crowd listened patiently. She exorcised pent-up frustration.

Moderator Betty Winston Baye (then with Gannett Westchester, N.Y., Newspapers) and panelists Dorothy Butler Gilliam and Thomas Morgan (both *Washington Post*), offered guidance to the younger journalists. Don't judge every perceived slight as racism, they said; it could be acts that were part of the rugged nature of the newsroom.

However, when ugly incidents could not be rationalized any other way but as racism, they had to speak up. Take the high road, they said. Define issues or incidents in journalistic, not personal terms. Appeal to editors or colleagues' sense of logic and decency.

NABJ had a coping session like this at its second convention in 1977. It was specifically relevant to 90 percent of the conferees because then they were in their 20s, were in the news business five years or less and were isolated in dozens of cities. At their coping session individuals realized, "I'm not insane." Entrenched bigotry and racism in daily newspapers and broadcasting lashed them all.

Seven years later on the last night of the Atlanta convention, banquet speaker Jesse Jackson said black journalists "operate with a needle in their backside and scissors in their chest:" great pain because white management often distrusted them, and they were often scorned by black communities that raised them.

The audience shouted and wailed its appreciation.

After Atlanta a fierce battle ensued to host the next convention, 1985.

Competing sites Philadelphia and Baltimore were ancestral homes for NABJ. The national was a direct descendant of the Association of Black Journalists (ABJ) of Philadelphia, organized nearly two years before NABJ.

Baltimore, meanwhile, was the site of the first big conference – NABJ's second – in 1977, where about 300 people came. The Association of Black Media Workers (ABMW) in Baltimore established itself months before NABJ in 1975 and maintained strong ties.

After written and video presentations by both chapters, the board voted 8-6 at its fall meeting to award the 1985 convention to Baltimore. This was the first time there was real competition and a close vote to host a convention, affirming the association's rising importance and relevance.

Feeling euphoric after the Atlanta convention, the NABJ board spread its wings by holding its fall meeting in Oakland, Calif. in early December.

In its nine years NABJ had never met on the West Coast. It was difficult to get a quorum of officers – most of whom were based east of the Mississippi – to come West. This time the board had two West Coast officers: Parliamentarian Marilyn Bailey of *The Oakland Tribune* and regional director Don Williamson of the *San Diego Union*.

The Bay Area Association of Black Journalists hosted the weekend of meetings. There was a reception at the home of the Robert C. Maynard, publisher of *The Tribune,* and his wife, Nancy Hicks Maynard, director of the Institute for Journalism Education.

At the board meeting Baltimore convention chairman DeWayne Wickham gave a progress report. Treasurer Tom Morgan gave final numbers on the Atlanta convention. Paid registration was 750, eclipsing the 334 the previous year.

At the Oakland meeting many NABJ officers met Djibril Diallo for the first time. He was United Nations information officer for Africa. Diallo was youthful looking, his face was dark and smooth, like obsidian. He wore flowing robes native to his Senagalese homeland. Diallo spoke resonantly. It was a pleasant mix of African roots and Western education. President Merv Aubespin befriended Diallo. He counted on Diallo to advise him on Africa and ways NABJ could play a significant role there.

The winter 1985 board meeting was in March in Minneapolis-St. Paul, the home of two board members, Denise Johnson and Walter Middlebrook of the St. Paul *Pioneer Press.*

In Minneapolis the board voted 8-4 to rescind its invitation to the South African ambassador to the United States, Bernardus G. Fourie, to speak at the Baltimore convention. The decision was in protest of repression, the bloodiest in 25 years. The ambassador had been asked to debate Randall Robinson, director of TransAfrica, a Washington-based lobby.

In May 1985 the city's bombing of the MOVE headquarters in Philadelphia traumatized many black journalists who covered the event or watched incredulously from around the nation. A group of mostly dreadlocked members, MOVE called itself a "back-to-nature" group, a contradictory description. Instead of settling in a rural area where their claims made sense, followers imposed their beliefs on working-class black residents living in a dense but well-kept rowhouse neighborhood in West Philadelphia.

MOVE people's beliefs resulted in bad sanitation that allowed vermin to multiply. "The rats and the roaches are our brothers and sisters," a MOVE member told neighbors who complained about infested homes.

As opposition to them grew, the radical group built a rooftop bunker and blocked access to the alley behind neighbors' houses. MOVE was preparing for another confrontation with police. The first one in 1978 resulted in a policeman getting killed. Evening news footage showed the police force of Mayor Frank Rizzo beating and kicking MOVE members lying in the street. The brutal images earned MOVE members sympathy from blacks. But they received little sympathy seven years later in 1985, at least in West Philadelphia. For 18 months MOVE tortured neighbors with late-night diatribes shouted from bullhorns urging the release of members convicted in the 1978 confrontation.

In 1985 the neighbors pressured W. Wilson Goode, Philadelphia's first black mayor, to do something.

He did. The result was disastrous.

Goode ordered police to extract MOVE members from their house on Osage Avenue. The neighborhood was evacuated on Mother's Day. Thousands of rounds of police gunfire were shot into the MOVE house. Police in a helicopter dropped a bomb on the house.

The house burned out of control, engulfing 60 others. Eleven children and adults died in the fire.

Residents watched in horror, disbelief, then anger. The only other time an American city bombed itself was in the 1920s when whites in Tulsa, Okla. bombed a rebellious black community. Many people doubted Goode would have tolerated the police bombing a white neighborhood.

A month later at Columbia University Graduate School of Journalism, a handful of black Philadelphia journalists described covering the story to about 40 members of the New York Association of Black Journalists. The Philadelphians' unsympathetic view of MOVE shocked the New Yorkers. "Not everyone in Philadelphia viewed MOVE as 'other brothers and sisters,' like the last time," *Philadelphia Inquirer* reporter William W. Sutton Jr. said.

Heshimu Jaramogi of black-operated WDAS-FM News said "The radical community didn't even come out for MOVE." Leon Taylor, a *Philadelphia Daily News* reporter, inflamed the journalistic audience: MOVE did what they said they were going to do, and they got what they deserved." Taylor summarized local reaction.

The MOVE story remained on people's minds for months. The complex story had dozens of angles.

The first 16 months of Mayor Goode's term was upbeat. But the MOVE fiasco crippled Goode politically.

Sutton of the *Inquirer*, NABJ Region 3 director, (Pennsylvania dominated that region) convinced the mayor to address black journalists on the opening day of the Baltimore convention. Goode accepted. About 600 journalists packed the city convention center on Aug. 1.

Did you err in delegating too much authority to police? a panelist asked the mayor. "It was a police operation," Goode answered. "I'm an expert in a lot of things, but not deploying police."

Panelist Joe Davidson asked, "The plan police gave you did not contain the main ingredient (the bomb). Why don't you question your subordinates for giving you such a woefully incomplete plan?" queried *The Wall Street Journal* and ex-Philadelphia *Bulletin* newsman.

Goode deferred the answers to a commission he appointed that was investigating the incident.

It was odd that Goode was reluctant to use his authority to learn why what looked more like a rogue operation was executed.

Many black journalists got their first up-close look at Goode in Baltimore. They were disappointed.

At the Baltimore convention, leaders of the Institute for Journalism Education (IJE) announced that a "quiet crisis" was occurring in the news business. Minority journalists, especially blacks, were leaving the field nearly as fast as they were coming in, according to the study by IJE.

The symptom was not a lack of interest in the work, but frustration. Journalists IJE polled demonstrated a burning desire to lead and crusade in journalism for balance, but they said their ideas or ambitions too often were blunted by white superiors. More than 40 percent of minorities tracked in the 10-year study expected to leave journalism because of perceived lack of opportunity. "Minority journalists ... are more likely than whites to say they desire careers in newspaper management. That desire seems to be linked to the aspirations of many minorities to effect change both within and outside the profession," said the study.

"While minority women are particularly desirous of a career in management, they are least likely of all groups to have been given managerial responsibilities."

The "Quiet Crisis" report propelled a new buzzword in the media industry: "Retention" of minority journalists.

Seventeen years after the Kerner Commission report that detailed the absence of blacks and black coverage in the media, many white editors and station managers were challenged to advance their thinking. It was not enough for them to hire a black or brown reporter and assume it was a great accomplishment. That reporter, and many men and women like that person, may want to be an editor, a commentator or whatever post their talent or ambition could take them. Did the IJE analysis and subsequent reports spur the media industry to act? When the report was released in summer 1985, 5.8 percent of newspaper journalists and 13 percent of broadcast journalists were of color. In the management or editing ranks, minorities represented 9 percent of the newsroom force.

Changes in the 1985 convention confirmed NABJ's complete break with its old era. Its awards program was no longer conducted at a banquet. Winners no longer competed with clattering dishes from waiters clearing tables.

An Academy Award-like production with dramatic video and audio and scripted introductions was staged in the Morris Mechanic Theater near the redeveloped waterfront. The awards show theme was a "Salute to Excellence."

Second, the job fair advanced in sophistication. The convention center was subdivided into scores of cubicle-type booths. News organizations purchased space, and NABJ members had to make appointments for job interviews. The year before, Aubespin recalled, NABJ's first job fair was a room in Atlanta where editors set up at a table and candidates could stop in and talk.

The third change was in the elections. Members were still smarting or were embarrassed by the tumultuous 1983 election in New Orleans. At least a year before the '85 election, the board of directors established rigid election procedures. Members voted at a polling place.

Unlike the last time in 1983, they did not cast pieces of hotel stationery at the business meeting.

By election time it was a three-candidate race for president: DeWayne Wickham, owner of a TV production company, Albert Fitzpatrick, minority affairs director with Knight-Ridder and Robert Tutman, a cameraman at CBS News. Wickham appeared to be the clear favorite. He was convention chairman of a smoothly run event. Fitzpatrick had a base of support. He was responsible for many people getting hired at Knight-Ridder newspapers and elsewhere. Some members however, expressed wariness over his corporate status. The long-time editor with the Akron *Beacon Journal* was at that time based at the home office in Miami.

Tutman was the maverick. Some members expressed doubt whether – as a television photographer – he was a full-fledged journalist. Video cameramen, a rarity in NABJ, were often seen as technicians, while print photographers were considered "photojournalists." He was a still photographer until 1968 when the first black news director at WBAL-TV, Baltimore, (NBC) hired him as a cameraman.

Bob Matthews ordered staff to train Tutman "or "I'll have him go out every day and (expletive)-up your work." In November 1969 Tutman tried out at WBBM-TV (CBS) in Chicago. "It was when (Black Panther) Fred Hampton was killed," he said. "I filmed it." Tutman was hired by WBBM, and two years later he moved to the network.

Some people liked Tutman's feistiness. NABJ, Tutman said, was getting too cozy with the very people it should be disturbing every day: corporate media heads, editors and station managers. Tutman preferred confrontation to diplomacy and negotiation.

Tutman had another motive. He wanted to be the spoiler to deny his childhood adversary Wickham the presidency. "I've known him since we were 4," said Tutman, age 38 at that time. "We've always had our differences. I ran around saying 'this ain't the right guy' (for NABJ president). People in Chicago and Baltimore said 'if you don't like the boy, run against him.'

"'But I'm busy.'

"'So shut up.'

"I waited until the last day (to file for office)."

The election for the most part lacked New Orleans' make-up-the rules-as-we-go-along hijinks. Ballot casting moved fluidly at the polls. Storm clouds moved in, however. A few dozen *Baltimore Sun* journalists – likely Wickham supporters – tried to vote but were disqualified. The journalists let the *Sun* pay their registration and assumed that the $150 registration included their $35 membership dues.

They assumed wrong. *The Sun* had not paid the membership fees. Fitzpatrick pulled an upset, edging Wickham 212 to 197. Tutman finished a distant third with 15 votes. Fitzpatrick's 15-vote margin of victory strongly suggested that the disqualification of host city journalists cost Wickham the election.

Years later Wickham said it was a "strategic mistake" not to verify that local supporters were members of NABJ.

"I bought into the notion that as convention chairman I should not use it to campaign," he explained. "I didn't campaign; my surrogates did." Nevertheless it was a bitter pill for Wickham.

Moreover, members worried that greater corporate influence was compromising NABJ's ideals.

At an undeniably successful convention, $120,000 in corporate contributions were earmarked for ballroom-sized luncheons, banquets and receptions. Yet, NABJ awarded only five scholarships amounting to less than $10,000. Scholarship support was an improvement from the three $1,500 awards the previous year. But placed next to the money spent for socializing, it alarmed many members.

"I'm dismayed by the extravagant waste of money this organization tolerates," said Reginald Stuart, a *New York Times* correspondent, at the business meeting. Aubespin explained that most media companies set conditions on how their contributions could be spent. Members like Stuart replied that if companies insisted that their money underwrite food and parties, instead of scholarships and other symbols of excellence, the money should be turned down.

The question was not settled in that meeting, however. It was a debate that would go on for years.

Chapter 12
Africa Outreach

In July 1993 Djibril Diallo glowed with satisfaction. It was the second day of the NABJ convention in Houston. Although no one declared it as such, it was an unofficial "Africa Day." The numerous Africa-related events were more than coincidental.

There was a well-attended symposium called "Africa in the Headlines." It attracted journalists, academics and government officials from North America and Africa. One of the panelists was Andrew Young, civil rights leader, former Atlanta mayor and U.S. ambassador to the U.N. in ·the Carter Administration. A local TV reporter, an African-American woman, noted that Houston had the third-largest Nigerian community in the world (Lagos was first, then London and Houston).

Second, NABJ awarded its first Ethel Payne fellowships, allowing two members, Michelle Singletary (*Washington Post*) and Karen Lange (Chapel Hill, N.C. *Herald*), to report from Africa. Payne was a foreign and Washington correspondent with the Chicago *Defender*. She covered black soldiers during the Vietnam war, witnessed Ghana's independence and traveled to Lagos to escort Whitney M. Young's remains back to the United States after his death there in 1971. Payne covered seven U.S. presidents, starting with Dwight Eisenhower.

Third, Bryant Gumbel, co-host of NBC *Today*, was in Houston to receive the 1993 NABJ "Journalist of the Year" award for his role in *Today's* week-long reports from Africa.

The broadcasts aired underreported realities and debunked long-lived myths and stereotypes about the continent and its people. Gumbel lobbied NBC long and strenuously for the project. NABJ now thanked him for the mighty journalistic feat.

In witnessing and sometimes facilitating the events on this day, Diallo was enjoying the harvest after planting seeds nine years earlier. Diallo had long cultivated African-American journalists who were interested in reporting on Africa.

Dozens of black American journalists lobbied for years to convince the white-controlled news organizations they worked for to cover Africa more thoroughly and accurately. After all, it was "the greatest story on the planet," said Kenneth Walker. He made two trips to South Africa for *The Washington Star* and ABC News in 1981 and 1985.

Diallo was born in Kolda, Senegal, in 1953, one of a dozen brothers and sisters. He called himself a first-generation literate, an understatement. Diallo is a Ph.D fluent in French, English, Spanish and Portuguese. His village valued education as a means to break out of colonialism.

As a secondary school student in Senegal he was an organizer with other students. They worked with American volunteers. "This achieved twin purposes," he said. "It made us involved in the community and it gave us an understanding internationally of the United States and Britain." This volunteer spirit would serve Diallo well when the opportunity came to work closely with black journalists.

Later Diallo studied and taught in England. While in Britain, Diallo founded the Pan African Exchange Scheme. The program sent black inner city youths to work camps in Africa. Recognized for his work with another organization, the International African Institute, Diallo was asked in 1980 to serve as an information officer for the U.N. High Commission on Refugees. Diallo then worked as a French editor in Geneva.

In 1983 he moved to New York as information officer in the U.N. Development Program for Africa.

In 1984 drought, then famine, swept across much of Eastern and Sub-Saharan Africa. Americans saw media images of skeletal children with bloated bellies and hollow stares. African children were dying.

"I said, 'How can I as information officer highlight the fight the continent was going through?'" Diallo said. He helped Dennis Bell, a *Newsday* correspondent and NABJ member. The newsman returned the favor. "Bell told me about the Atlanta convention" that summer, said Diallo.

"I got to Atlanta, walked in and started discussing (the drought calamity). My impression? Individuals here and there were committed to Africa. But while people sympathized with Africa, the members as an organization could not afford to devote time to Africa. NABJ was made up mostly of (people) concerned about survival in the newsroom. There were very few foreign correspondents."

Before 1984, only a handful of African-American journalists reported from Africa for major news organizations. Les Payne did it for *Newsday*. In 1978 he was a Pulitzer Prize finalist for his reporting from South Africa. Leon Dash of *The Washington Post* was a Pulitzer finalist too. He did three special assignments in the mid- to late-'70s. This included living with rebel forces in Angola and covering 2,100 miles on foot in two months. Thomas A. Johnson of *The New York Times* filed dispatches from a number of African nations. And so did Randy Daniels of CBS News. In the early 1980s Daniels left CBS and established a TV production company, Jacaranda, in Nigeria. The company shut down after a 1983 military coup.

In 1984 the drought in Ethiopia and neighboring countries was a big story. So too was unrest in South Africa. Black and so-called "mixed race" people were not citizens of their native land. They denounced and resisted apartheid (again) and died at the hands of well-armed white minority and black surrogates.

In the meantime South Africa was being isolated internationally. There was a U.N.-sponsored cultural boycott of South Africa. Next, college students and grass-roots organizations began pressuring U.S. institutions to divest themselves of financial holdings in South Africa.

At this time the Reagan Administration took a supply-side approach to the South African government. The policy was called "constructive engagement," maintaining diplomatic ties with Pretoria. These were supposed to be "carrots" but there was no evidence of any "stick" to prod South Africa to change.

More black American journalists became interested in news from Africa. In Atlanta a few dozen members attended a workshop on Africa coverage. Such a workshop was normally scheduled at annual conventions. This one, however, was special. The panelists included the leading (white) editors of major newspapers that had the resources to have foreign correspondents. Members asked the panelists, why were there so few black U.S. Africa correspondents?

"I don't think it's a good idea to send black reporters to Africa," Ed Kosner, editor of *Newsweek* magazine, told Les Payne circa 1980. "I don't think they can be fair." The editor, however, said he was comfortable with sending Jewish reporters to Israel or Irish reporters to report on Ulster.

A.M. Rosenthal, executive editor of *The New York Times*, was in the room in Atlanta. "People (journalists) were pumped up," said Sam Fulwood. "The king of the white folks (Rosenthal) was there, and they wanted to show their stuff. People asked tough questions but tried not to be offensive. They were very direct."

Diallo said the feared editor of the world's most powerful newspaper was jolted. "I didn't know there were so many black journalists in this country," Rosenthal said.

"Second, even if you wanted to report (from Africa) you didn't have uncontrolled access." Rosenthal's point could not be dismissed. There were more dictatorships than democracies among Africa's 50-some countries. Many governments tried to muzzle foreign reporters. And South Africa, one of the freest on the continent for the press, barred U.S. journalists by race in the '70s. Tom Johnson of *The New York Times* was denied a visa.

Les Payne of *Newsday* said he tricked South African authorities in order to get into the country in 1976.

Rosenthal's observation was not lost on Diallo. He saw an opportunity to give African-American journalists access to his native continent.

"My work has been giving access (to journalists) without clouding it with the agency I work for," said Diallo. "Having understood how NABJ functions, we had to build a constituency for Africa."

Diallo planted seeds and worked the soil. After the Atlanta convention, he said, "I started going systematically at my expense to all NABJ board meetings. I found that any member could go, not vote, but sit and observe.

"I got a mailing list and put members on it for *Africa Emergency.*" This was a newsletter that Diallo and other U.N. officials created. It carried information on international relief efforts and development issues in Africa that were overlooked, particularly by the U.S. press.

"Now, said Diallo, "One thousand members were getting it. U.N. members and NABJ members, however, said this may not be a good use of my time.

"At a second level, I suggested, 'Let us try to have a symposium on Africa media coverage in the U.S.'"

In 1985, 300 journalists participated in a conference at Howard University. Diallo suggested, "Why don't we have an NABJ fact-finding trip to Africa that would report back to the symposium? I found the money."

Fourteen black American journalists from the mainstream and black-owned press took the trip. They included Michael Cottman and Clem Richardson (*Newsday*); Denise Johnson (St. Paul *Pioneer Press*); Marcia Slacum Greene (*Washington Post*); Mervin Aubespin (*The Courier-Journal*); Marilyn Marshall (*Ebony*), and Wilbert Tatum (New York *Amsterdam News*).

The group did reporting from drought-stricken areas and met with African journalists in Senegal. The newsmen and women also met with leaders from the Organization of African Unity (OAU). The field reporting was unlike anything the American journalists experienced at home. They often worked in open countryside until 1 a.m. They got their first look at semi-lagoons called "niayes" that were relied upon for gardening. Desert encroachment rendered many niayes useless and made farmers migrate to towns.

The coverage by African-American journalists brought a different perspective. The differences were not necessarily stark, but textured. The standard way to cover the calamity in Ethiopia was to show the people as victims at the mercy of international relief efforts. Black U.S. journalists reported this too because this was the reality.

But they also reported other realities. They wrote about governments building water lines and setting up agricultural projects to grow food instead of depending on the West. They also wrote freely about dictators who used food as a weapon, starving out ethnic rivals to keep power. Other media picked up the stories and stepped up their own coverage.

U.S. Africa coverage had been as barren as the land ruined by drought. African-American journalists who were now reporting from that continent turned on a news faucet.

In the United States the news from Ethiopia spurred people to action. A rainbow coalition of recording artists – Michael Jackson, Ray Charles, Bruce Springsteen, Bob Dylan, Diana Ross, Dionne Warwick and dozens more – formed a mass choir. Led by Quincy Jones, they recorded "We Are the World," a song to raise money for the starving Africans. "Live Aid" concerts in London and Philadelphia in 1985 raised $70 million for famine relief.

"We are the World" inspired a tasteless parody by John Bloom, a white movie critic for the Dallas *Times Herald*. It was swiftly challenged by the NABJ chapter in Dallas-Fort Worth.

Bloom, who wrote under the pseudonym Joe Bob Briggs, wrote a parody called "We Are the Weird." In his April 12, 1985 column he called starving Africans "the scum of the filthy earth." He said the song would aid "the United Negro College Fund in the United States 'cause I think we should be sending as many Negroes to college as we can, especially the stupid ones."

Members of the Dallas-Forth Worth Association of Black Communicators protested angrily. A letter signed by the officers was printed in the *Times Herald*. It called for the termination of the "Joe Bob Goes to the Drive-in" column.

Members, both from broadcasting and newspapers, confronted *Times Herald* management: How could they afford to have a pretend "good-ole boy" movie critic gratuitously insult a large segment of black readers and at the same time ignore or cover the black community so badly? Sixteen percent of Dallas was black; 25 percent of the Dallas-Fort Worth metro area was black and brown.

The *Times Herald* management was embarrassed by Joe Bob's column. He picked on a vulnerable topic and provoked a mighty roar of anger. Bloom's column was canceled. More important, the *Times Herald* promised to hire 10 more black journalists and sponsor scholarships.

The Joe Bob Briggs incident was an early sign that NABJ was building a constituency for Africa and growing stronger at the local level.

In 1985 the New York Association of Black Journalists held a forum in which three NABJ members talked about recent reporting assignments in Southern Africa. They were Frank Dexter Brown (an editor with *Black Enterprise);* Jill Nelson (a free-lance writer for *Essence* and *The Village Voice)*, and Sam Fulwood III of *The Baltimore Sun.*

Nelson told about 60 colleagues that South Africa was "50 times different" than what she had expected. After landing, she watched security police armed with Uzis patrol the airport baggage area. She did not fear for her safety in the black townships, but because of the paranoia of white South Africans, she "was more conscious of fear in my hotel room" in Johannesburg.

"I crumpled newspaper and put it by the door to hear if they were coming. When I sent a crossword puzzle from one of the newspapers to a friend (in America), the envelope was slit and crudely taped back together."

Reporting in the townships, said Nelson, was difficult because "black leadership (was) is constantly changing. It is fluid."

Frank Brown spent time outside South Africa in the frontline states, neighboring countries engaged in undeclared regional war with Pretoria. "Bandit organizations" like Renamo in Mozambique, said Brown, were responsible for bombing villages and killing and mutilating civilians.

Back from a five-month assignment, Fulwood said "South Africa was better and worse than anything I imagined. I was treated well because I was a journalist. But by being a journalist, I was able to go into places and see things that were bad. I remember seeing people get shot at and beat up and not see it just once. Funerals were like a football game; 50,000 people gathered to bury 15.

"You get caught up in all the enthusiasm. It's extremely exciting and frightening. There was always the police presence; tear gas, guns and armored vehicles."

Grass-roots opposition in the United States stepped up the pressure for more coverage. Sam Fulwood attributed it to getting his overseas assignment. He was a business reporter at the *Baltimore Sun* when Randall Robinson, Mary Frances Berry and Walter Fauntroy got themselves arrested for demonstrating in front of the South African Embassy in Washington, D.C.

"The anti-apartheid activists were very clever," said Fulwood. "They opted to get arrested on Thanksgiving Day. The got on the front pages because turkeys, parades and football were the only things going on on Thanksgiving. *The Sun* editors didn't know what to make of it."

Black journalists like Nelson, Brown and Fulwood got a chance to report from Africa. Many more black journalists who were unable to go engaged in activities in the USA. The Philadelphia chapter and WDAS-FM, a black-owned radio station, raised $9,300 for Africare, a relief agency, during a 36-hour radiothon in early 1985. Other chapters – NABJ had grown to a dozen affiliates – adopted village schools in Africa and sent supplies such as books, magazines and clothing.

At the midpoint of the 1980s, black South African challenges to apartheid were at a fever pitch. Whites had the guns, the bombs and the laws, compared to rocks in the hands of children, but looked less invincible than they did a decade or so earlier.

White South Africans were winning the shooting war – hundreds of blacks were killed compared to a handful of whites – but they were losing the war of world opinion.

Black journalist Kenneth Walker of ABC News accompanied anchor Ted Koppel and the *Nightline* staff to South Africa for a series of live broadcasts. "Reporting on the incomprehensible nature of apartheid is the best running story on the planet," Walker told New York Association of Black Journalists members in spring 1985.

A CBS *60 Minutes* broadcast on South Africa convinced ABC to do a week of live *Nightline* reports from South Africa. Morley Safer's report was kind to the government. Reforms were coming, said South African officials. It would transform apartheid's brutal side.

"After *60 Minutes*," said Walker, "blacks in the U.S. wrote and called ABC and the other networks en masse, something that doesn't happen very often. Also, black South African resistance had escalated to the point where it could no longer be ignored."

Traditionally defensive Pretoria, said Walker, gladly complied with *Nightline's* request to send in a team in light of what Walker termed the "international credibility" the *60 Minutes* coverage provided.

The South African government delayed telecast of the ABC broadcasts each day in South Africa in order to screen the shows and register objections with the network.

It was Walker's second visit to South Africa. In 1981 he raised funds to go while a reporter for *The Washington Star*. The journey started in 1978. While Walker was reading about the Soweto uprising at his desk, the metro editor walked by. He said "I see we're finally getting rid of some of you people."

The bizarre stab at humor moved Walker to act. "I sensed," said Walker, "there was an inescapable link between the amount of anti-black racism practiced here and anti-black racism practiced there. I wanted to inquire and see did this link exist and what was it.

"It took three years of lobbying and a change of owners (to Time Inc.) to convince them to let me go."

By 1981, Walker, 30, was helped by Percy Qoboza, a South African journalist who was writer-in-residence at *The Star*, and Roger Wilkins, nephew of NAACP director Roy Wilkins and an associate editor with the newspaper.

Eight thousand dollars was raised for Walker's trip; $3,000 of that total was Walker's money.

At local meetings African-American journalists got chances to hear from colleagues who experienced reporting from Africa and from African journalists who told what it was like while standing on U.S. soil.

In June 1986 Rich Mkhondo of *The Johannesburg Star* (and previously the *Rand Daily Mail*) described the dangers of his work to Philadelphia journalists. Mkhondo spoke six days after the South African government imposed a second state of emergency that allowed sweeping police powers and muzzled the domestic and foreign news media.

By then South Africa had 180 laws governing what could and could not be printed. A section of the Internal Security Act said the press could not publish information unless it was sure it was true. Police had six months to confirm the truth.

"You can't write anything subversive," said Mkhondo. "But nobody knows what subversive is."

Mkhondo was a 30-year-old in the United States on an Al Friendly Fellowship for international journalists. He had been a reporter for four years. Mkhondo's family wanted him to get out of the business. He had been shot at three times while on assignment. Once, Mkhondo was wounded and had to be hospitalized for a month. He was arrested six times.

At the *Star*, Mkhondo was one of eight black journalists on a staff of 70. White journalists rarely covered the dangerous assignments, but they were promoted and given raises faster than the blacks, said Mkhondo. *The Star* published five editions daily. Most blacks read the Africa edition and most whites saw the later editions, which carried less news of bloodshed in the black townships.

By the mid-1980s African leaders, activists, journalists and U.S. foreign policy experts got chances to tell their stories to large, inquisitive NABJ audiences. At the 10th annual convention in Baltimore, Randall Robinson, director of TransAfrica, Assistant U.S. Secretary of State Frank Wisner and Neo Mnumzana, chief U.N. observer for the African National Congress, debated U.S. foreign policy and South Africa's state of violent upheaval.

The South African ambassador had agreed to take part in the debate, but three months before the convention the NABJ board voted 8-4 to rescind the invitation.

The decision was in protest of repression, which was the bloodiest in 25 years. Dissenting board members said an accepted invitation should not be taken back and, furthermore, the ambassador would be given a chance to shed light on the crisis.

At the Baltimore convention, Wisner said the way to end apartheid was not with sanctions but through public and quiet diplomacy. To prepare black South Africans for larger roles in their country, U.S. tax dollars were bringing 200 South African students to America each year for university training and the United States was investing in South African black businesses. Wisner called the Sullivan Principles "a beacon" inside South Africa. The principles, crafted by the Rev. Leon Sullivan, an African-American minister in Philadelphia, asked U.S. corporations operating in South Africa to pledge to pay blacks equal wages with whites and provide equal working conditions.

Robinson and Mnumzana strongly disagreed with U.S. policy. Said Robinson: "This administration and this president is soundly on the side of the white minority. I say this reluctantly because President Reagan has reduced our nation before the world to a tremendous disgrace."

Robinson noted that the night before the debate, U.S. Senate and House conferees had repudiated Reagan administration policy of "constructive engagement" in South Africa. U.S. government sanctions followed.

"South Africa had been in a state of emergency since 1948," said Robinson, the brother of NABJ founder Max Robinson, to hundreds of members. "It's a shame that the president of the most powerful democracy in the world has to be dragged kicking and screaming to the right position."

Mnumzana called apartheid "a hazard for whites, and a veritable inferno for blacks." He said 5,000 to 7,000 black children were dying each year because of subhuman living conditions. "There is no historical evidence that apartheid will ever be dissuaded to change," said Mnumzana.

"The time is now to isolate them."

Two days later, John Qwelane of *The Johannesburg Star* addressed NABJ members. He belonged to the Union of Black Journalists in South Africa, which was banned by the government. To get around the ban, an alternative organization, the Black Media Workers, surfaced. Like Rich Mkhondo a year later, Qwelane described the difficulties of reporting in his country:

• Official lies and deliberate misinformation stoked great hatred of the white minority regime by the disenfranchised black majority.

• All newspapers geared to black South African readers were owned and managed by whites. (Since the story selection was often different in the editions black readers received, it was naive to assume that the reports were credible.)

• Foreign correspondents frequently exploited black South African journalists: Native journalists caddied foreigners around the country, interpreted and introduced them to sources. When it was time to be paid for the services, foreigners often disappeared.

Qwelane's work included coverage of riots in Soweto. His reports exposed and ended the practice of white police instructing migrant blacks to kill other blacks living in townships.

At NABJ's awards program in 1985, the interest in stories about Africa was clear. Of the 18 nominations in five categories (print journalism, TV journalism, radio journalism, photo journalism and international reporting), seven nominations were related to Africa. They included dispatches from South Africa by Nathaniel Sheppard Jr. of *The Chicago Tribune* and Kenneth Walker's *Nightline* reports. Nominations also included stories done on U.S. soil, like "Rev. (Jesse) Jackson Confronts South African Consulate in Beverly Hills" by Kwaku Lynn of KPFK-FM in California or "Apartheid and the Dancer's Anguish," a Style section piece by Carla Hall of *The Washington Post*.

The Journalists of the Year were co-winners Dennis Bell of *Newsday* and Kenneth Walker of ABC. Both were recognized for Africa coverage.

Black journalists kept joining and expanding NABJ. They joined for the camaraderie, the networking and the chances to better their journalism skills. Throughout the 1980s at national conventions, members had the opportunity to hear and question international newsmakers – particularly Africans – and improve their understanding of that continent.

The Rev. Allen Boesak, co-founder of the United Democratic Front, was a keynote speaker at the 1986 convention in Dallas.

"I am pleading with you – fight for us for our sakes, and for your own sakes," said Boesak. "You shall never be free until we are free." He told the NABJ audience that black South Africans "already are knee-deep in blood," because of the repressive state of emergency. There is an attitude that "white privilege and the maintaining of apartheid is worth the death of black children," said the minister. "Apartheid has to be fought with more than words of condemnation." Dozens of people wept openly, dabbing watery eyes with luncheon napkins after Boesak's desperate appeal.

A few days later, the Journalist of the Year, Charlayne Hunter-Gault, wept openly too. She accepted NABJ's highest honor for her PBS series "Apartheid's People." Hunter-Gault noted that the cameraman who shot the pictures could not share the praise; He was killed in South Africa while reporting the story.

Boesak told his story at a time when the struggle to slay apartheid seemed most intense because there was so much more U.S. press coverage. The coverage was largely showing a discredited and repressive white South African regime and black and so-called colored people living under unjustifiable segregation and second- and third-class status.

The white regime struck back at the foreign media. Five journalists were expelled in the last six months of 1986. During this time the regime imposed restrictions three times on the press, threatening imprisonment or deportation.

In the United States, the U.S. Justice Department filed a criminal complaint against Michigan publisher John P. McGoff. He was charged with failing to register as a foreign agent. In 1979 the South African government acknowledged that it delivered $11.4 million to McGoff for him to try to buy *The Washington Star* and take other steps as part of a $72-million propaganda campaign to improve Pretoria's image. The revelation led to the resignation of Prime Minister John Vorster of South Africa.

In 1988 NABJ demonstrated continuing interest in Africa by establishing the Percy Qoboza Award for Foreign Journalists. Qoboza was editor of *City Press*, a black-oriented newspaper, and had been editor of *The World* and *The Post*. Those papers were closed by the government for attacking apartheid. Qoboza, 50, died Jan. 17, 1988, from a heart attack. The first winner was Zwelakhe Sisulu, a Nieman Fellow and journalist with *The New Nation*, a Catholic-owned newspaper in Johannesburg. Sisulu was honored in absentia. He was imprisoned for writings that condemned apartheid.

The son of Walter Sisulu, president of the African National Congress, was behind bars when a prison guard brought a plain-wrapped package to his cell, dropped it, then left without comment. Sisulu opened it. The package contained the NABJ Percy Qoboza award. Black prisoners in the teeming cellblock roared their approval.

Sisulu and others were locked up, but not forgotten by Americans. He was released a few months later.

Successive Percy Qoboza winners came from black-majority African countries that were struggling with military rule, democratic agitation and censorship. NABJ gradually turned some of its focus away from South Africa. An often-asked question of black Americans was why they protested so loudly about white South African repression against blacks but seemed mute about black repression elsewhere in Africa?

The answer was simple, some argued. South Africa bragged that it was a democracy (albeit for whites) – as America did when it sanctioned slavery and later Jim Crow segregation. South Africa was a modern, prosperous, capitalist society like the United States.

With the legalizing of oppression of South African blacks in the 1940s, many African-Americans saw a mirror image of their country during the civil-rights era. The same could not be said of several dozen Sub-Saharan African countries that did not share a Western democratic tradition.

The innumerable instances of brutality and repression and press censorship, however, were unacceptable to Americans.

As more African-American journalists studied and visited the continent, they began to question black leaders there and critique black-majority states.

In 1993 on that day of three Africa-related events in Houston, Djibril Diallo said "Having understood how NABJ functions, we had to build a constituency for Africa, like the Sports Task Force.

"We are at certain times or places in history where our contribution accelerates a process. We don't expect (NABJ) to be uncritical supporters of Africa. We showed Africa needed NABJ and NABJ needed Africa."

Chapter 13
Reston

A new president, a new home base for the National Association of Black Journalists. After Albert Fitzpatrick was elected in August 1985, he set up a temporary national office at Knight-Ridder headquarters in Miami.

During the just-ended Aubespin era it was understood that NABJ could no longer live like a nomad and expect to thrive. Aubespin and Treasurer Tom Morgan, now a *New York Times* reporter, sought a permanent address. They wrote funding proposals to media organizations.

Several media and educational institutions came forward. Aubespin and Morgan visited the University of Chicago, and Dow Jones showed them space in Silver Spring, Md., a Washington, D.C., suburb.

The most appealing location was Reston, Va., another Washington suburb. It was home of the Newspaper Center, which housed the American Society of Newspaper Editors (ASNE).

Jerry Friedheim, head of the ASNE Foundation, was eager to have NABJ as a tenant. Why? "They wanted as many media organizations (as possible) under one roof," said Aubespin. "And with ASNE's commitment to diversity it would be a good move to assist us." ASNE conducted an annual census of minority journalists and set a goal to achieve racial parity in mainstream newsrooms by the year 2000. It was also attractive to NABJ officers: In addition to office space near Washington, the center had an extensive media library, meeting space and the national offices of other industry associations just doors away.

Friedheim and Aubespin negotiated an inexpensive rent. ASNE, he said, understood that NABJ did not have much money. Its members were working journalists and the organization at age 10 was still young. The New York Times Co., Washington Post Co. and Knight-Ridder, Inc. were among the news organizations that granted funds to open and operate the office. The Gannett Co. was the biggest giver: $100,000.

In November 1985, Albert Fitzpatrick, elected the previous summer in Baltimore, opened the office on Sunrise Valley Drive. With the permanent address settled, at least one other missing element remained to be filled: hiring a salaried, full-time executive director.

NABJ never had one in its 10-year history. Yes, Paul Brock, the man singularly responsible for finding journalists through his contacts as a communications director with the Democratic National Committee and getting them together to found NABJ in 1975, carried the title executive director through the '70s and early '80s. Brock however, was a volunteer, and after 1980 his role diminished as he became estranged from a number of board members.

In the meantime, NABJ tripled its membership to at least 1,000 in two years, grew from having two to about a dozen affiliate chapters and was managing finances in the six figures. The Baltimore convention, said treasurer Morgan, took in $225,000 in member registrations and corporate sponsorship, and $143,000 was subtracted to pay for the convention. After $30,000 was put aside to pay Louisville office expenses, $52,000 remained to run NABJ.

"NABJ has gone beyond the point where it can exist as a volunteer body," Morgan told fellow board members at the fall meeting. "It (NABJ) needs professional help." Executive board and regional directors spent more time as clerks and administrators, answering letters, mailing applications and licking the stamps, than setting policies and charting a course for the blossoming organization. Most of the board agreed that a full-time salaried administrator was necessary.

Lafayette Jones was eager to ride in and assist. His Chicago- and Washington-based Smith, Jones & Associates performed managerial services for a number of professional organizations.

Board members listened to Jones' pitch but were for the most part cool to the idea. Most officers doubted that a managerial firm could satisfy the special needs of a journalists' organization. This attitude by many newspeople existed just before corporatization of newsrooms and journalism became apparent in the 1990s. Newspeople were repelled by the notion of non-journalists managing their associations. It did not matter whether the instinct was rational or not. Journalists by training and instinct were reluctant to do business with business-type people, even when it involved their institutions.

During the board meeting, officers were presented with three future national office sites: Downtown Baltimore, Washington, D.C., and Reston, Va.

The Baltimore proposal included free use of a computer and printer. The District of Columbia site could put NABJ in the center ring of news media powers, but it was the smallest space and the most costly to lease.

The Reston site had the poorest access to Washington, D.C.; It was 45 minutes away. But the rent was one-fifth the cost of rents for the Washington and Baltimore sites, and NABJ could have support services of 50 newspaper organizations in house.

The board chose Reston.

Albert E. Fitzpatrick grew up in Elyria, Ohio, 27 miles west of Cleveland. Elyria's population was 27,000, and 5 percent of the inhabitants were black. His journalism career began midway in high school. He became manager of the local high school sports team. The *Chronicle-Telegram* in Elyria asked him to call in statistics for $5 a game.

Fitzpatrick went to Kent State University. He received an internship and became sports editor of the college newspaper. After graduation, Fitzpatrick went to the suburban desk of the Akron *Beacon Journal*. Fitzpatrick was part of a 1971 Pulitzer Prize-winning reporting team at the *Beacon Journal*, a Knight-Ridder newspaper.

Fitzpatrick said during his 29 years there he held every editing position in the newsroom, which included farm editor, copy editor, assistant news editor, city editor and managing editor. In 1977, he became executive editor of the 157,000-circulation daily.

Fitzpatrick joined NABJ in 1976, only months after it was established. He was elected president nine years later. He was Knight-Ridder's vice president for minority affairs, based at the company headquarters in Miami. In that role he recruited and mentored scores of minorities for the company's 30-plus newspapers in 1985.

His status as a corporate news executive gave pause to a number of members, most still in the reporters ranks. Many NABJ people were wary of management or corporate types from big media influencing NABJ goals or policies.

Fitzpatrick's corporate status, however, was an asset for NABJ as it prepared to reach out to industry powers.

Aubespin, his predecessor, had an avuncular style at meetings. The immediate past president could get the 15 other officers to reach a consensus after a period of coaxing and negotiation.

Fitzpatrick was accustomed to board rooms. He had the blunt, semi-impatient attitude normal for top-level editors. At board meetings he would let the officers air out a number of issues, but curtly, Fitzpatrick would reel in debate when it seemed to veer off a specific point. Executive and managing editors, extremely busy juggling numerous staff meetings and projects, want reporters and middle managers to make their points succinctly. That was Fitzpatrick's style.

He also was a tenacious fund raiser, another habit not uncommon to corporate leaders.

Fitzpatrick initiated a "president's club" and leaned on high-profile NABJ members to donate $500 each to build an endowment fund for scholarships.

Other members of more modest means were encouraged to give $250 or $100 to build the fund.

During Fitzpatrick's two-year term, 1985-87, the organization raised $105,000.

In March 1986, when the board met in Cambridge. Mass., for its winter meeting, it adopted its first 12-month budget. Treasurer Tom Morgan introduced and explained the $371,000 plan. It was financed with member dues, convention revenues and corporate grants. Instead of planning a few months ahead, NABJ had a blueprint for at least a year of programming and services.

In the blueprint was money to hire an executive director to run the office in Reston full-time. A search committee brought four finalists to the Dallas convention for interviews with the entire 16-member board. On a Wednesday afternoon when the board conducted business before the convention opened, the officers chose Dennis Schatzman of Pittsburgh.

At that time he was a deputy comptroller of the city public school system. Before that he was a municipal judge and before that a newsman with the *Pittsburgh Courier* and *Afro-American* in Baltimore. The board wanted a journalist in the executive director's position. Schatzman's legal and administrative experience, plus journalism background impressed the board.

On paper and in person Schatzman had triple talent and skill. He was the man for the job.

The convention was a window on bold, brassy initiatives black professionals were taking in media. Black filmmaking burst on the convention scene.

In the 900-seat hotel theater-auditorium, a packed house previewed the PBS documentary "Eyes on the Prize," a six-part epic on the Civil Rights Movement from 1954-65. Director Henry Hampton combined footage of the demonstrations and conflicts in the South with recent interviews of the heroes, heroines and villains of that time.

Interviewees included New York *Amsterdam News* newsman Jimmy Hicks, who died shortly after being filmed. On film Hicks described what it was like to cover the Emmett Till trial with other black press colleagues and face the hostility of Southern whites. Hicks was honored posthumously at the convention with the Lifetime Achievement Award.

The Dallas-Fort Worth Chapter showed movies from the Tyler Film Collection, a rare collection of black films discovered in a warehouse in Tyler, Texas, in 1983. It included the work of Oscar Micheaux, who made several dozen black-oriented films from the 1920s through 1940s. Micheaux's Westerns and urban tales of lost or forbidden love were remarkable.

In the present, "New Jack" filmmaking debuted. Spike Lee, a wily 29-year-old filmmaker from Brooklyn, N.Y., previewed "She's Gotta Have It," a sex farce about a woman and three men who satisfied her needs very differently. "She's Gotta Have It" propelled Spike Lee into the national spotlight. For NABJ, debuts by Lee and Hampton and the reintroduction of Micheaux set the precedent for black-oriented film to premiere at future conventions.

The convention mixed fun with history and lore. There was a Black Cowboy rodeo at the Dallas fairgrounds. It was staged to remind or introduce visiting journalists to American cowboys of African descent and Buffalo soldiers who protected the West in the 19th and 20th centuries.

The rodeo plus cookout was a rousing success, so much so it alarmed Treasurer Morgan. He discreetly summoned four board members to his hotel room. Morgan was carrying at least $20,000 cash from rodeo and other on-site convention revenues.

He was scared. Morgan did not have a means to secure the money in an account. A robbery or burglary at the hotel could rob NABJ of crucial funds. Morgan could be forever scandalized trying to explain the disappearance of funds. Board members sat on the bed and counted $20, $10, $5 and $1 bills, confirming the amount for the treasurer.

"I often walked around with a big tan briefcase," said Morgan. "There usually was money in it. "Mal Johnson (former treasurer) turned over bank records of $56,000. There were some conventions where we had that much in cash. We had a sudden jump in convention registrants. We didn't have experience handling money of that size."

A previous summer when Morgan brought more than $10,000 in convention cash home to Brooklyn and tried to

send the money to the NABJ account in Washington he had
to fill out federal forms. To deter money laundering by drug
dealers, the government had recently instituted a requirement
to document movement of large sums of cash.

Starting with the Dallas convention, Morgan began
applying the cash directly to NABJ's hotel bills for big
expenses such as meal functions, meeting room charges and
audio visual expenses. Said Morgan, "When I applied it to
the hotel bill I'd count it with the hotel staff behind closed
doors then get a receipt for it. It was too much to count, and
I didn't want to count it."

Protecting large sums of money far away from
headquarters was one of many surprises in managing a
growing association in the late 1980s. "We learned these
things as we went along," said Morgan. "We were
journalists; we knew how to write and edit, not run an
organization. It was a big experiment for us."

Another experiment, short-lived, was the result of a
generational split. Joseph Perkins, in 1986 age 26 and an
editorial writer with *The Wall Street Journal,* touted a
"Young Black Journalists" movement within NABJ. It was
formed in January 1986 and was open to print journalists
under age 30. Older NABJ members, said Perkins, were a
"Post-Civil Rights era" generation that was more liberal than
many of the 20-somethings coming of age in the politically
conservative Reagan-era 1980s.

Perkins said he was bothered that "successful blacks
feel they have to capitulate" to prevailing thought in the black
community. "I don't think I have to come here with a special
mission to interpret my community any more than a black
doctor has to interpret his community," said Perkins. "I have
an obligation, but it's not a professional obligation, it's a
personal one."

Richard Prince, one of the post-Civil Rights era "old
heads," wrote in the Rochester, N.Y. *Democrat and
Chronicle* that Perkins and his followers "feeds fears the
group represents more than youthful arrogance; that it has
ideological overtones. Add to that the naivete and selfish
sense of mission that many detect in their younger
colleagues."

Young Black Journalists evaporated in less than a year. Nevertheless, it did show that many factions or branches were sprouting within NABJ.

Dennis Schatzman was born Feb. 6, 1950, in Pittsburgh. He said Mildred Berry, a seventh grade teacher, got him interested in journalism. "She gave us book reports. I went to see Percivell Trattis, managing editor of the *Pittsburgh Courier* from the 1930s to 1960. I went to see if he'd give me a book. He gave me *The Jungle* by Sinclair Lewis. I got an "A.""

"Got any more (books)?" he asked the editor.

"He gave me a Lincoln Steffens book *(Shame of the cities)*. I was hooked," on journalism.

He wrote for his high school newspaper. Schatzman attended the University of Pittsburgh. He ran track and wrote for the college paper. "I read the *Courier*, (Chicago) *Defender* and (Philadelphia) *Tribune* on microfilm in the library. I studied (Robert L.) Vann, (George S.) Schuyler, Ethel Payne.

He said he met Ethel Payne with Buthelizi in '86.

He was a cub reporter with the Baltimore *Afro-American* from December 1973 to June 1975. From 1977 to 1980 he was city editor of the *Pittsburgh Courier*.

"I got into a car accident," said Schatzman. "Eighteen months I was disabled. I certified myself to be a special court judge. I was elected in 1981 and 1984. At the same time I was a free-lance writer. I was named school controller for the Second Commonwealth for Pittsburgh. I uncovered a large board of education scandal involving computers."

Between the *Afro-American* and *Courier* jobs Schatzman worked in public relations and was a lobbyist. He did public relations for Carnegie Mellon University when he met and befriended Arlethia Perry. In 1986 Arlethia worked for Penn State University. The University that year hosted the NABJ Region 3 spring conference. Schatzman was invited to speak. He said, "Mike Days was regional director. I took a cake. I really had a good time. Someone mentioned that the executive director's job was open.

"I was trying to get out of Pittsburgh."

Schatzman said he received death threats because of his investigation, and he was mourning the deaths of his father and stepmother. His fraternity, Kappa Alpha Psi, and the NABJ convention in Dallas were meeting the same week. Schatzman flew to Dallas.

"Do you really want this job?" Mike Days asked me. I beat (out) three others with Pittsburgh ties, Carl (Morris), Francine (Cheeks) and James (B. Parks)."

Schatzman said his successes were opening the Reston office and getting NABJ on the map. He was involved in organizing the first Unity board meeting, a joint session of NABJ and the National Association of Hispanic Journalists boards in fall 1986 in Philadelphia.

He said "I was able to get Mangosuthu Buthelezi to see the Washington chapter and get good publicity.

"We got good deals in Miami (for the '87 convention). Al backed me. (Michael) McQueen and his wife helped me."

Schatzman lasted less than seven months in the job. "In all fairness," said Schatzman, "three-quarters of the board was supportive from afar. I took it for the wrong reasons. I was trying to get out of Pittsburgh. There was the pressure from dad's death. I had problems with the abuse of illegal drugs. I did not do a good job.

"Some people cut me down. I took a draft report to the meeting instead of the final report by mistake. I took the wrong information and was embarrassed by these people."

Shortly after the Chicago board meeting in March 1987, Schatzman tendered his resignation to Al Fitzpatrick.

"I thought I could do it (executive director's job) because I was a newsie. But I came from the Black Press and I was dealing with some (black) primos in the White Media. Being a journalist and administrator is different from being an administrator of journalists."

Two months after Dallas, Schatzman and Brenda Gillis, administrative assistant, opened NABJ's new headquarters in Reston, Va. Sept. 15, About 25 miles away in Washington, D.C., *The Washington Post* was also having a grand opening and a bad day.

Its Sunday magazine debuted Sept. 7. The cover story, "Murder, Drugs and the Rap Star," was a gritty account of a black New York rap performer charged with the murder of a Howard University student. Inside the same glossy magazine, critic-at-large Richard Cohen wrote a defense of barring young black men from retail shops. "White assailants are hard to find in urban America. Especially in cities like Washington and New York, the menace comes from young black males," wrote Cohen. "As for me, I'm with the shopkeepers." Adding insult to injury, no advertisements in the 112-page debut had black people.

"An accidental coincidence," said Publisher Donald Graham, an amazing one, considering that Washington, D.C., was at least 70 percent black. At the urging of black radio personalities and pastors, outraged black Washingtonians employed a return-to-sender tactic: In four weeks of Sunday afternoon demonstrations, they dumped nearly 50,000 copies of the magazine, a supplement of the Sunday paper, at the door of the *Post* on 15th Street N.W. Most of the protesters arrived in their church clothes. On Oct. 5, Executive Editor Benjamin C. Bradlee wrote an apology. William Raspberry in his *Post* column called the magazine debut "a disconcerting combination of bad luck, bad judgment and racial insensitivity."

NABJ was nearly 11 years old and 1,400 members strong, but not alone. Other American journalists of color were pounding the door to be included in the major news media. In 1983 the National Association of Hispanic Journalists formed using NABJ as a model. In two years it grew to 500 members. Regional press associations of Asian Americans and Native Americans (Indian) soon flowered into national groups.

Minority journalism association leaders knew their groups were competing against each other for newsroom jobs and foundation support. Whether it was deliberate or unintentional, a number of white editors and broadcast news directors engaged in divisive hiring tactics.

"They say, 'We've already hired our minority this year, and we don't need any more,'" said Manual Galvan, a *Chicago Tribune* newsman and president of NAHJ in 1986.

In Philadelphia, William W. Sutton Jr. and Juan Gonzalez were city hall bureau reporters for their respective papers, the *Inquirer* and *Daily News*. Patrisia Gonzalez was an *Inquirer* reporter. Sutton was NABJ parliamentarian, Gonzalez and Gonzalez were active in NAHJ. The trio arranged a joint meeting of the NABJ and NAHJ boards in Philadelphia the first weekend in November.

Thirty people assembled. "The statement we want to make to the news media is, 'don't divide us,'" said Fitzpatrick. Galvan of NAHJ told board members from both associations that the message they needed to get to white managers was "'Minority' doesn't mean 'black.' Nor does it mean 'Hispanic.' Neither should be used solely to describe an Asian American or Native American. Don't pit us against each other." After a three-hour round table, both boards agreed to appoint a liaison to examine 15 areas including:

• Scholarships, internships and a job bank exchange;

• Monitoring coverage of minority communities and issues, and exposing racist and biased coverage, as well as presenting examples of good coverage and excellent public service journalism. Also, spotlighting media organizations with good or bad records for hiring minority journalists.

• Jointly serve as guest editor and publish an issue devoted to minority affairs in 1988 in *Social Education*, a national journal of social studies.

• Begin an advertising campaign and produce a video geared to youth, encouraging them to pursue careers in newspaper and broadcast journalism.

• Hold a joint convention in 1992, the 500th anniversary of the Columbus voyage to the Americas.

More minorities – black, brown, red, yellow – were competing for newsroom jobs. That did not have to mean a larger pool had to be funneled to limited opportunities. The minority population was expanding. The pool of available whites, especially white males, was shrinking. The 1980s was a boom time for the media just as it was for Wall Street. A lot of newsroom hiring was done. At the close of the black-Hispanic summit, Fitzpatrick told a black radio interviewer that to achieve parity the associations could not expect to see white people go. However, the associations could create a framework to bring more minorities in.

Chapter 14
Kerner Plus 20

At the Chicago board meeting in March 1987, a 9-8 board vote decides who will host the 1988 convention. It is the closest vote to date in NABJ's first 12 years. St. Louis edges out New York City. The board meets with the *Ebony/Jet* editorial staff at its South Michigan Avenue headquarters. Shortly after the meeting Schatzman resigns as executive director. Carl Morris, minority affairs director of ASNE, is appointed the replacement.

That spring NABJ Region 9 gets Leroy Williams of the *Rocky Mountain News* in Denver to fill the representative's post, which was vacant for 2 1/2 years. It was vacated in 1984 when Rhona Williams left TV news in Denver to work in public relations. The Rocky Mountain or Big Sky states was NABJ's largest geographical territory (10 states, more than 1 million square miles) but least populated (about a dozen members) district.

NABJ seriously considered folding Region 9 into West Coast Region 10 and Midwest Region 8, but Leroy Williams' arrival was fortuitous. As that region grew rapidly in the late 1980s and early '90s, (it was one of Nesbitt's Megatrend areas) black journalists began settling in Denver, Phoenix, and other cities).

In 1987 the news media were seriously analyzed by experienced black and other minority professionals. In March the Institute for Journalism Education sponsored a conference in Washington called "Racial Diversity: A Blueprint for Action." Two hundred journalists participated.

"Exclusion of people from the news industry hurts our entire society," said chairwoman Dorothy Butler Gilliam. "If we continue our current course, it won't be long before people don't care about news. The big loser will be the news industry itself."

The participants were saying it was time to get beyond simply desegregating the mainstream news media, it was time to truly integrate it. "Diversity" was a word used in the conference theme. The word was fresh, used at least five years before it would become a '90s buzzword.

Charles Martin, IJE president, said at the conference that nearly 20 years after the 1968 Kerner Commission report on Civil Disorders, news organizations were shifting their mission "from social responsibility to the bottom line."

If that statement was true, it posed a double-edged sword to black and other minority journalists. If print and broadcast news outlets were less socially responsible, it probably meant reluctance or resistance to hiring and promoting from minorities; it could also mean inflammatory or neglectful coverage of minority communities. There was plenty of anecdotal evidence of that.

However, news companies mindful of the bottom line could not help miss this reality: Twenty percent of America consisted of racial minorities – black, Hispanic, Asian and Native American – and that population was projected to grow to 25 percent in the 1990s. Soon, 75 percent of new entrants in the workforce would be people of color – members of minority groups and women (including whites). The market and workforce pool changed.

Industry leaders had to learn to manage in a new environment. Opportunities followed.

And as their numbers grew, American ethnic and racial minorities were more assertive in defining themselves. By late 1987, the ethnicism "African-American" crept into newspaper columns and was heard here and there on black-oriented radio programs. Black-owned Unity Broadcasting and National Black Network used African-American as a matter of style. "By attaching African-American, you bring all of our history, not just spawned in the Civil Rights movement," explained a spokeswoman for Unity Broadcasting. "Saying 'black' does not focus on our rainbowness (including Caribbean and Latin American people). We are more than the definition of a color."

Another evolutionary word concept was "multiculturalism." In the early 1980s Pam McAllister Johnson defined it as a synthesis of the racial, ethnic and gender differences that together are assets, not liabilities, in the workplace. Most newsrooms lack an adequate balance of blacks, Hispanics, Asians, women or people who approach news with a multicultural understanding, said proponents like Johnson, publisher of the *Ithaca Journal* (Gannett), the and the first black person to attain that top rank at a mainstream daily newspaper.

A few years later in the '90s, the backlash to the concepts of diversity and multiculturalism and redefinitions like African-American came in the form of accusations of "political correctness." Often the indictment was hurled by members of the white male status quo. At times the "political correctness" critique had merit. Some mischief makers or misguided people redefined words to whitewash American English. "Learning disabled" and "differently abled" arrived.

But in most cases wasn't redefinition in order? What did they say to racial crudity like this: At the University of Missouri Journalism School, a black instructor asked a white instructor why few blacks were featured on the campus TV station? The reply: "Do you know any watermelon dealers I should know?" The black woman instructor shook off the remark; she had heard worse. But black students protested and said the remark was a symptom of the callous attitude at the university. The J-school had faculty members participate in mandatory "awareness" training.

In January 1987 in Rochester, N.Y., radio station WHAM-AM dropped its policy of identifying crime suspects by race at the urging of the Rochester Association of Black Communicators. Richard Prince, an editorial writer at the *Democrat and Chronicle* newspaper, questioned the station's policy after hearing a crime suspect described in a broadcast solely as "a black man in his 20s" with no further distinguishing characteristics. Radio station management contended using race was essential to the "word picture" it must convey to its audience.

RABC was not satisfied and persisted with its complaint. One, race and age was an incomplete description of a crime suspect. Including height, weight and distinguishing facial features gave a more compelling "word picture" and reason to tell a story using race.

Furthermore, Prince showed the danger in writing or airing incomplete racial IDs. One week after the Rochester broadcast the Associated Press filed a story about a 14-year-old white girl in Southern New Jersey who said she was sexually assaulted by a "black man in his 20s." The girl later admitted she was attacked by a 14-year-old white boy. She made up the black composite, said authorities, because "she didn't think anyone would believe her."

WHAM's new guidelines read: "Make no reference to race, creed, color or nationality unless that information is absolutely essential to the story."

Racial identity and how to use it, especially in crime stories, continues to be a dilemma. The greater presence of black journalists in these newsrooms meant racial IDs were often challenged for their relevance in stories. It was an example of the positive effect organized black journalists accomplished. This check was hardly foolproof. It was against most journalists' instincts to have an ironclad rule. But the more racially mixed a newsroom the more likely people called attention to these sensibilities.

In 1987 two surveys, one conducted in Boston and one in Central Florida, assessed news coverage of black people. After examining 3,200 television, radio and newspaper stories, the Boston report said 70 percent of news reports in the white-owned media on two primarily black communities concerned crime or accidents; 85 percent of the stories reinforced negative stereotypes about black communities. In the Orlando, Fla., metropolitan area, a one-month analysis of local TV news said most black-oriented stories were about crime (46 percent); politics (24 percent); sports and entertainment (10 and 9 percent); international news (16.5 percent); crime (12 percent) and politics (7.5 percent).

Such scrutiny was important because of another new word: "underclass." People left behind in gutted cities ravaged by street crime grew more hostile with expanding local, national and international media. Critics insisted there was never any positive coverage of these urban centers.

In 1987 race and journalism went to trial. Four black New York *Daily News* journalists sued their newspaper for discrimination. A six-member federal jury on April 15 ruled in favor of plaintiffs David Hardy, a political reporter; Steven W. Duncan, an assistant news editor; Joan Shepard, Manhattan cultural affairs editor, and Causewell Vaughan, a copy editor. The jury awarded a $3.1-million settlement. It was the climax of a seven-year legal struggle.

It was one of the few times a race discrimination suit against a major news organization was contested at a trial. News organizations before that settled race or sex discrimination suits out of court or were able to prove cases did not have merit. But the *Daily News* case stuck. Some thought that *Daily News* owners gambled on a hunch that the four black journalists would lose easily in the hostile, anti-black, Reagan-era atmosphere. But the crude newsroom antics exposed in court stunk too much to the jury.

The eight-week trial exposed testimony about editors of the nation's largest metropolitan newspaper casually referring to "niggers" and "spics" – and numerous tales of unethical journalism practices. The jury agreed that in the mid-1970s to early 1980s the newspaper discriminated against black journalists in salaries, promotions and assignments and retaliated when those employees complained. After the trial the *Daily News'* management team was overhauled and about 10 black journalists joined the paper during the change, said editor Gil Spencer, a newcomer himself from the *Philadelphia Daily News*, another gritty city tabloid. Spencer said about 50 of the newsroom's 425 employees were black or Hispanic.

As there was minority growth at at least one big newspaper, studies reported decline elsewhere. The Radio and Television News Directors said the percentage of minority people on broadcast news staffs slipped to 13 percent from 15 percent nine years previous. Black men were endangered: 400 of them dropped out of radio and TV news in the last two years, said the news directors.

On the college campuses, minority students majoring in journalism declined to 7 percent from 11 percent, said a study. Educators at the time were not sure what was causing the decline. In the 1980s, college enrollment increased for all racial and ethnic groups, except black students.

In 1987, Miami was young, restless, bold, explosive, wildly colorful and of course tropical. NABJ held its 12th convention in this rainbow city, home of "black Americans, white Americans and recently arrived Americans," said Mayor Xavier L. Suarez. The metro area included 800,000 Hispanics, 400,000 African-Americans, 250,000 Haitians and 250,000 Jewish Americans. There were many new faces among the 1,400 convention goers: Young journalists and new members working at their first newspaper or TV station alongside news veterans who came to reacquaint themselves with NABJ after an estrangement.

Mental stimulation, source-building, fellowship and recreation nourished them. They jousted with Chicago Mayor Harold Washington; were scolded, then rallied on by victorious "Daily News Four" plaintiff David Hardy, and inspired by U.S. Appeals Court Judge A. Leon Higginbotham Jr. "This will recharge my batteries for another six months," said a copy editor from an Ohio newspaper

DeWayne Wickham, Gannett News Service columnist and owner of Vanita Productions, was elected president, besting Robert Tutman, a network TV photojournalist. Wickham rebounded from a humiliating defeat in 1985. Outgoing President Albert E. Fitzpatrick pointed to a fast-growing association that in two years had:

• Opened a national office in Reston, Va.
• Added a dozen affiliate chapters.
• Increased its treasury 150 percent, to $500,000 from $200,000.
• Raised $100,000 for a scholarship endowment

fund, Fitzpatrick's personal crusade.

During the opening session Chicago Mayor Harold Washington, fresh from his re-election, told NABJ members, "You're on the right quest when you talk about parity in the media. The media need a shot of adrenaline. Not to wake up, but to be honest." Washington complained that coverage of his hometown was biased and hostile, instead of critical. Washington said the advantages of a Jesse Jackson presidential candidacy in 1988 outweighed any disadvantages. "Some of the other (Democratic candidates) are good, but I don't think they speak clearer on issues than Jackson. He's an education, not just for black people but for everyone. Jackson's 1984 campaign, said Washington, were responsible for the election of two black congressmen.

The mayor had a spirited exchange with several reporters. He said he was trying to reform a city housing authority at a cost of $1 billion that the federal government allowed to defer maintenance for 28 years. Previous administrations, said Washington, used the authority as a patronage haven to control voters.

"You can fight city hall and win," said Steve Duncan, one of the Daily News Four journalists telling another packed room of journalists about the seven-year legal battle. The panel that included Hardy was moderated by Myron Lowery, former Memphis TV journalist (and NABJ's first vice president/broadcast in 1981) who successfully sued his station for discrimination that fall.

Hardy urged journalists to get copies of the court transcript. Much of the white-owned media, he said was waging "a campaign of misinformation that is absolutely hysterical."

Hardy was mad at NABJ. He said while the Daily News Four case was winding through the courts, the association gave a news reporting award to Sam Roberts, a white, former *Daily News* political reporter. During the trial Roberts showed off the award, unconvincingly, as proof the News' black journalists didn't have a good case. Also, former *Boston Globe* editor Thomas Winship, an expert witness for the *Daily News* management, accused black

journalists of "jumping from job to job for pay raises."
Winship gave the first W.E.B. DuBois lecture to NABJ.
Hardy's revelation was a bitter pill.

But after scolding NABJ, Hardy offered advice:
Establish a legal defense fund. "Time's past due for black
people to organize and confront the system," he said. "On
the 200th anniversary of the Constitution, it's not the
government that needs to be confronted, but the media."

A month before the 200th anniversary of the U.S.
Constitution, Federal Appeals Court Judge A. Leon
Higginbotham, also an author and historian, urged black
journalists to tell stories about the evolving document and
moments in history when people served justice and equality.
Higginbotham, author of one of the 100 most important
books of the 20th century according to *The New York Times*
(*In the Matter of Color: Race and the American Legal
Process*, 1978) was the third person to give the annual
W.E.B. DuBois lecture. "If DuBois were here,: said the
judge, "he would say there are several unresolved issues on
our nation's agenda. You (NABJ) are willing to be more
than the traditional critic . . . you will be the ones to
determine fact from myths. In 1987 the "We the People"
Bicentennial of the U.S. Constitution struck many black
Americans as a patriotic orgy for whites. Higginbotham
counseled that the issue was not *whether* to celebrate the
Bicentennial, but *how* to celebrate it.

"It's whether we identify with the plantation owner
or 'We the Other People' (blacks, women and Indians) who
were written out of the original document.

"You and I have to be serious scholars. We have to
know as much about DuBois as we know about Aretha
(Franklin). We have to know as much about John
Russwurm as we know about Reggie Jackson."
Higginbotham urged the thousand assembled in the hall to
avoid trivializing the news.

The 1986 newsroom numbers: broadcast 13 percent
minority, newspapers, 6.5 percent minority; 56 percent of
daily newspapers did not have minority journalists.

Carl Morris, NABJ executive director, said ASNE, which set a goal for racial newsroom parity by the year 2000, was losing the numbers game. When its first newspaper census was taken in 1978, 16 percent of the U.S. population was black, brown and yellow. The minority population was 20 to 25 percent through the 1980s and projected to be 30 percent by the year 2000.

If the goal did stretch out of reach, it did not stop black and white NABJ participants from forging ahead for parity like Olympic runners.

Loren Ghiglione, the white editor of *The News* in Southbridge, Mass., and other small New England weeklies, directed an aggressive minority recruiting drive at his papers. One third of the reporters were minorities. For his effort Ghiglione received that year's Ida B. Wells Award. The previous year he was chairman of the ASNE Minorities Committee. It organized a task force of more than 30 professional newspaper groups to increase minority hiring, and it expanded industry job fairs from four to 19.

John L. Dotson, a black journalism pioneer and new publisher of the Knight-Ridder owned *Daily Camera* in Boulder, Colo., (30,300 circulation) urged young black journalists to apply to small newspapers that are "easier to get into," and where they can "report on important stories very quickly." The lack of parity in the news media, said Dotson, Ghiglione and others, had many causes and required many solutions.

Internally, NABJ members voted to change their dramatically expanding association. Members voted by a 9-1 ratio to ratify a revised NABJ Constitution and Bylaws. The second and most critical proposal was a 4-1 vote by members to realign 10 regions. The change was necessary to deliver services effectively and adjust to dramatic population shifts in the South. Relief was needed in Region 5, with eight states which covered one-third of the members and stretched about 1,200 miles. The South trimmed down to a six-state region. Other regions absorbed new states. The changes took effect in 1989.

Conventions 1981 and 1982 entertained members with three-hour riverboat cruises. Miami upped the ante: NABJ put on a day-long cruise to Freeport in the Bahama Islands. A year earlier the board signed a contract and put down $20,000 to reserve a vacation cruise ship. Many people grumbled privately that the fun event was inappropriate. Nevertheless, 1,000 members sailed before dawn. They swam, sunbathed, drank, shopped, danced, did the limbo and did heavy politicking for the election.

While some members wrung their hands about one day of conspicuous revelry, a trend became apparent: More NABJ members brought their spouses and children and turned the professional meeting into a combined family vacation. While the board wrestled with staging relevant journalism workshops and forums, it also had to be attentive to child care and site-seeing venues.

On October 19, 1987, the stock market crashed on Wall Street. It was the worst financial collapse since the infamous 1929 crash that wrought the Great Depression.

NABJ was not immune from financial losses. The plunge eroded about $80,000 of $459,000 in investments.

Treasurer Morgan and other board members accepted the 17.5-percent erosion as "paper loses" that NABJ would recover over time.

At the end of February, the board met in Los Angeles, its second meeting ever in America's largest state. At a reception sponsored by the *Los Angeles Times,* there was groping silence when *Times* Publisher Tom Johnson told NABJ officers that of 1,208 newsroom employees, 33 (2.7 percent) are black. "Did he really want to let us know this?" some board members whispered among themselves. "The numbers," said Johnson, "indicate we must do better."

At the board meeting NABJ announced membership grew 18 percent since the August convention in Miami to nearly 1,000 full, associate and student members. A two-month spring new-member drive was to kick off and award rebates to chapters that attracted the most members. Meanwhile, the board approved professional chapters in Denver, Seattle and Birmingham, Ala., and student chapters at Eastern Illinois and Texas Women's universities. NABJ grew to 22 professional and 13 student chapters.

On March 17, 1988, President DeWayne Wickham led "Kerner Plus 20," a symposium in New York City examining the impact of recommendations to the news media made 20 years ago by the U.S. Commission on Civil Disorders. The two dozen participants included founding NABJ president Chuck Stone and Lawrence A. Still, former deputy director of information for the Kerner Commission.

At the May board meeting in St. Louis, Nashville and Lansing (Mid-Michigan) became the 23rd and 24th professional chapters.

A computerized Job Bank began operation in April. Nearly 150 members were registered in the bank and 40 news organizations were initial subscribers. Newspapers, TV and radio stations and media chains paid a fee according to size from $150 to $1,000. After a month, 34 jobs were posted and 23 people were matched or hired.

The scholarship committee received a record 92 complete entries, a 50-percent increase over the previous year. Eight winners were to receive $2,500 each.

During the visit the 17-member board went to the University of Missouri at St. Louis and were treated to a local lesson in Afro-American history.

On display were pictures and letters telling the story of Lucille Bluford, an elderly woman and St. Louis native working in the black press in Kansas City. For six consecutive years beginning in 1938, she petitioned the University of Missouri (at Columbia) Graduate School of Journalism for admission. Each time she was rejected by the chancellor and admissions director.

As a result of Bluford's efforts to break the color barrier the state established a journalism program at Lincoln University, a historically black college in Jefferson City, Mo. Many black journalists were Lincoln graduates. Years later the University of Missouri began admitting black journalism students.

In May, NABJ Region 2 (New York, New

Jersey, Connecticut) expanded its reach two ways. It met in Rochester, N.Y., in an affirmative act of keeping and attracting members in areas of New York that were not New York City. People came from Rochester, Buffalo and Syracuse. The regional was NABJ's first handshake with Canada, an often overlooked part of the African Diaspora.

Rochester was a 3 1/2-hour drive from Toronto, population 3.1 million and home to 300,000 black people, mostly of Caribbean descent. Toronto also had the second-largest Chinese community in North America (San Francisco was first). Minorities made up 11 percent of Canada's population, and their numbers were growing, said black Canadian journalists who participated in a forum.

"Not far in the future," said Dwight Whylie of the Canadian Broadcasting Corporation, "the majority of Canadians will not be of English or French origin. There will be greater linguistic, cultural and ethnic diversity. It will be different from the U.S. melting pot. Canada is evolving literally as a multicultural environment."

That said, Whylie and Ricardo Smith of the Institute of Multiculturalism in Canada said its Canadian media, like the United States', need to reflect the general population.

Minorities made up less than 2 percent of the media staff, said the Canadians. Whylie was one of two blacks on the 100-member CBC news staff. *MacLeans*, the *Time* magazine of Canada, had three blacks on staff, but none were journalists. Moderator Dwight Ellis, vice president for minority and special services for the National Association of Broadcasters, urged journalists and entrepreneurs to take note of opportunities in Canada.The northern neighbor was the United States' No. 1 trading partner.

The spring St. Louis board meeting was the inspection before the August convention. At the end of August, 1,316 were coming to the city. The convention theme was "Kerner Plus 20: Moving Ahead or Slipping Back?" At a general session, moderator Ruth Allen Ollison, assistant news director at WTTG-TV (Fox) in Washington, D.C., looked out into a sea of black faces in the main ballroom of the Adams Mark Hotel and asked "How many

of you own media outlets?"
One woman stood up.
Two decades ago the Kerner Report criticized the media for employing so few blacks. In 1988 the emphasis remained pushing more minorities through the door. But also, managing, and even in some cases, owning the house.
In a decade, minorities on daily newspaper staffs more than doubled to 3,900 (7 percent of 55,000) in 1988 from 1,700 in 1978. Minorities on these staffs who were managers or supervisors amounted to 13 percent, a quantum leap from 20 years ago when it was 1 percent or less.

Civil Rights warriors pressed NABJ members to press their employers harder. "If the patient (large segments of the black community) isn't getting better, he's getting worse," said former Black Panther Bobby Seale.
Dick Gregory, a forum panelist with Seale, said, "You're sitting out there working for white racists. You can leave here now and go back to where you work and say, 'I'm not going to tolerate these things anymore.'"
"These things" must have included the crack cocaine epidemic and the street crime and mayhem it wrought in black communities. They also included the benign acceptance of a black and brown "underclass" that grew angrier, disillusioned and self-destructive. Even the black middle class – which included most journalists – battled with overt and covert racism in offices and board rooms.
For the first time in four years, the DuBois lecturers were a couple, Tim and Daphne Maxwell Reid, co-stars of Frank's Place, a CBS-TV "dramedy." In the spirit of DuBois the Reids were more than mere entertainers; they were cultural crusaders lobbying for and presenting multidimensional black characters on the small screen.
Said Tim Reid, "I remember (partner Hugh Wilson) saying to me: 'We can just do a simple sitcom, not take any chances and probably have a big hit and make a lot of money. Or we can take this opportunity to portray the South and blacks and whites in a way that's rarely seen on television, dare to do something different.' Without a moment's hesitation, I said, 'Let's do it.'"

Daphne Maxwell Reid accused many creators of TV programming of "purposely trying to undermine the basic unity of the black family." She called for "more black women in prime time who are neither oppressed nor abused by black men or depicted as tools of pleasure for men in general."

At the convention NABJ members paid an emotional tribute to former ABC News anchorman Max Robinson. The normally robust, resonant NABJ co-founder and 1981 Journalist of the Year was frail and his voice cracked. Robinson was fighting a losing battle with AIDS. He died four months later in December at age 49.

A session on blacks in sports included Major League Baseball Commissioner Peter Ueberroth. "Continue to be critical," said Ueberroth about the paucity of blacks in baseball management, "and don't listen to an odd voice from some whining, sniveling, malcontent who doesn't know what he's talking about." A year before, Los Angeles Dodgers executive Al Campanis said blacks were near non-existent in management because they did not have "what it took" to qualify. Campanis' interview on ABC-TV's *Nightline* got him fired. His words drew greater scrutiny of sports employment beyond the playing field.

That session was a triumph for the sports task force, which demanded a large role in the association and became a force offering Saturday symposiums on sports and society.

"I wonder," wrote Betty Winston Baye, "whether the founders ever really imagined that their small tribe would one day grow into a nation."

The intimate group of 200 or so reporters and a few editors of gatherings a decade earlier now included informal and sometimes formal caucuses of sports journalists, editorial writers and op-ed columnists, business journalists and middle- and upper-level news managers.

Professional diversity altered NABJ culture.

St. Louis was the last time NABJ tolerated typos in its highest awards. The Frederick Douglass prizes, busts of the editor, orator and abolitionist, were missing an "s" from his last name.

This was too much for Kenny Walker, then with ABC News, and an awards presenter. Visibly annoyed, he offered to pay NABJ's cost of having new awards made.

For years, Merv Aubespin, a skilled painter himself and an art collector, said NABJ could not alter the work by Long Island, N.Y., artist Inge Hardison.

It was a plaster cast replica of work done in the 1960s for a series called "Negro Giants."

Eleven table-top sculptures included images of George Washington Carver, Sojourner Truth and Harriet Tubman.

NABJ had handed out this award since 1976. Scores of replica busts for future winners filled Aubespin's garage.

Nevertheless, it was time to get the name right.

After all, NABJ did not want Douglass, the abolitionist, confused with his contemporary Stephen Douglas, Lincoln's opponent who favored letting the states decide whether to continue slavery.

In 1989 the Frederick Douglass Awards were gold medals of Douglass embedded in acrylic.

Chapter 15
Shaping the World View

Two years times two associations equals four.

On Oct. 15, 1988, in Baltimore, the associations of Black, Hispanic and now, Asian American and Native American (Indian) journalists convened a summit.

The first summit in 1986 brought together the boards of NABJ and NAHJ.

DeWayne Wickham said the four associations were sending a historic message to white-owned media companies that "multiculturalism is not only something we believe in, but it's something we're committed to work toward."

Wickham and presidents Evelyn Hernandez (NAHJ), Lloyd LaCuesta (AAJA), Mark Trahant (NAJA) and about 60 board members (combined) issued a joint statement:

"While the minority population is projected to reach 35 percent in 13 years, the minority voices in the media are at dismal levels with no prospects of a rapid increase. Our united efforts are crucial to bring more minority people into the profession, to dramatically increase their promotion and advancement to all levels of the industry and to stem the alarming trend of their flight from the profession."

At lunch speaker Mary H. Futrell, president of the National Education Association, said her field faced future crises. By the year 2020, 35 percent of U.S. schoolchildren will be black, Hispanic or Asian, meanwhile there was a tailspinning decline in minority teachers from 18 percent to a projected 3 percent by 2000. She called for a relentless campaign to recruit minority teachers.

The journalists resumed their business. In three hours they discussed three issues:

• The possibility of the four associations holding a joint convention.

• Funding and fund raising. There was concern that some media companies that underwrite programs for minority associations want to "write one check, throw it in the middle of the room and have us fight for it," said a participant. The consensus was against the "one-stop shopping" corporate funding concept.

• The boards created an Executive Leadership Council of the presidents, immediate past presidents and executive directors to coordinate joint projects.

Later that weekend, when NABJ met exclusively, it announced the sites of three professional development seminars held in conjunction with the American Press Institute. A seminar on "Public Policy and Its Impact on the Underclass" was set at Hampton University in January 1989; "Research Techniques" was scheduled at API in Reston, Va., in May and "Management Techniques" was set at Jackson State (Miss.) University in October 1989. Three dozen journalists participated in the sessions.

The board approved a $612,000 operating budget for 1989 and voted 7-6 to allow a regional funding allocation based on membership. Small regions received a minimum $1,000; larger regions received proportionately more. Previously, each of the 10 regions, regardless of size, received $1,500. The Garden State (N.J.) and Austin, Texas, Associations of Black Journalists were approved as the 27th and 28th professional affiliate chapters.

Affiliates challenged their local media. In Tampa, Fla., the Suncoast Black Communicators (Tampa/St. Petersburg/Clearwater) questioned the firings of a handful of black *Tampa Tribune* journalists. Protest letters sent to executive editor H. Doyle Harvill, other media organizations, government officials and community groups were so pointed that they placed chapter members in the position of being critical of the hands that fed them.

"The risk of losing our jobs is worth it," said Karen Brown, a University of South Florida communications professor, and chairwoman of the ad-hoc committee that drafted the letter. "We run the risk of being chastised if we speak out, but we are still being chastised even when we don't say anything." Sun Coast Black Communicators reacted to the firing of bureau reporter Cathy M. Jackson in August and termination of at least four black journalists since 1985. Two months later in October, two black women journalists were fired. Harvill refused to answer the letter, citing the firings as "an internal personnel issue." But in an interview with the *NABJ Journal* he denied that black journalists were singled out for failure. Harvill said the paper was in the midst of a "full-blown recruitment effort."

Through 1988, the Tawana Brawley case tested the ability of black journalists in the mainstream press to get to the truth. In November 1987, the black teen-age girl from a northern New York suburb, said she was raped by six white men and dumped in the woods. Feces was smeared on Tawana. "KKK" and "nigger" were etched on her stomach. Cotton was stuffed in her mouth and nose.

It was the latest in a series of racial crimes in Greater New York that brought out sharp racial divisions and introduced the region and nation to a new generation of black activists. Lawyers C. Vernon Mason and Alton Maddox rushed to Tawana's aid. So did the Rev. Al Sharpton. Brawley's charges made her an instant cause celebre.

But Tawana's story had problems. Her legal and civil rights team refused to cooperate with a state investigation. And reporting by a number of black journalists in the New York-area media pointed out contradictions and inconsistencies in her story. Tawana may have lied to cover up parental abuse or other problems.

Black-owned media meanwhile defended the activists and Tawana. *The City Sun,* a Brooklyn weekly, published a copyrighted investigative story backing several of the girl's assertions. Black news and talk radio aired Mason, Mattox and Sharpton's views uncritically and regularly.

The trio used the audio platform to announce press conferences and demonstrations almost daily.

Maddox, Mason and Sharpton retaliated against black reporters who did not buy the racist-white cops-did-it story without evidence. Tension between the black community and black journalists peaked when Maddox, Mason and Sharpton denounced black *Newsday* reporters from the pulpit in a crowded Brooklyn church.

"Put them out!" shouted people in a congregation-turned mob. Red bow-tied security staff told *Newsday* representatives to leave. "If *Newsday* leaves, everybody leaves," announced Don Terry, a *New York Times* reporter. When a security staffer put his hands on a 21-year-old *Newsday* woman intern, eight journalists picked up their notebooks and cameras and filed out of the church.

"It was emotionally draining," said *Newsday* reporter Clem Richardson. "We were tired of bring lied to and were tired of being referred to as 'Rent-a-Toms.'"

Mason called the reporters "arrogant" for walking out. He was unable to recognize the act of self-respect.

Sharpton accused the press of disrupting the rally. "The press isn't supposed to show solidarity," he said. "They're supposed to be covering us."

Black journalists were shell shocked by the abuse they absorbed from black New Yorkers in the street and pews and from white editors in the office who doubted their ability to be aggressive but balanced. Said Richardson,"We had to fight battles on both sides."

That fall, a 23-member special grand jury concluded that Brawley fabricated her story of abduction and rape. The media overlooked the fact that she was nevertheless a victim of parental abuse or political manipulation.

In 1985 and 1987 minority journalists warned of a "quiet crisis," hundreds of members falling out of the field, especially in broadcast news.

More data and some answers emerged. A 1988 survey by University of Missouri professor Vernon Stone for RTNDA reported that from 1979 to 1986, black men accounted for a 2 percent drop in the number of non-whites in TV news and a 1 percent drop in radio. In a one-year period 300 blacks were no longer part of the broadcast news force. NBC News correspondent Noah Nelson said many black male correspondents no longer "wanted to go through the trouble of fighting a very sophisticated battle of racism and misconceptions of what a black journalist ought to be."

Fred Brown, black and news director of KYW News radio in Philadelphia, said if white managers are told by superiors to hire more blacks and women, they were apt to "double dip" by hiring black women who satisfy two federal equal employment opportunity goals at once.

Moreover, black men were caught in the broadcast news tailspin of the mid- to late-1980s. ABC, NBC and CBS changed owners. Jobs were sheared from news divisions, 1,000 between 1986 and 1987. The Fox network emerged as a fourth power. Rupert Murdoch crafted a news division under a new set of rules. Many experienced blacks who left established independent companies.

Dwight Ellis of the National Association of Broadcasters said whites as well as blacks were affected by the cuts. As the pool of jobs grew shallower, the "old-boy network" that traditionally controlled the apportionment of jobs, and which blacks were not part of, grew tighter.

In spring 1989 ASNE reported minority employment at daily newspapers in 1988 inched forward one-half of one percent to 7.5 percent of the work force. NABJ and other minority associations answered, that's not good enough.

At the spring board meeting, a "Partners in Progress" award was presented to Mary Sparks, a white woman and head of the Journalism and Broadcasting Department at Texas Women's University in Denton, Texas.

"She's at every convention with at least six students," said DeWayne Wickham. "This small college dominates our scholarship and internship programs."

Also that season, Albert E. Fitzpatrick became the first African-American to win the Ida B. Wells award in its 7-year history. The award was bestowed by NABJ, the National Conference of Editorial Writers and National Broadcast Editorial Association. Fitzpatrick, assistant vice president of minority affairs at Knight-Ridder, was recognized for exemplary leadership in moving the news media toward racial and cultural diversity. Fitzpatrick was instrumental in hiring and promoting minorities within Knight-Ridder and outside the Miami-based company.

By spring 1989 nearly 125 people served on the New York Convention Committee. They met monthly in United Negro College Fund offices on East 62nd Street. New York had come a long way from 1982 when a regional caucus consisted of five people gathering under a canopied table. New York in the early years was an underachieving chapter. It had about a dozen very dedicated members, but it did not achieve as much as communities that did not have the distractions of the most-populated U.S. city.

The New York Association of Black Journalists wanted this convention badly. It rallied members and associates. Two years ago, losing the 1988 convention to St. Louis by one vote still stung. New York lost because many board members were wary of the hotel expense. The one-year delay increased guaranteed hotel costs anyway.

New York faced a dual burden: It was expected to put on a great show. The venue after all was the media capital of the world, a cosmopolitan city of art, fashion, intellect and culture. Meanwhile, there were doubters. Can the New Yorkers pull it off? Do they have their act together? Like wide-eyed visitors who fret about New York's notoriety for crime, high prices and rude behavior, NABJ members in the hinterlands harbored convention fears.

Meanwhile, there was a battle of wills among President Wickham, Executive Director Carl Morris and convention co-chairs Charles Moses and Linda Waller. In soliciting and securing corporate underwriting, who had authority, Reston or New York? Leaders in New York and Washington (Reston) wrestled for control not unlike the way New York, the center of money, traditionally battled with Washington, the center of government.

No wonder NABJ leaders fought. Stakes were high. It stood to gain or lose the most revenue ever from a convention, attract the most people ever and attract the most publicity, for better or worse. Charles Moses was a long-time NABJ member and veteran newsman. He fondly remembered the 1977 Baltimore convention. Moses learned his craft at Community News Service in New York and worked at the Rochester *Times-Union*, then *Newsday*. After working many years in news he studied for an MBA. By

1989 Moses left newspapers to work for Bristol-Myers. Linda Waller had been involved with NABJ a dozen years too. She was from Lawnside, N.J., a Philadelphia-area suburb and incorporated black town. She decided at age 14 to become a journalist inspired by watching trailblazer Edie Huggins anchor the news on WCAU-TV in Philadelphia. In 1968 at age 14, Waller wrote a letter to the Philadelphia *Bulletin*. She challenged an editorial criticizing Olympian John Carlos for raising his fist in a Black Power salute during the National Anthem.

"They printed it," she said, "I was emboldened by it. But, we got these harassing calls. My mom said I was too smart to be a journalist. I should be a lawyer. I told her I didn't want to be a lawyer because they lie for a living. A (school) counselor told me to be a teacher."

At age 16 Waller wrote to *Bulletin* columnist Claude Lewis seeking advice. Lewis recommended she contact the Dow Jones Newspaper Fund. Waller used the career center to select a college with a journalism program. Waller attended the University of Bridgeport and went to work at Gannett Westchester-Rockland Newspapers, first as an intern and later in a number of reporting and editing positions for a dozen years.

By 1989 she was working for the Newspaper Fund in Princeton and was NABJ Region 2 deputy director.

New York Convention organizers promised an international event focusing on the African Diaspora, whether it was Harlem, Haiti or Harare. "Shaping the World View" was the convention theme.

New York was an opportune laboratory: The city was absorbing great waves of immigrants, as it did a century ago. This time they were people of color from Latin America and the Caribbean and Asia. New York City was in the middle of a mayoral campaign. David Dinkins, a courtly long-time political figure, was favored to become the city's first African-American mayor. Dinkins was counted on to salve racial wounds opened in the late 1970s and 1980s.

Hundreds of NABJ members engaged in an expensive campaign to pick their next president in August.

Four candidates emerged: Tom Morgan, treasurer and *New York Times* reporter; Ruth Allen Ollison, assistant news director, WTTG-TV, Washington; Robert Tutman, cameraman for CBS News in Chicago and Tony Cox, TV correspondent for Los Angeles-based news service, NIWS.
    Cox dropped out of the race by spring. He lacked the money. His company would not bankroll him. Tutman said he did not ask his employer for money to campaign "on principle." The campaign money, he said, "could be better used on scholarships and on some of the other things we say we're all about." Tutman traveled to two spring regional meetings by car. He was relegated to longshot status.
    That left the battle for president to Morgan and Allen-Ollison. WTTG gave Allen-Ollision $10,000 to cover cross country trips, mass mailings, receptions and buttons and banners. Of $5,000 Morgan spent two months before the election, at least half came from *The New York Times.*
    Outgoing president Wickham said he did not accept any money from his employer when he ran successfully in 1987. "If we expect news organizations to pay the way," said Wickham "they're going to expect that we dance with the one who brought them." Members were already uneasy about NABJ dependence on corporate contributions for conventions and operating expenses. Bankrolling election campaigns was alarming. "It's a much larger statement," said Vanessa Williams, a *Philadelphia Inquirer* reporter and Region 3 director. "It's more symbolic (for companies) to say 'We put that person there.'"
    Two former presidents said the integrity of the office was not in danger. "The ethics is in the people who hold the office," said Mervin Aubespin. "If they allow themselves to be unduly influenced, I'm sure membership will vote them out." Immediate past president Albert Fitzpatrick added "I would hate to think anybody who would be elected to office would succumb to such pressures."
    Nevertheless, candidates in 1989 spent five to ten times more to run for president of this non-profit association, an unpaid position, than what Aubespin spent in 1983 in the first truly competitive NABJ election.
    Many members reacted one of three ways: One camp

wrung their hands, troubled about company funding of individual campaigns. Two, supporters in the Allen-Ollison and Morgan campaign played politics like the pros they covered. Three, there were smear and whispering tactics. Pressure by supporters was applied to popular and respected members to endorse one of the leading candidates.

About one-third of the 2,000 convention participants voted for president and other officers. Morgan won with 337 votes to Allen Ollison's 244. Tutman earned 46 votes.

Beginning his seventh year of board service, this time in the top position, Morgan vowed to bring "stability and continuity" to the office. "NABJ used to feel like a family," he reminded members. "It's time to get back to that and stop this bitterness."

But at the convention anger shifted to the handful of paid national staff in Reston. Had it become too independent of the volunteer elected officers? The question arose during the business meeting, sparsely attended by about 200 people (check) but held in a cavernous hall at the Hilton and Towers. A member asked board members at the dais who had approved the Central Intelligence Agency setting up an employment recruiting booth at the jobs fair? It was present with scores of news organizations. No elected officer seemed to know who invited the CIA.

The CIA asked to participate and the national office in Reston accepted its job fair fee. Furthermore, CIA participation was listed in the July/August *NABJ Journal* published before the convention. Outraged members apparently overlooked the fine print in their journal. Executive board members from President Wickham on down agreed the agency's participation was a bad idea.

Modern-day black journalists feared being labeled or used as spies by the white-majority government, or worse yet, becoming the spy and police agencies of government. NABJ asked the two black women CIA representatives to leave. The intelligence agency money was returned.

This was a high-tech convention. Moses, Waller, Todd Beamon of the *New York Times* and their legion of convention committee members patrolled the convention floors with two-way radios, on the lookout for overcrowding or problems with service. For the first time, computers were used for writing and editing workshops.

Diane Abbott gave the W.E.B. DuBois lecture at this diaspora-inspired convention. She was a British Member of Parliament. In 1987, Abbott and three others became the first Britons of African descent elected to the body. Immigrants rebuilt London after World War II, she told a ballroom filled with journalists. Abbott asked "What does it mean to be a black journalist? Three components to a black world view: A sense of history; international perspective and a degree of self-respect and self-love as black people."

When Michael Manley of Jamaica spoke it was the first time NABJ was addressed at its convention by a foreign head of government. The prime minister made a case for his country and black people everywhere.

Regarding Third World debt, he said: "A lot of you (journalists) are led to believe it's because a lot of lazy people don't work hard. . . ."We're told it's our problem – but it's your problem too. Detroit can't sell enough tractors (to the Third World)." We need a program, he said, "that gives borrowing countries a chance to breathe (and respects lending countries). We have to end the economic paralysis."

The other keynoter was an American from the Bronx and son of Jamaican immigrants: Gen. Colin L. Powell. The four-star general was national security advisor. Seven days before NABJ convened, President George Bush nominated Powell to be chairman of the U.S. Joint Chiefs of Staff, making him the first African-American in the post.

At the convention Powell paid tribute to black soldiers who defended America for two centuries. He said they made his achievement possible. Then Powell veered into the conservative dogma of the Reagan administration. Urging military preparedness, Powell said: "When you are beginning to see signs of victory and success, that's not the time to quit . . . history has told us that many wars have been lost because the guard was let down."

The convention was as deep in substantive forums and workshops as the Empire State Building and World Trade Center were tall. But a first convention in New York required showcasing the flash and charm that make New York, New York. There were receptions at the United Nations and the Metropolitan Museum of Art. At the hotel, a darkened ballroom turned into a fashion runway. Thirteen designers paid tribute to the industry's top models in a "Soul of Seventh Avenue" show. But these social events were not enough. The hosts made arrangements with the City of New York to rent a subway train to take fashionably dressed convention goers to the Apollo Theater for the "Salute to Excellence" awards program. "The 'A' Train is the quickest way to get to Harlem," said Duke Ellington and Billy Strayhorn. The hosts promised to prove it.

Behind the scenes there was anxiety. Could a dreamlike journey from midtown 70 blocks to Harlem turn into a nightmare? The night before, at the fashion show, an excited crowd tried to push its way into the ballroom. A number of doors were barricaded, creating a fire hazard if the crowd already inside had to flee. The reception area was so crowded and stuffy that a few women fainted. Linda Waller watched in horror then radioed volunteers for help. The crowd was guided into the ballroom without incident.

But Waller and Moses saw the potential for trouble the next evening. Rain was forecast. The 1,350 Apollo Theater guests staying in the hotel had to walk a few blocks to a special subway stop to catch the A train and schmooze at a reception. Travelers had to have their Apollo tickets, no excuses. But if people were fumbling with umbrellas and rainwear, how could the crowd be moved on schedule and without harassment or hassles?

The convention committee for weeks rehearsed how it would provide security, but it was time to alert the board about more plans. An emergency early morning meeting was convened in the hotel presidential suite, where Wickham roomed. Like commanders in a war room, Waller and Moses briefed the board on several scenarios for moving hundreds of people on time, safely and comfortably, even if the weather turned foul. The weather behaved. Visitors in elegant dresses and tuxedos whisked to 125th Street and Eighth Avenue on the chartered subway train. In the theater, anchorman Bernard Shaw of Cable News Network was honored as Journalist of the Year. Lifetime Achievement was awarded to Peggy Peterman of the *St. Petersburg Times*. This year, honorees accepted Frederick Douglass awards with the name correctly spelled.

The convention cost $661,000. A record $95,000 in cash was handled on site. Net profit was slightly less than the $183,000 in revenues from the St. Louis convention. This was a victory. "The dire predictions that New York would be a money-loser didn't happen," said Waller during a fall report. "The convention succeeded in a city much more expensive than St. Louis. "It brought money, relationships and stature it never had before (i.e., Kodak supplying film to photojournalists, and use of 20 Atex computer terminals for editing, layout and pagination instruction)." Final paid attendance was 1,991, up 30 percent from the 1,395 people who came the previous year and more than double participation two years before that. "NABJ realized that when it committed to New York City, the cost in such a major urban center was going to exceed other cities," said Waller. "But the tradeoff was an exciting program."

In December, President Thomas Morgan and 60 NABJ members participated in an international conference of Caribbean, African and North American journalists in Jamaica. Weeks before a new decade, the National Association of Black Journalists was shaping a world view.

In 1989 NABJ closed its second era; the first was 1975-1983. In the mid- to late-'80s a national office made the association visible and accessible to media powers, money interests and young journalists or students getting started or pondering a career. At the start of the second era, Mervin Aubespin promised that the members working in the Paducahs and Peorias of America would feel connected to NABJ; it was not just for folks in New York, Washington, D.C., and Chicago. Albert Fitzpatrick opened the national office and expanded NABJ as a player in the media industry. Wickham developed the association from within and set a foundation for self-sufficiency. Morgan opened the next era with handshakes in the African Diaspora, a conference in Jamaica and the truly international convention.

Why journalism?

Did I choose or
did it choose me?

Carole Bartel (Not interviewed)

Her whereabouts were unknown. Natalia Aberdeen of the Congress of Racial Equality (CORE) said that the man who would have known of Bartel, Wendell Garnett, died recently. He was CORE's unofficial griot.

Furthermore, a fire five years ago destroyed much of CORE's archives. It occurred at the office on Flatbush Avenue in Brooklyn.

Carole Bartel's work can be found in bound copies of *CORE* magazine at the Schomburg Center for Research in Black Culture in New York City. In five 1975 issues Bartel was listed as one of three assistant editors.

Edward H. Blackwell Jr. (Interviewed March 22, 1991.)

Born in 1919. He grew up in Minneapolis. Blackwell lives in Madison, Wis.

How he became a journalist? "It evolved," he said.

"I never thought of myself as being a journalist.

"The next thing I knew I was doing it.

"I came through the money door. I came in because there was a story that needed to be told.

"My background was labor. I used to sit at the feet of my guru, Harry Bridges. My father was a sleeping car porter.

"I never took a journalism course in my life."

Blackwell attended the University of Minnesota while working as a dining car waiter and cook. Blackwell completed course requirements in political science but did not receive the degree. Blackwell's first newspaper job was with a longshoreman's paper in Seattle in the late 1940s.

In the 1950s he was a reporter for eight years with the black-owned *Minneapolis Spokesman.*

Blackwell was hired by *The Milwaukee Journal* in 1963. He stayed 15 1/2 years until January 1979.

"I wrote stories if I was in Mississippi or wherever I was. I was an expert on riot coverage. I knew what the police or demonstrators would do.

"The whole period of the Mississippi struggle was important. There wasn't many of us (black journalists), maybe 15 or 20 black reporters (in the early 1960s.)

"In the early '60s editors relied on preachers to keep them informed. They (preachers) could not do that (so newspapers began hiring black reporters.)

"I finished my career as a columnist.

"Later, they (editors) thought the era of black journalism had passed. For example, interest in the central cities.

"There was more impact from the business side of newspapers. For example, in Chicago, advertising departments realized there were tens of thousands of black middle-class families. They would sponsor Urban League conventions."

When Blackwell left *The Milwaukee Journal,* he said "I felt like I was just spinning my tires in the mud."

Reginald Bryant (Interviewed April 22, 1991.)
Native Philadelphian. Born Oct. 17, 1950.

"We were catalysts for the (founding) Washington meeting," he said. "There were loose organizations. Philadelphia had a 'rat pack' of TV-radio-print people.

"Then, black journalists were at best adornments.

"My association with journalism was as an independent contractor in broadcasting. I was not in it for a glorification of the media, but unification of the people. The D.C. meeting had a mixed bag of on-air types. Max (Robinson) was singularly the most visible, most passionate.

"The Philadelphia contingent led the organizational process. NABJ was modeled on the way we did things in Philadelphia. We came together out of necessity, not a boutique or professional organization.

"Every time Acel (Moore) and I went to a city (or state) -- places like Minnesota and Alabama -- for 'Black Perspective on the News,' we met a journalist we could use on the show.

"'Black Perspective on the News' started in summer 1973 as a replacement show, a step-up program. It was national from 1974 to 1978 in 160 cities."

Bryant remained active with NABJ and the Philadelphia chapter through the 1980s.

In 1991 he was doing communications and public relations work for Local 1199, health and hospital workers union. Bryant was also the host of "Catharsis," a talk show on WRTI-FM in Philadelphia.

Maureen Bunyan (Interviewed Feb. 22, 1991.)

Bunyan's family is from Guyana. They emigrated to Waukeshaw in Southeast Wisconsin.

"We were the only minority family in the town or county," she said.

"I read a lot. I had relatives in many countries. I always liked what we now call 'communications skills: reading, writing and speaking.'

"I thought I wanted to be a newspaper or magazine writer, for example, for *The New Yorker*. I was a free-lancer at *The Milwaukee Journal* and in 1968 an intern. I felt comfortable with them.

"I wanted to be a journalist, but I didn't choose broadcast journalism. I was identified after Kerner (Commission Report) to go into broadcasting. I was living in Milwaukee and going to college.

"I was in a play 'Who's Got His Own," by Ron Milner.

"At the second performance, Tony Brown was in the audience. He asked me, 'Ever thought of going into TV?' This was 1969. He said 'Why not enroll in the Columbia Summer Program?' Tony Brown set up a meeting with Gary Gilson at WITI-TV in Milwaukee. (ABC-Storer)

"Gilson said if Columbia accepts you, we will accept you. The station never had a black presence on the air.

"But the manager said 'I didn't look black enough or sound black enough. Why don't you cut your hair and change your name -- to King.'

"I was put off. I went to the Summer Program, but I did-

n't go back to WITI. I talked to Tony Brown. There was a
position at WGBH-TV in Boston. I got it. I worked a
month in Milwaukee and went to Boston in October 1970.

"In Boston I covered labor and education. It (WGBH
broadcasts) was a roundtable format. I went to WCBS-TV
in New York in Spring 1972."

Since fall 1973, Bunyan has been in Washington, D.C.
with WTOP-TV (CBS). In the late 1980s the station was
bought by *Gannett Co.* and renamed WUSA-TV.

Crispin Campbell (Interviewed Oct. 9, 1991.)

Born Jan. 29, 1952, Savannah, Ga. Campbell said that
she is 6-feet tall.

Her father was a minister and Campbell's mother was an
English professor.

Campbell moved around like an Army brat, from Savannah to Albany, Ga.; Grambling, La.; Jefferson City, Mo.;
New Orleans; East Lansing, Mich.; Oakland, Calif.; Denver; Marshall, Texas and New York City.

She said "My family was 'book poor' (like Southern folks
who are 'land poor' because they have a lot of property but
not much else.)

"When I was bored, I read the encyclopedia.

"Journalism chose me. I began writing since I was six or
seven. When President Kennedy was assassinated, I was in
the sixth grade. People fainted when they heard the news.

"I went home and wrote an essay. It got published in the
church newspaper.

"In the ninth grade, I wanted to be an astronaut, or Lois
Lane.

"When I got to college, I thought it was more fun to be a
reporter.

"I went to Dillard College one year as a pre-med major
with a journalism minor -- an indication that I was trying to
please my mother and myself -- and finished the last three
years at Michigan State.

"I worked one summer for *UPI* (*United Press Interna-
tiononal*) in Chicago."

How I got to the founding meeting?: "Paul Brock called

us all together.

"I don't remember why we were there. We just felt we had to do this. We did not have our own organization and there was no reason why.

"Just like the white old-boy network, we needed an organization where we could network. For years I was the only black at MacNeil-Lehrer. Most of us were the (only) voice of blackness wherever we were.

"Many people then were coming out of the Michelle Clark (summer) program. We were all having the same problems at different levels.

" A lot of blacks were being programmed to fail, for example, young blacks with degrees from white universities.

"At one point (at the founding meeting) some of us said, 'wait a minute, where does this brother (Brock) come from? How did we get a p.r. person (Democratic National Committee) to come and form us?'

"I joined SPJ (Society of Professional Journalists) and Women in Communications and all the organizations to be hooked in before there was 'us.'

"I was a member of Women in Communications since 1971 when I was a sophomore. Seven years later I was at a meeting in Washington. A white woman asks me, 'who invited you?' I said no one. She says, 'oh, a new member!'

"I asked myself, why do I have to pay my dues and go through this? A white woman is trying to make me a sub-third-class person. White male SPJ members did not seem threatened by me.

"When I was interviewed by a white man for a job at *AP* (*Associated Press*), I had to wonder, 'how dumb can you be?' When I told him what my parents did he said, 'Oh, you're from one of those few black families where the child was encouraged to read.' Do I curse this man out? I didn't.

"He was one of the whites who was trying to be fair, but he (like others) had this attitude, like when Reagan would tell stories that he never witnessed overt racism.

"I love people. I love telling people stories. I became a writer because nobody could tell the story better than me."

Campbell was a reporter with "MacNeil-Lehrer" from 1975-78. From 1978-81 she was a producer with WETA-

TV, Washington, D.C. Later she was with "America's Black Forum" with Julian Bond, also on public TV.

After that, Campbell free-lanced for *The Washington Post* (Tom Morgan was her editor), then ran a newsletter, *Drug Enforcement Report.*

In 1983 she went to Nigeria (Benin) for three months to do public relations work for a church.

In 1988, from February to November, Campbell was election relief (a reporter/editor) for *Associated Press.*

Crispin Campbell became a born-again Christian.

The past two years she had been recuperating from surgery. She had an auto transplant. Her right kidney was removed and put back in her body. "I hope to jump out in the world early next year," she said in a 1991 interview.

Charlie Cobb (Interviewed Aug. 30 and Sept. 1, 1991.)

Born June 23, 1943, Washington, D.C. He grew up in Washington and Springfield, Mass.

How I became a journalist?: "I backed into it.

"I bumped around Africa, writing stuff for black newspapers and *Negro Digest* (renamed *The Black World.*)

"I saved my own money to do it. I began in 1970-71.

"I met a lot of black journalists from the Civil Rights movement. Earl Caldwell, Gerald Fraser, Larry Still and Lerone Bennett were regularly on the scene.

"I went to Mississippi in 1962 with the Student Non-Violent Coordinating Committee and stayed five years. I was a student for a year at Howard (University.)

"I was still associated with SNCC. The late Bertrand Russell began organizing a war crimes tribunal in Stockholm.

"In that context, he was curious as to what young black people might have in common with guerilla organizations like the Viet Cong (that is, in organizing people and communities.) He wrote SNCC.

"Myself and Julius Lester wound up going to Hanoi for four weeks. On the way back I decided, rather than fly over Africa, I would go there.

"I traveled with Cortland Cox on fourth-class (dormitory

class) on a boat from Marsellies. African laborers often traveled on these boats. Fifty dollars. Sixty men to a room. Everyone got a tin plate, tin cup and a bed.

"I went to Guinea, Morocco and Liberia. I was just curious about Africa. SNCC with help from Harry Belafonte sent some people to Guinea.

"I went back to Tanzania to live from 1970-72. Before that I helped organize Drum and Spear bookstore in (Washington) D.C. and I taught at Federal City College (now, University of the District of Columbia.)

"I worked as a foreign correspondent for NPR (National Public Radio) from late 1975 to 1979. I began free-lancing for *National Geographic* (the opportunity arose when support for a free-lance project on Zimbabwe fell through.)"

Cobb became a staff writer in 1985.

Marilyn Darling (interviewed Aug. 1, 1991)

She is a native of Atlantic City, born in December 1934.

Darling grew up in the Philadelphia-Wilmington, Del. area. "I traveled a lot as a kid," she said. "Delaware is narrow and much more segregationist. It radicalized me.

"I tended to be a bookish, thoughtful kid. I'd ask, 'who am I?' I decided there was a way to empower people. With information. Black journalists owe a lot to people who hit the streets. People were sick of distortions and were not going to let non-blacks in the community cover it and make money from it.

"In the '60s people began to seek you out. I was a writer. I was interested in film. I studied communications. (Circa 1964) I did various free-lance jobs. I took a job doing research for WOR-TV (in New York City.)

"WHYY was aware of my work and it was under pressure (to integrate) for license retention. It was 1970-71 when I went to WHYY. I worked as a producer. I was there until 1978-79.

"I agreed to work for DuPont for five horrible years in corporate communications until 1985."

Darling now runs her own business out of her home and takes care of her mother. Her father died when she was very young.

How Marilyn Darling remembers the NABJ founding: "Some people arrived on scant budgets. Others heard about the meeting for the first time. Connie Chung (who worked with Max Robinson at WTOP) was interested in joining. A quick decision was made: 'no.' That was a mistake.

"I'm not a joiner. I don't surrender to groups easily. I happened to be covering that (political) conference and I was invited to the room. I became a founder.

"That was (too) casual and serendipitous."

Leon Dash (Interviewed November 1990 and Sept. 12, 1991.)

Born March 16, 1944 in New Bedford, Mass. When his father returned from World War II, the family moved to New York City when Leon Dash was age 2. He grew up in Harlem and the Bronx.

Dash developed an interest in journalism and writing while at Rhodes Preparatory School.

Dash enrolled at Lincoln (Pa.) University then switched to Howard University. He studied African History. He found out that *The Washington Post* had a copyboy opening on the 8 p.m. to 4 a.m. shift.

"No one wanted that job. But it was perfect for me," said Dash. He could go to school and work full-time. It was better than the work he was doing, steam cleaning buildings from a scaffold. He took the newspaper job Nov. 5, 1965.

Five months later, April 1966, the city editor asked Dash if he wanted to try out for the summer reporters internship program. "I understood his concern," said Dash. "He didn't have any black reporters in case a riot broke out." Dash worked as a reporter while a student at Howard.

Shortly after Martin Luther King's death, Dash went to Kenya as a Peace Corps volunteer to teach in at a rural high school. That was from 1968 to 1971. Dash returned to the paper in 1971.

He was a member of the Metro Seven (Richard Prince, Michael Hodge, LaBarbara Bowman, Penny Mickleberry, Ivan Brandon and Dash.)

The Metro Seven presented executive editor Ben Bradlee

with specific complaints and insisted that the paper institute an anti-discrimination program. A complaint was filed with the EEOC and EEOC found in the Metro Seven's favor. *Post* lawyers demanded that it be withdrawn, citing errors. EEOC decided not to prosecute.

The protest fizzled but it motivated women at *The Washington Post* to file a sex discrimination suit.

Joe Davidson (Interviewed in fall 1990 and April 20, 1992.)
He was born April 26, 1949 in Detroit.

"My junior high school journalism class (eighth grade, 1962-63) got me interested. The English class was a journalism class. We didn't have a (school) paper (it was eliminated because of citywide budget cuts.)

"What drew me (to journalism)? I think it was the process: Gathering information, putting pieces of the puzzle together so that a wide group of people could learn something from it. Putting something on a page (for example, layout). Those kind of things interested me.

"In high school I had another journalism class.

"I was heavily involved in student government." Davidson graduated in 1967.

"I was an Eagle scout. There was a day when we went out with someone in the profession. I spent the day with a sportswriter from *The Detroit News*. He covered racing.

"I was told that I didn't have to go to journalism school (to become a journalist.) I worked for the college newspaper at Oakland University, then a small, state-supported school (located in Rochester, Mich.)

"My father suggested that I talk to my professor about getting an internship. My political science professor spoke to the chancellor, who knew the editor of *The Detroit News*. I got a job as a copy aide.

"I made a point of not being called 'boy.'" Back then stories were typed on carbon books with six copies. Journalists would yell "boooy!"

Davidson said, "I'd wait until they yelled 'copy!'"

Davidson was an intern at *The Detroit News* in 1969-70 and joined the staff full-time in 1971.

In 1972 Davidson went to graduate school, Michigan University, and earned an M.A. in Public Policy Studies.

In August 1974 he became a reporter at *The Philadelphia Bulletin*. When the paper folded in 1982, he went to *The Philadelphia Inquirer* briefly then to *The National Leader,* where he was managing editor.

When *The Leader* folded in 1984, Davidson went to *The Wall Street Journal*. He was a Washington correspondent who covered the Department of Health and Human Services. From late 1990 to early 1992, Joe Davidson was a correspondent based in South Africa.

Allison Davis (Interviewed Jan. 11, 1991.)

Born April 7, 1953. Davis grew up in Teaneck, N.J. and later Silver Spring, Md., where she went to high school.

Current events were normal discussion around the family dinner table. Her father, the late Walter Davis, was a labor leader in the AFL-CIO and later was an official in the federal Equal Employment Opportunity Commission in the late 1960s.

Walter Davis was the EEOC's first deputy director.

He led and encouraged discussion of issues. Ideas and issues became an interest of Allison Davis.

"My father traveled a great deal. Whe he came home he'd tell us what he had done. He was very much involved in civil rights as a labor leader. He marched in Selma. He strategized with Bayard Rustin.

"My two brothers and I would draw on our father's experiences and on current events we'd learn in school and see on TV.

"We wanted to see if we saw him (their father) on TV.

"From the first grade, current events became my favorite activity. I always knew I wanted to get into newspapers from junior high school on."

Allison Davis went to Boston University, where she majored in journalism. She finished her studies in 3 1/2 years.

She was set to apply for jobs in newspapers. But in April 1975 she got an offer to work at WBZ-TV, the NBC affiliate in Boston, as a writer/producer.

She called it "a lucky kind of thing."
She worked for three years at WBZ then went to KDKA-TV (CBS) in Pittsburgh in 1978. In 1981 Davis went to NBC News. She was a producer for "Nightly News" and later TV magazine shows.

Sandra Dawson (Long)   Interviewed July 11, 1991
She is a native of Annapolis, Md. Born June 25, 1952.
"I chose journalism. I majored in journalism in college and worked on the high school newspaper.
"I was always an avid reader. Growing up in Maryland, it was still very segregated. The newspaper I grew up read-eing (*The Evening Capitol*) would read 'John Doe, a Ne-gro from . . .'
"We were always in the crime news. There was nothing positive. It was never 'John Doe, a white male.'
"I decided if I ever could get a job on a newspaper I'd try to change that.
"I saw journalism as a vehicle of social change.
"The turning point was when I was a high school senior. A couple of friends and I cut class and heard Alex Haley speak at the community college. He was already known for the *Autobiography of Malcolm X.*
"He talked about the research on his own life. How he slept on a ship to feel what it was like to be on a slaveship.
"I took notes and wrote a story. It made the front page of my high school paper. I had the bug.
"In college, I switched to journalism from English my junior year. DeWayne Wickham was in my class.
"I didn't write for the *Diamondback* (the campus paper). I did for the *Black Explosion* (a new campus paper).
"It became part of the black student union. We moved it from occasional publication to (publication) every two weeks. That took a lot of work."
In 1974 Dawson began work at the Wilmington *News-Journal.* She stayed at the *News-Journal* until 1977, then she worked for *The Philadelphia Bulletin* from 1977-82. *The Bulletin* closed in January 1982 and she took the rest of that year off. Dawson joined *The Philadelphia Inquirer*

in 1983.
When interviewed in 1991 Dawson was deputy suburban editor for Pennsylvania. She was age 39 and a 16-year veteran of three papers.

How Dawson remembers the NABJ founding meeting:
I came specifically for the journalist meeting. I got the *News-Journal* to pay for it. Very few black women were in the business.
"A number of us were very young and right out of college. We were trying to cope with the racism. We talked to vets like Chuck (Stone) and Les (Payne) who offered advice. There was that feeling of camaraderie."

Paul Delaney (Interviewed Dec. 12, 1990.)
Born in Montgomery, Ala. Delaney grew up in Cleveland during his teen-age years.
"I always wanted to be a writer. (But) I didn't want to take English and Literature and become a permanent student or teacher."
He majored in journalism at Ohio State University. He graduated in 1958.
Delaney applied to dozens of daily newspapers but was turned down.
"I never thought about being most likely the only black in the newsroom. I had heard about Carl Rowan and Ted Poston of the *New York Post* and a handful of others. I knew by their experiences everything would be OK."
When he did not get hired by a newspaper, Delaney went to the Baltimore *Afro-American.* He didn't like it.
Delaney moved to Cleveland and drove a cab for a year.
In September 1959 he went to work for the *Atlanta Daily World.*
"I was in the South at a critical time in history. It was the first job I was fired from for a disagreement over civil rights. I'd argue with the editor every day." (The black-owned and conservative *Atlanta Daily World* was anti-movement, said Delaney.)
"I stayed in Atlanta from 1961-63 and worked as a pro-

bation officer.
"I went to the *Dayton Daily News.* The papers that were hiring blacks were in the big Northern cities."
Paul Delaney moved on to *The Washington Star,* then to *The New York Times.*

William Dilday (Interviewed June 11, 1991.)
He was born Sept. 14, 1939 in Boston.
"In my high school yearbook (Boston Latin H.S.) I wrote that I wanted to be a sportswriter. But, there were very few sportswriters who looked like me."
Dilday went to Boston University. After college he worked for an electronics company. He started at IBM and stayed about five years. He turned down a transfer to New York and went to work for EG&G/Roxbury.
"I sent resumes to all the electronics companies. I made 100 resumes and I had a few left over. I was interested in television and I sent resumes to all three networks.
"WHDH-TV 5 (CBS) Boston called." That was in 1969 (that station lost its license because of media concentration and was defunct. The WHDH call letters came back recently, replacing WNEV-TV, also CBS.)
Dilday went from WHDH to WLTB in Jackson, Miss.
"We (my wife and I) were proper Bostonians. I hadn't been further South than (Washington) D.C., and my wife, Tarrytown, N.Y."
Dilday said that to sum up the culture shock they felt in Mississippi.
He left WLTB in 1974 for WJTV, also in Jackson, Miss.
When interviewed in 1991, he was corporate vice president of the *News Press and Gazette* and managed six TV stations.
How Dilday remembered the NABJ founding meeting?:
"The driving force was Paul Brock. It was thoroughly his idea of getting people to talk about it. He never let us get too far from it.
"Paul was a real pusher. He kept us in focus.
"We met early in the day and again that evening. It seems like a thousand years ago. I had been at WLTB-TV

(NBC) since 1972 as a general manager.

"I technically wasn't a journalist. My job was in management. But the TV station itself was a news operation.

"At the meeting people were defining narrow guidelines (for eligibility.) We talked of black-owned media vs. major media and print vs. broadcast.

"I was writing and doing TV editorials. I doubt I would have qualified (for membership) had I not been."

Sandra Dillard (Rosen)   Interviewed Feb. 25, 1991.

"I chose to be a journalist.

"I made the transition from a third-generation schoolteacher to a first-generation journalist.

"I had sort of given up on journalism but journalism found me. I realized how much I enjoyed it when I was following Shirley Chisholm around.

"I wrote my first newspaper article when I was 9 years old. It was a story about my campfire group and I wrote the article for a black newspaper. I was living in Sacramento." Sandra Dillard moved to Denver.

"When I was 12, I represented Colorado and Wyoming in the National Spelling Bee. A young reporter from *The Rocky Mountain News* (Denver) was my chaperone and she covered my trip to the national contest in Washington, D.C.

"I had a 'Welcome to Washington, D.C.' badge on.

"The reporter hooked up with a colleague to go to a cocktail party and dropped me and another girl contestant at a movie house. It was OK for the (white) girl to go in, not me. 'We don't let niggers in here,' I was told. The girl decided to stay with me. We had to find our way back to the Willard Hotel ourselves.

"This was the 1950s and Washington was still segregated. I told the reporter: 'You should do a story on this.' She disagreed.

"She preferred to do a story on the number of steps at the Washington Monument.

"That's when I suspected a whole lot of news was being missed.

"In high school I wrote for my high school paper. I was told I couldn't be editor because I was a girl."

Dillard majored in journalism at the University of Denver. When she was a 17-year-old freshman she was a stringer for the *Kansas City Call* . She filed news stories about Colorado.

"I wrote for the college paper. I was the only black. I got no encouragement. I became a teacher, like my mother and my grandmother.

"As a young divorcee, I went to the University of California at Santa Barbara to work on a master's in theater. I got a job at the Center for Black Studies in fall 1970. We started a newspaper in 1971.

"In 1972 I applied to the Summer Program for Minority Journalists at Columbia University.

"I was selected from 500 applicants. Twelve of us were in the class."

Dillard went to the *Denver Post* and has been there since August 1972.

"I've done everything I've wanted to do here. I worked in the Washington bureau, was a fashion writer, got a chance to use my master's degree in theater. I am now the entertainment/theater writer. I cover everything from Omar Sharif to M.C. Hammer."

How Dillard recalled the NABJ founding meeting:

"A lot of us were covering the black political conference.

"After the event, we were told 'If you're interested (in forming a black journalists group), come up to the room.'

"About nine people were in Paul Brock's room. It was very casual. Some of us were sitting on the floor. I remember Brock, Stone, Jarrett, Luix Overbea and another guy from a big Eastern newspaper.

"People were talking about burying egos, about waning interest and why it was not a good idea for one black man to bring his white wife.

"At the Houston conference, about 100 people -- the number 116 sticks in my mind -- attended. One-third of them were students. We tried our best to encourage and welcome them.

"The eligibility debate? You should be making a living

in journalism. I still think the standards are too lax."

Joel Dreyfuss (Interviewed in fall 1990.)
Born in Haiti, Sept. 17, 1945. He grew up in the Caribbean, West Africa, Europe and the United States.
His father published a small English-language newspaper in Haiti.
In the 1960s while a student at City College of New York, Dreyfuss complained to the school sports editor about a story riddled with errors.
'Can you do better?' the editor huffed.
A week later, Dreyfuss got his first byline.
He went to work for *Associated Press, The Washington Post* and the *New York Post* , and he was the first New York bureau chief for USA TODAY.
In the late 1970s to early 1980s Dreyfuss was executive editor of *Black Enterprise* magazine. In the late 1980s he was an associate editor with *Fortune* magazine. He was the magazine's Tokyo bureau chief for two years.
Dreyfuss is an expert on computers and the impact of technology.
He is a man of many interests. He was a past member of the musicians union, Local 802, and a member of the Council on Foreign Relations.

Sam Ford (Interviewed April 25, 1991.)
Ford was born and raised in Independence, Kansas.
"I'm a person with a small-town outlook.
"You're not reaching Black America until people in Independence, Kansas, know what you're up to. (In small towns) you have murder, poverty and people who have dropped out of society.
"I chose (journalism.) Ever since I could remember (age 6) I wanted to be on TV. I wanted somebody looking at me.
"I was always a lover of history. What is it but yesterday's news? My mother told me stories about World War II."
Ford graduated from high school in 1971.
"I went to J-school at Kansas University -- Sam Adams

was one of my professors -- and the University of Minnesota (graduate school of journalism.)" Ford worked two years at WCCO-TV (CBS) Minneapolis. He began there in 1976. He was with CBS News for nine years. When Ford was interviewed in April 1991 he had worked the last four years at WJLA-TV in Washington, D.C.

David Gibson (Interviewed Oct. 3 and Oct. 7, 1991.)
Hometown: Chicago. Born Aug. 1, 1951.
"I kind of wanted to be a disc jockey.
"While I was studying to be a lawyer, I decided that I wanted to be a newscaster.
"At the end of my sophomore year, while I was working packing books at Moody Bible Institute, there was an opening for an announcer at their radio station. They didn't have any black announcers.
"I worked there while finishing school. For a non-profit place, it had some of the best facilities I've seen. They were able to do radio dramas. I learned to edit tape there.
"I was a general announcer. I took a speech course in school and other courses. After a couple of years I decided that I preferred it.
"With time, I gravitated toward news.
"I've worked 15 years at ABC Radio Network, since November 1976. Before that, four to five years at Mutual Black Network and KGFJ (Los Angeles), KYLK (Houston) and WMBI (Chicago), a non-commercial radio station. I started there while majoring in criminal justice at the University of Illinois at Chicago."
How Gibson remembers the NABJ founding meeting?:
"I was a founder? That's very interesting. I was there. I didn't have a lot to do with the formulation. (My NABJ involvement) was essentially at that meeting.
"Being at Mutual Black Network, I'm sure someone told me about the NABJ meeting. It sounded like a good idea. I should have followed up, but I didn't."

Sandra Gilliam-Beale (Interviewed on Oct. 24, 1991.)
Born in Dayton, Ohio, Jan. 26, 1945.

Graduate of Ohio University with a degree in psychology. Gilliam-Beale was a weathercaster and special features reporter for WHIO-TV 7 (CBS) from 1971 to 1976.

"I found out about NABJ by accident. I was in town for a convention (American Women in Broadcasting.)

"I was buttonholed in the lobby about NABJ; I believe the person was Chuck Stone. Chuck and I were at the registration desk."

She was the first NABJ Region 6 director (Midwest) from December 1975 to November 1976.

"I didn't think of my situation as a career, it was a job."

Journalism definitely chose Sandra Gilliam-Beale.

"I had just purchased a new car and I was working as a service representative for Blue Cross and Blue Shield.

"The car broke down. I needed a place to cool off. I went to a nearby office building. To stall, I asked for an employment application.

"When I tried leaving, the receptionist said 'you have to talk to our general manager. I'll get in trouble if an applicant leaves.'

"The general manager, Joseph B. Whelan, told me that they did not have any openings but if they did they would be in touch. I left.

"When I got home, my phone was ringing. It was the general manager. He was offering me a job." Gilliam-Beale was hired as a receptionist. The job paid twice what she was making at Blue Cross-Blue Shield.

"When Taffy Douglas (the first black newscaster at the station) left, she strongly recommended me for her job." Gilliam Beale got it.

"It was a convenient time to be black and speak 'white' English. Whelan once said, 'our listeners don't know you're black.'

"Some people thought that was a compliment. I didn't. I decided to make a lot of personal appearances (so people clearly knew that I am black.)

"It started out as a new experience, a honeymoon experience. It was made in heaven. Then there was a big management change by the principals in Atlanta. A very bigoted,

racist man came in. He was responsible for my leaving.
"When I left, Ohio Bell offered a job paying two times
what I was making. I turned down (TV news) offers from
CBS in Chicago and Metromedia (which later became
FOX.)"

Gilliam-Beale has been a customer service representative
since 1976.

"I'm really part of another world."

She lives in Trotwood, Ohio, a Dayton suburb, and cares
for her invalid mother and three grandchildren of a crack-
addicted daughter-in-law.

View of NABJ: "I really thought it had great possibili-
ties, the tip of an iceberg waiting to be recognized.

"Chuck (Stone) was very knowledgeable and eager to
share his knowledge. I knew in his heart he was no loser."

She follows NABJ in news accounts and what people tell
her. "NABJ has not matured as rapidly as I had hoped. It
needs more press.

"A lot of people (still) know nothing about the organization."

Bob Greenlee Interviewed July 8, 1991.
Born Sept. 12, 1940 in Washington, D.C. He was raised
in New Haven, Conn.

"I chose journalism. I wanted to be a writer (author/
playwright.) I was told that one of the quickest ways to
reach my goal was to get a job on a weekly or daily newspaper. I served in the U.S. Air Force in Germany (1961). I
had plenty of time to write. When I came home I went to
work and to night school.

"A black coalition of 54 organizations in greater New
Haven got together and started a newsletter, *The Crow.*

"I submitted a couple of articles. After a year it evolved
into a tabloid. The executive director hired me as an administrative assistant.

"Barbara Winters and I approached the director about
buying it. The organization said OK. We had to get loans to
open an office."

The paper published from 1967 to December 1970.

"The real irony was that *The Crow* was widely read in the black community, but read much more widely in the larger (white) community (based on surveys and where subscriptions were coming from.)

"I wasn't sure if it meant not enough blacks read or that whites were interested in knowing what was going on.

"After the paper folded I worked in a factory and went to college. In 1971 I took a press release from the college to *The New Haven Register.* I had a chance to meet with an editor who knew me.

"He asked me if I wanted to work for them. He first offered after *The Crow* folded but I strung him along.

"I met the city editor and the editor. He hired me in January 1971.

"I took two positions (stands): I wasn't going to chase ambulances or do crime stories. There was more to do in the black community than that."

Greenlee said he took that stand because "I couldn't control what happened after I wrote the story (for example, editing, headlines, placement).

"I never had any trouble. I came at a time when everyone needed 'one' on their staff.

"I was older (mature, age 31). At first I covered the black community and later became an education reporter, then covered zoning and planning, environment and municipal politics. I created an urban affairs beat."

Greenlee stayed with *The New Haven Register* 10 1/2 years until May 1982.

Martha Griffin (Interviewed June 9, 1991.)
Griffin grew up in Gloucester County, Va.
She chose journalism.

"I was interested in writing. I studied journalism at Ohio University. I had a job at *The Sun* (Baltimore Morning) for a few months.

"I went to WHUR-FM News. I worked at National Public Radio from early 1974 to 1976."

How Griffin remembered NABJ's founding: "At the founding meeting, I had just turned 26. I had been in Washington, D.C. nearly three years.

"I had the desire to know and talk with other black people who were covering news. I felt it was important to belong to that community, know what problems they had, expectations, and measure myself against them."

After NPR, Griffin did some free-lance writing for magazines. She went back to Howard University in 1978, then to graduate school. Later years she worked in public relations. Since 1989, Griffin has been doing public relations and corporate communications for Prodigy Service, a partnership of IBM and Sears that markets on-line computer services.

Bob Hayes (Interviewed Aug. 28 and Sept. 5, 1991.)

Robert L. Hayes was born Oct. 24, 1933 in St. Louis. He grew up in Seattle. He is a graduate of the University of Washington (B.S. in Political Science, 1960.)

"How I became a journalist? I had gotten involved in political things.

"I was president of the San Francisco NAACP chapter, headed up a Ford Foundation pilot project in education and I wrote a black travel book.

"During that time I got involved with Randolph Hearst, a benefactor of mine (he was chairman of the board of the Hearst Foundation.) He was an investor in my business: The Black American Travel Association.

"In the process of socializing, we'd talk about political things. Our views were polarized. Hearst's views were very conservative.

"When I'd give my opinion he'd say 'I don't see that in my newspaper!'

"I'd say, 'well you're staffed by people who don't have access or sensitivity to Third World views.'

"Hearst said: 'Would you like to write for us? When do you want to start?'"

Six months went by. Hayes did not want to be a reporter chasing fire engines. Hayes began in October 1971 (around his 38th birthday.)

"Not the usual way of getting into the newspaper business. I came on as a columnist. I did three political columns a week and features.

"I traveled a lot in the U.S., Africa and the Far East."

Hayes was with *The San Francisco Examiner* from late 1971 to 1977.

"The experience was frustrating in a sense. I came at a time when a lot of sensitivities were questioned.

"The media became highly sensitive to the fact that it was not hiring and promoting blacks in the same way that it castigated others (institutions.)

"At that time Patty Hearst, the publisher's daughter, was kidnapped. The family was going through their own soul searching.

"Willie Hearst the reporter prodded Randy (Hearst) to hire more minorities. There was a recommendation that there be a moratorium until enough minority journalists were hired to meet parity in the newsroom.

"The paper would only hire experienced black journalists (five years' experience or more). This was threatening to many whites who worried about losing seniority.

"White journalists contacted (Randy) Hearst and said Willie and me were trying to turn the *Examiner* into a minority tabloid.

"Also, Randy was reacting to the Symbionese Liberation Army (Patty Hearst's kidnappers), who called him a 'pig.' Hearst put things on hold. I made plans to move on in a couple of years."

How Hayes remembered the NABJ founding: "I was very impressed with the people I came in contact with.

"All of them were basically reporters, not in decision-making positions. they talked about getting blacks into the business.

"They seemed to be so concerned, terribly concerned, about paving the way for the younger generation. I felt like for the first time since joining the *Examiner* that I met some real reporters."

When Hayes was interviewed, he was director of public information for the Los Angeles Board of Public Works. He had been there since 1987. Before that he was public information officer for the Los Angeles County Bar Association. From 1977 to 1981, Hayes was owner of Lockeroom Enterprises, a sporting goods business. He had stores in San Francisco, San Diego, Berkeley and Sacramento.

Derwood Hall   (Interviewed Nov. 14, 1991.)

Derwood Franklin Hall was born Dec. 26, 1949 in Providence, R.I. He grew up in New Rochelle, N.Y. Richard Roundtree ("Shaft") was a childhood friend.

Hall attended Johnson C. Smith University in Charlotte, N.C. He was an offensive tackle on the football team (Hall said he is 5-feet 10-inches tall and weighs about 300 pounds.)

Hall and some colleagues put college radio station WJCS on the air. In 1971 he became assistant director of public affairs for WSOC-TV, Charlotte, N.C. Hall was host of "Quest," a public affairs program.

"I guess journalism chose me. I came from a progressive family. I was active on campus and I was outspoken about drugs (Hall said his father was a heroin addict.) WJCS was a springboard kind of thing."

At the NABJ founding meeting, Hall was in Washington, D.C. to conduct interviews at the black political conference. Hall completed studies for his degree while at WSOC-TV. He stayed at the station until 1979.

Hall became a minister, an ordained Presbyterian and Baptist. He studied at Morehouse Divinity School. Hall has been a minister for 19 years.

He said it happened after he interviewed the late Martin Luther "Daddy" King Sr. on his TV show. "Hall," King told him, "I think you're going to preach." When Derwood Franklin Hall was interviewed, he was pastor of Seven Star Missionary Baptist Church in Los Angeles.

Hall is also a deputy probation officer. He is involved with a Regimented Inmate Diversion (RID) program in the San Fernando Valley area.

Vernon Jarrett   (Interviewed in spring 1991.)

Of approximately 100 people who were at NABJ's founding meeting there were 43 confirmed members. Forty two of them signed the membership list that the 43rd member, Mal Johnson, was custodian of.

Nevertheless, Vernon Jarrett is undoubtedly an NABJ founder.

He was on a 16-member interim committee that set up the Dec. 12 Washington meeting.

Jarrett was born June 19, 1921 in Saulsbury, Tenn. His remarkable childhood in a small Southern town is featured in *The American Dream -- Lost and Found* by Studs Terkel. The narrative was dramatized in a play based on selected chapters from the book.

Jarrett earned his B.A. degree at Knoxville College. He did post-degree work at Northwestern in journalism and at the University of Kansas City, where he studied TV writing and producing and the University of Chicago, where he studied urban sociology.

Jarrett's journalism career began in the black press in 1946 as a reporter for the *Associated Negro Press* and later the *Chicago Globe* and the *Chicago Defender.*

In 1968 Jarrett became a commentator on WLS-TV (ABC) in Chicago.

In 1970 he went to *The Chicago Tribune* as a columnist and worked there until 1983.

Since 1983, Jarrett has been a columnist at the Chicago *Sun-Times.* In addition to newspapers and television, Jarrett was one of six owners of WVON-AM, a black-owned talk radio station.

Mal Johnson   (Interviewed Jan. 31, 1991.)

She was born July 4, 1934 in Philadelphia. Mal Johnson's maiden name is Hooser.

"Journalism chose me. I wanted to be an artist, but my mother told me I wouldn't make any money at it. Black mothers then made up your mind for you. I was told I could become a nurse, teacher or undertaker. I chose teaching."

She studied at Temple University and earned a B.A. in Education and a Masters in Community Dynamics and Intergroup Relations.

Mal Hooser married Frank B. Johnson, a native Philadel-phian and career Air Force officer. They lived overseas. She taught school in the South Pacific (Guam and Mariana Islands) and four years before that in Europe.

Mal Johnson returned to the United States when her husband died, about five years after they married.

"I was running the civil rights movement for the North City Congress (Broad Street and Columbia Avenue in North Philadelphia), an umbrella organization for 450 non-profit organizations.

"In 1965 I got a call from Channel 48 (WKVS-TV, Kaiser Broadcasting.)

"I didn't know the station. They wanted someone to run the public/community affairs department.

"The person who interviewed me (John Gilmore) didn't realize I was a black person until I got there. You could see he was startled. But I wasn't going to let him off the hook. The person who called me was his boss.

"After about an hour he said he'd get back to me. I wasn't home 30 minutes before my phone was ringing and Gilmore was begging me to take the job. He said *his* job was at stake. We later became friends.

"Though I am a product of the civil rights movement, I don't have as much animosity for all whites as others do. I know some are good and others are not. I refuse to have my life narrowed by hating all whites."

Johnson worked at WKVS-TV until March 1969.

"At that time I was giving a speech to women broadcasters in Houston. I was giving them a hard time because they turned down a $150,000 grant from HEW (U.S. Department of Health, Education and Welfare) to train minority women for broadcasting jobs.

"Their reason was, if we train them, they'll take our jobs.

"The president and CEO of Cox Broadcasting, J. Leonard Reinsch, was the next speaker. I didn't know.

"In order to shut me up, the group named me to the board of American Women in Television and Broadcasting.

"At the next meeting, Reinsch was the only male there. He hired me.

"He became my guiding mentor. I went to Cox as a Capitol Hill correspondent.

A few months later, I became White House correspondent. I worked for 21 years (1969-90) in radio and television, broadcasting to 22 stations.

"Reinsch was the man who brought us the (FDR) fireside chats. He taught Eleanor Roosevelt how to speak (on the air) and taught Truman to speak." Reinsch died in 1991.

Toni Jones (Interviewed June 4, 1991.)

She is a native of Detroit. Jones was interviewed shortly before her 44th birthday.

She grew up on Edison Street on the West Side. "A pleasant place when I was growing up," she said.

"I chose it (journalism.) It was something I happened to do easily. My parents were very encouraging."

She went to Wayne State University. After graduation Jones went to New York City. She worked for a year at *Time-Life Books* as an assistant.

She applied to *The Detroit Free Press*. She was hired in 1973 and stayed until 1979.

In between, Jones worked a couple of years as a writer for "The Elgin Baylor Show," sponsored by Chrysler, based in Detroit and broadcast nationally.

She moved to New York in 1979. Jones was a newswriter for WABC-TV, and later became a public relations specialist. Since 1987 she has been a p.r. specialist for the Newark, N.J. Museum.

How Jones remembered the NABJ founding:

"I went to Washington for that meeting, not to cover an assignment. I thought it would be worthwhile or I wouldn't have been involved.

"It was time to have an organization at that time."

Howard Chuku Lee (Interviewed Nov. 18, 1992.)

"I scarcely remember the organization," he said when he was reached in Brooklyn, N.Y. by telephone.

Lee described himself as "office manager, national distributor, public relations man, strategist and chief flunky" for London-based *Africa* magazine. Lee appeared in the staff box as a correspondent in September 1974. For most of his time with *Africa,* he was listed as an assistant editor. Lee was with the magazine 9 1/2 years, until January 1984.

Lee currently had a Brooklyn-based trading company, Trade Resources International, that does business with a number of African countries.

He is also a real estate appraiser. He is married to Pat Cummings, an illustrator and publisher of children's books.

Howard Lee was born Feb. 14, 1948 in Denver. The family moved to Los Angeles, the city where Lee grew up.

He majored in Political Science at the University of Redlands. He did graduate work at George Washington University in Washington, D.C. It was under a Ford Foundation program that helped recruit and train minorities for the foreign service. The U.S. Information Agency provided part-time work.

Lee's master's degree was in international communications. His master's thesis was called "Use of Satellite TV as an Instrument of Presidential Foreign Policy."

Lee entered the foreign service. "I wrote press releases for the ambassador. I was doing journalistic-type things"

Lee said he traveled to 40 countries. He was based in Paris. "In Paris, I really became interested in Africa." That was 1972-74.

Lee saw a lot of Africans who wanted visas to go to the United States. He did not have authority to grant them, but Africans would knock on his door and approach him since he was a black face in a sea of white ones.

"I noticed the treatment of Africans was different.

"They had to have all kinds of letters and bank accounts. Someone else could walk right on the plane.

"After a while, American brothers would come through. Some of them demanded things, others asked. I got more and more interested in the African beat. There were so many Africans in France. Francophone Africans ignored you. Anglophone Africans greeted you and (black) Americans would nod (in acknowledgement.)

"I had leave time. I was surrounded by whites. Why not go home?"

A friend from Ghana arranged a meeting with Raph

Uwechue, a former Nigerian ambassador. Uwechue had just acquired a magazine.

"Raph was recruiting. We believed a lot of the same things.

"Based on that common ground," a relationship began. Uwechue asked Lee to run *Africa* magazine's U.S. office in New York. It was a spacious apartment on West 82nd Street, across from Central Park. Lee had one of the two bedrooms converted into an office and hired a secretary. He got writers like John Henrik Clarke to write for *Africa*.

Lee conducted numerous Q&A interviews around the country with leading African-Americans in politics and business. They included Charles Rangle, PANAF co-founders Darwin Bolden and Emiko Amoye, Maynard Jackson, Andrew Young, Jesse Jackson and Abdul Haleem (Louis) Farrahkan.

The other part of Lee's job was getting *Africa* to U.S. readers. "I had wholesalers in 43 cities," he said.

"Ten to 20,000 copies would come (monthly.) I'd clear them through customs and break it down (into bundles for distribution)."

Lee said he got the magazine on 450 newsstands and into bookstores in Tri-state New York. "We'd carry it on our backs (to the local outlets) and ship to 43 cities.

"*Africa* was a Pan African entity. We went about collecting news from an Afrocentric point of view. We did not talk anybody down. We were getting advertising support from multinationals."

Indeed, copies of *Africa* averaged about 100 pages of monthly editorial and advertising copy.

Editor-in-chief Uwechue said that at its peak *Africa* magazine circulation was 160,000 and 86 percent of the sales were to African countries.

Lee changed his given name on his 29th birthday to Chukwuemeka. It is Ibo for "God has dealt kindly with us." Lee shortened his name to Chuku (he notes that Chuku is acceptable in the United States but in Nigeria, Nigerians would not use the shortened version because it would be translated as "god." Lee would be addressed as "Emeka.")

On NABJ: "I remember it vaguely. We tried to do the right thing and define ourselves as black journalists.

"At the founding there was a real need to communicate between ourselves and amongst ourselves about what was happening in our writing and our work.

"We put an emphasis on positive reinforcement of who and what we were. For example not saying 'non-white' but 'black' or 'African-American.'

"Some brothers (journalists) had been through fire; others were timid. I was cynical and suspicious. I was looking for the handkerchief heads. I didn't notice any."

Lee drifted away from NABJ after about two years.

"I was never a journalist-journalist," he said. I was doing publishing."

Claude Lewis (Interviewed Feb. 13, 1991.)

"I was born in the Bronx and I grew up in Harlem.

"Langston Hughes came to my school and invited us -- eight to nine students -- to write poetry.

"We mailed it to him.

"Hughes' responses came by mail. He said mine was bad.

"I sent a second poem. He said it was worse. 'One thing I like about you,' Hughes told me, 'you're persistent and you could be a newspaperman.' I later became friends with Langston Hughes and James Baldwin.

"I chose to be a journalist. I worked for *Newsweek* from 1954 to 1964. I began as an editorial assistant, then became a researcher, then writer / reporter covering national affairs, science, sports and religion."

Lewis went to the New York *Herald-Tribune* in 1965. He was one of the writers of the "New York City in Crisis," series that appeared nearly every day for eight months at the beginning of the John Lindsay years.

From 1966 to 1969, Lewis worked for NBC News in Philadelphia. NBC lost a suit to Westinghouse and was faced with moving to Cleveland.

"I didn't want to go to Cleveland, so I stayed three years. KYW (Westinghouse Broadcasting) came in (replacing NBC as owners)."

Lewis went to *The Philadelphia Evening Bulletin* as associate editor. He became the first black columnist at *The Bulletin* (1969.)

"Stokely (Carmichael), Huey (Newton) and H. Rap Brown demanded to speak to black journalists. They said that was the only way they would be treated objectively. They helped create the need for black journalists.

"Martin Luther King was in the news, Vernon Jordan was complaining.

"They (daily newspaper editors) created instant journalists. When I was a city hall reporter for *The Bulletin* I remember Marian Perry walked into the room with a mike in her hand and asked: 'How do you create news?'

"She worked in the administrative office of her television station. She didn't succeed. She was treated unfairly.

"At the Lincoln University Conference (1970), many black men (journalists) showed up with white women.

"Francis Ward's wife (Val) asked: "Who's this white woman in the back?

"'That's my wife,' answered William Hilliard of the *Oregonian* (Portland).

"'She's going to have to leave. This is a conference for black people.'

"That just about destroyed the conference. People had to defend who they slept with. Some cried."

Race and stereotypes made people hypersensitive. Lewis gave this example: "I remember carrying two watermelons. Earl Caldwell refused to get on the elevator with me. But he ate the watermelon upstairs in his room."

Claude Lewis worked at *The Philadephia Bulletin* until the paper folded in January 1982. That year he became founding editor of *The National Leader,* a black-owned weekly published in Philadelphia.

The Leader folded in 1984. Lewis joined *The PhiladelphiaInquirer* as an editorial writer and columnist.

Pluria Marshall (Interviewed Aug. 1, 1991.)
Born in Houston Oct. 19, 1937.
"I took pictures in the military. I was a medic on inde-

pendent duty in Japan from 1956-58.

"If you didn't take advantage of the photo craze in To-kyo, you were crazy.

"When I returned to the United States I found my (photo) work was just as good as the professionals. I continued with photography in the military.

"I got out of the service in February 1960. I worked at the post office and enrolled at Texas Southern (University).

"I became a photojournalist. I worked in the newspaper business 17 years (before NABJ was founded). I did work for black publications in Houston and Washington, D.C.

"I was with the National Black Media Coalition (NBMC) two years prior to NABJ (1973). Jim McCuller of Roches-ter, N.Y. was the organizing chairman."

Marshall replaced him in 1975 and established a national office.

"I found out about the NABJ founding from Max Robin-son, Simeon Booker and some *Jet* people.

"I would not qualify to be a member (of NABJ) today. The eligibility issue did not come up. People were too busy worrying about getting (the organization) formed. People were so glad to see something form.

Marshall said that barring Texas Southern Communica-tions Department Dean Carlton Molette from being a mem-ber in 1976 "was the dumbest thing I ever heard."

"We're (NBMC) more responsible for black broadcast journalists getting jobs than any organization in America. We have the real leaders of the industry at our conferences. They (NABJ) resent the work we do.

"It's a case of egos and ignorance.

"NABJ is appealing to black print members from white newspapers.

"It is an organization of black journalists who work for the white press.

"They've become a contradiction to black folks in the black community. It's a miracle that NABJ's around.

"NABJ's staple should be employment of black journal-ists in all levels of media. I've been on Capitol Hill and at the FCC to testify for nearly 18 years. Ben Hooks (a former FCC commissioner) used to refer to me as the 'ace commissioner.' There may have been one thing that (NABJ) has been included in. They have no presence at the FCC.

"There is a lot about what they do that is very weak. They're walking in place. We (NBMC) should have a strong relationship with NABJ.

"They have a strange notion that they can fight the people they work for. They can get to the moon quicker.

"We (NBMC) sue many of them (media companies). We sued Westinghouse. They do a lot of good things but they had no niggers at their station in Philadelphia. All these companies know: Ain't none of them safe.

"Problem with the organization (NABJ) is there is no leadership. Every administration starts all over. NABJ elects people who know how to write a story or a column or produce the news, but not much else," Marshall says.

Acel Moore (Interviewed April 6, 1991.)
Born Oct. 5, 1940. Journalism chose Acel Moore.

He grew up in South Philadelphia. Moore played musical instruments from age 7. He lived in the same neighborhood with future jazzmen Ted Curson, Jimmy, Percy and Albert Heath and Charles Earland. Moore played in Earland's band and played a recital in the second grade.

Moore was a schoolboy who liked to read, sketch and play music.

He went from high school to the Army. He was stationed in South Carolina, Texas, Seattle and Alaska. He finished in Washington, D.C. There he took some college-level courses.

Planning to go on to college, Moore took a copy boy job at *The Philadelphia Inquirer* in the early 1960s.

His plans changed. He apprenticed for six years and became a reporter.

That was at a time when the apprentice system was ending. Times changed, Moore said, because journalism schools proliferated from 1965 to 1975. In 1967-68, Moore said he was one of three black professionals out of about 350 people in the *Inquirer* newsroom.

Moore became active with Black Communicators (1967-

68), a forerunner of the Association of Black Journalists (ABJ) of Philadelphia.

Acel Moore was president of ABJ in 1977. In 1978 he helped organize the NABJ conference in Chicago.

In 1983 Moore lost a run for president of NABJ.

"I thought I'd make a good president and I would have something to offer. I think I made a contribution.

"Most of the people who supported me were elected to the board. I forwarded the proposal to have an executive director (full-time)."

Luix Overbea (Interviewed March 26, 1991.)

His first name is Latin or Creole for "light."

Overbea was born in 1924, the son of a father and mother from Louisiana and Mississippi. He grew up in Chicago.

"I got into it (journalism) in protest.

"I was attending DuSable High School (1939) and I did not like the way the school newspaper covered us. It should have had more students covered in the paper and be recognized beyond cheerleaders and the football team. My senior year, I decided to join the school paper.

"The first article I wrote was horrible. The teacher told me: 'It does everything a news article is not supposed to do.' But when the paper came out, my piece was ranked third-best. I felt vindicated.

"I went to junior college in Chicago because I didn't have the money for four-year college. I worked on the school paper. I was upset that they did not make me editor.

"I entered the military near the end of World War II. I was a schoolboy soldier with high grades. I was in the Army specialized training program.

"There was a captain who liked me. He knew I wanted to be a journalist. I went to Germany, then to the Philippines. I became a military journalist on Laity Island. On the side, they taught me to be a librarian.

"I went to Northwestern (University) on the G.I. bill. I didn't realize (then) that I was the first black graduate from the news sequence and the second from Medill (the first was Fletcher Martin, a magazine sequence major who went to the *Chicago Sun.*)

"I went to work for *Associated Negro Press* (where he worked alongside Vernon Jarrett.)

"It didn't pay well. I couldn't marry my sweetheart. I went to a black newspaper in Tulsa.

"On July 4, I received a letter from the *Winston-Salem Journal.* The black residents there told the editors that they wanted more than crime news about themselves. There was a Negro news page in the paper that was written by a schoolteacher.

"They (the editors and readers) were looking for a journalist. Northwestern's dean participated in a conference at Wake Forest (University) and he was asked if there were any black Northwestern graduates he could recommend. I was hired in 1956.

"They told me that I was the first black to work in a (daily newspaper) newsroom in the South. I did some of everything. Tom Wicker was the sports editor. He let me write.

"Then I knew I was staying in journalism. The pay was better. I was getting more than I had asked for. (But) I found out that I was the third lowest-paid reporter on the staff. A few women were paid less.

"That was an issue that made me join NABJ. Black journalists might be taking less than what they were worth."

Overbea worked in Winston-Salem from 1956-68.

He moved from editing the Negro news page to covering general news.

He returned to the black press as managing editor of the *St. Louis Sentinel* from 1968-70. Overbea left when they were unable to pay him for a while. To get by he ran up all of his credit cards.

Overbea went to the St. Louis *Globe-Democrat* (1970-71). He was assistant makeup editor.

Overbea is a Christian Scientist. A friend told *The Christian Science Monitor* personnel director that he knew a good journalist.

The director interviewed Overbea in St. Louis.

Overbea said he was commited to the *Globe-Democrat* for a year, but if *The Monitor* was still interested, call him.

The Monitor did. Overbea went to the newspaper near the end of 1971.

When *The Christian Science Monitor* changed its newspaper format, Overbea was among three black journalists who were phased out.

When interviewed he was host of "Inner City Beat" on Monitor TV.

Les Payne (Interviewed in winter 1991 and July 1, 1991.)

Born July 12, 1941 in Tuscaloosa, Ala. Payne learned to read at age 3. At age 12 his family moved to Hartford, Conn. "In Hartford, I grew up with three papers: *The Hartford Courant, Hartford Times* and (national editon of the) *PittsburghCourier* (my stepfather would bring it).

"The only journalist I knew was Bill Matney (the NBC newsman. Payne didn't know then that Matney was African-American because he was so light-complexioned).

"I chose journalism. I wanted to be a writer. I started in the 10th grade. In my junior year of college I was thinking of how I could make my living writing. The University of Connecticut did not have a journalism major. I graduated with an English degree.

"The problems I faced in 1964 were what black journalism aspirants faced: Journalism was never a career accessible to us. I was interested in daily journalism. Once out of college I had no hope of getting a job in Hartford. I delivered *The Courant*. But I didn't apply.

"I went into the Army. *That* was open to us (blacks.)"

Payne trained to be a commissioned officer. He became a military journalist and was on Gen. William Westmoreland's staff in Vietnam.

Bill Nack, described as a "brilliant writer" and "good friend" by Payne, went to *Newsday*. "I never heard of it," said Payne. *"Newsday* was looking for black reporters. Nack recommended me in a classically written three-page letter. "But Bill, I'm going to Columbia (University)," I told him. He told me 'you can come here.

"I flew up, in uniform, and took the test.

"I was offered a job on the spot.

How Payne remembered the NABJ founding meeting: "Chuck (Stone) was the driving force. He was the locus, the generator. Chuck told us: We (journalists) were late. Now is the time to organize. We need a structure, constitution and bylaws.

"I decided to run for president (in 1981) because we needed someone to gain a foothold, who was senior and achieved in the industry.

"Journalists respect that. We needed someone who had respect.

"I was just named national editor in March 1980, and I was a strong national editor, not a figurehead. I directed national and foreign coverage and hired staff.

"I certainly had more than enough to do.

"I tried (unsuccessfully) to get Tom Johnson (*New York Times* newsman) to run. People were walking away from the organization. I ran almost belatedly. I pretty much came to the convention and announced.

"Ben Johnson was running and that would be a disaster. I checked into his background at the Louisville paper. He had the scent of the sharper. I didn't believe he could deliver on all the promises he made.

"When Ben knew I was running he said he'd drop out. It sounded like a deal. I said no, let's give the people a choice.

"I thought the group needed something else. I was outraged by ASNE (American Society of Newspaper Editors) saying they want parity by the year 2000. I blasted them. They can do it in an instant. Blacks should not be taken in by 'on-the-horizon politics.'

"Two, (we needed to) establish relationships with black journalists abroad in the Caribbean and Africa.

"A Third-World extension.

"Louisville was the first election I remember where people began political campaigning. Marilynn Bailey organized people (for Payne's candidacy) in a big way.

"Ben Johnson ran like he was running for mayor of a major city. He reminded me of the slave dressing in the master's clothes when the master was away. I'm from Alabama.

"A lot of imitating was going on. And, Roberts Rules

tended to be immobilizing.

"It was tough juggling demands of my *Newsday* column, being national editor, speaking engagements and family. In 1982 my daughter was 16 and sons were 8 and 10. There was no national office or activist regional directors.

"I had to lend money to some regional directors to assure a quorum.

"Vernon Jarrett told me about Mal Johnson: She's honest, hard-working and can be trusted with the money.

"I knew she was nettlesome. Too often black organizations mess up with the women and the money. I didn't tell people I'd raise $10,000.

"Merv Aubespin was my vice president. I supported Acel Moore (as successor). He (Merv) never forgave me. I felt we still needed some firepower.

"But Acel did not come to talk to the New York delegation and was too cliquish with the Philadelphia group. He huddled too much with them.

"Those early administrations, we look back at the chaos. But we achieved tax status, the Ida B. Wells award, internships and newsletters paid for by other means."

Alex Poinsett (Interviewed in spring 1991.)
Born in Chicago, Jan. 27, 1926.
Poinsett was a World War II Navy veteran.
"I went to the University of Illinois on the G.I. Bill. The aptitude test said I was suited for history, but I had developed a flair for writing in the Navy. I was a sportswriter for *The Exploder* in Hawaii.

"At the University of Illinois, I took every creative writing course available. Then I considered making a living while pursuing the great American novel. I learned a lot about methods but not content. I worked on a master's in philosophy. I got married and forgot about dreams to pursue a doctorate. It came time to get a job and we moved to Chicago.

"I canvassed all the publications. The usual reply: 'You have excellent credentials but we don't have any openings.'

"Walgreens interviewed me on the phone and just about

offered me the job as its house organ editor. 'I was the person for it' -- until I showed up.

"I took a job working in a pig sty factory spraying wooden pig stys for $40 a week. Meanwhile I sent a resume to *Johnson Publishing Co.*

A couple of months went by. No response. The factory was near *Johnson Publishing.* Spontaneously, I decided to go see him. I had my paint-smeared clothes on. I managed to see Mr. (John H.) Johnson.

"I asked him if he read my material. He hadn't. He said I had no experience. I said, 'How do you and these other people expect me to get experience if you don't give me any?'

"I think he was struck by my temerity."

Johnson: 'I have a position in the library (morgue) for a file clerk. If anything opens on the writing staff, we'll try to work you in.'

"I worked there a month. A *Jet* writer was fired for accepting $750 from gospel singer Clara Ward.

"She called Johnson and asked, 'Where's my story? I gave your man the money.' I replaced that writer.

"I stayed seven years at *Jet* (1952-59) then went to *Ebony* (1959-81.) I was assistant editor and later senior staff editor. I went to Grumman in Long Island in 1981.

"After a year and a half, I returned to Chicago."

Claudia Polley   (Interviewed July 16, 1991.)
Born in Indianapolis, circa 1950.
"I chose journalism, sort of.

"I was brought up as a musician. I played violin 16 years -- since age 4 -- and sang." Polley is a mezzo contralto.

"This (voice) is the way my mother and other members of my family speak. It worked on the air."

In 1968 at age 18, Polley was attending Julliard.

"I was being a fairly active and serious concert singer. I went looking for a part-time job. I applied to all three (broadcast) networks.

"At ABC, the interviewer said he never heard of Julliard.

"Julliard is across the street. I walked out.

"CBS didn't have openings. NBC hired me as a news

assistant on the early morning shift at WNBC. I figured it would be something different, something exciting.

"The world was our oyster in 1968. We could do no wrong, example, the Black Power movement, Vietnam.

"I stayed at NBC until graduation in 1971.

"I became politicized too much by New York City friends who were involved in the anti-war and Black Power movements. '(Why not) just go and be a diva?' I said no.

"I was living in a house with people in the McGovern campaign. I joined the senior staff.

"I was one of the three Texas coordinators with Bill Clinton (now President Clinton) and Taylor Branch (a Georgia native who wrote the Pulitzer Prize-winning *Parting the Waters,* the epic on the Civil Rights movement).

"It was a chance to learn about the South. I lived in Texas three months. I returned to New York City before the 1972 election.

"A friend in Indianapolis (Frank Lloyd) bought WTLC-FM. I became a morning drive anchor in 1973. It won a lot of black music awards.

"I stayed a year then went to NBN (National Black Network). I was their first woman anchor/reporter. I found it stifling. I went to Mobile, Ala. to work as press secretary for Jay Cooper, mayor of Pritchard, and head of the Southern Conference of Black Mayors. I stayed four to five months. It was very different. I didn't feel as comfortable as I should have.

"I took another offer: A two-hour talk show on WNTS in Indiana. All news, talk and sports. It was September 1974. David Letterman was at this station.

"I stayed six months. I went to News and Information Service (NIS). NBC called and I accepted. I was at NBC one and a half years (circa March 1975 to July 1976). I went from radio to TV and TV sports."

Polley said she was comfortable reporting sports because she was familiar with it. Her grandmother handled business affairs for the varsity teams at Oscar Robertson's high school in Indianapolis.

And when Claudia Polley was age 4, she was the team mascot.

How Polley remembered the NABJ founding: "There were a lot of us from different places. What was going to work for everybody?

"Nineteen seventy five was not the most united of times. Nixon was just forced out of the White House. In the political world, everybody was staking turf.

"We wanted to maintain our integrity in what was a black journalist. There were not that many p.r. people, but, should they be included?

"There were a lot of points of friction but we worked through it.

"The room felt hot. It was close and very emotional. We were happy about what we were doing but we wanted to make it better. I remember Max Robinson being very vocal and a tempering influence.

"I was elected treasurer. It took us (NABJ members) a while to figure out what we were going to do. I resigned and moved to France in July 1976.

"Some Julliard friends were doing work on the Bicentennial and asked me to come sing for three months (classical music and background on disco tracks).

"I was working at NBC as an independent contractor. NBC was not ready to offer me a contract. I stayed (in France) four years until 1980."

When Polley was interviewed, she was working at National Public Radio as a weekend news anchor and reporter. She's been there since July 1989.

Richard Rambeau (Interviewed May 11, 1991.)

Native of Detroit. Date of birth circa 1938.

"My mother was involved in community service. I went to Catholic schools. I told my mother that my innate calling was to be an advocate.

"I didn't like bullies. I didn't mind throwing my body at one; intellectually too.

"I worked at the North End Family Center. It had a Black Panther breakfast program. The Republic of New Africa met upstairs.

"We were very politicized. My brother David was already involved in broadcasting. I came into the radio group. "What attracted me to journalism? The power. This was a way to pry people loose from positions. I pulled a person out of Marion (prison). You could use that information to benefit your people. It wasn't about being a wannabe with a credit card, BMW or a contract for life, it was taking something back to the community. I got involved with Project BAIT (Black Awareness in Television). It was radio and TV programming for, by and about black people."

How Rambeau remembered the NABJ meeting: "We (some of us) were concerned that no one from *Muhammad Speaks* was present. People were primarily colored representation of the white media. We argued about that then.

"I didn't feel that those who worked for the majority media could really reflect what was going on in the black community because they were paid by the majority.

"Pluria (Marshall) and I were into license challenges. If it wasn't about that, it wasn't black.

"Oldtimers said we shouldn't be that shrill. But we were.

"Project BAIT got bogged down in license challenges for six years. We lost broadcast time at the public TV station. We regained it elsewhere.

"I became disillusioned and walked away about 10 years ago. We didn't get meaningful support from the community, (even though) we walked many people through interviews." Rambeau called them "mashed potato" interviews. "What am I doing now? Nothing. Absolutely nothing."

Willie C. (Curtis) Riddle (Interviewed Feb. 1, 1991.)
Born circa 1950. He grew up in East St. Louis, Ill.
"I chose journalism. I enjoyed writing and reading short stories. I was an English Literature major at Southern Illinois University.

"I chose journalism as a minor in 1968 when things were happening, example, campus demonstration. I wrote for the campus daily newspaper. I became editor by my senior year. I stumbled into it, but I chose.

"While in college, I was a part-time reporter at the East St. Louis *Metro East Journal* (now defunct, one of six papers owned by Lindsey Schaud). I wrote for the *East St. Louis Monitor* (black-owned) too.

"I had three or four job offers in March 1972. I went to *TheCourier-Journal* in Louisville, Ky. right out of school.

"There were no black reporters on staff. Merv Aubespin was in the art department (Aubespin went to the Columbia journalism program that summer.)

"In 1974, I covered the National Black Political Assembly in Cincinnati. I met Ellis Cose and Reginald Stuart. That was the first hint that there were efforts to organize.

"I went from *The Courier Journal* to *The Baltimore Sun.* I was counties editor."

Riddle became an editor at USA TODAY, then he became a publisher in Gannett, first at the *Journal-Courier* in Lafayette, Ind. and later the Lansing (Mich.) *State Journal.*

Charlotte Robinson (Roy) Interviewed May 30, 1991.

Born in Institute, W. Va., circa 1947. Her father taught economics at West Virginia State College (a predominately black institution then, integrated now).

"When I was nine I decided I wanted to be a famous playwright. My father was in the diplomatic corps. We were living in the Philippines.

"My aunt sold a story I wrote to a children's magazine. I was paid for it and I bought a bicycle. A light went off in my head -- I can make money from this."

Charlotte Robinson lived in Rangoon, Burma; Manila; Ankara, Turkey. She went to high school (boarding school) in Leysin, Switzerland. When she returned to the United States, she went to Fisk University.

"I realized I was black." She said that self-mockingly.

Living overseas, said Robinson "gives you a perspective on affairs of this country. You can see the forest and the trees. Being a writer I wanted to share that perspective.

"You learn tolerance. An important trait (is) for newspeople to be fair.

"I got married at age 19 and transferred to the University of Delaware. I worked at the Wilmington *Morning News* on weekends while in school, and continued full-time after

graduation." Her husband then was working for DuPont.
"I was the first and only 'Negro' at the Wilmington paper.
"The first thing they sent me to was a black power con-
ference in Newark (Del.) I was the mole."
Robinson was a reporter for nine years. She went from
Wilmington, Del. to the Madison, Wis. *Capitol Times,*
then, three years at *The Detroit Free Press.*

How Robinson remembered the NABJ founding: *The
FreePress* sent us to write about the political convention. It
was an exciting period for black journalists. It felt like the
first time that there was enough of us in the black media
and the general market media.

"There was debate that those in the black media . . . (she
pauses to measure her words) that the (new) group should
be very, very exclusive.

"Boy, that was a heated topic.

"And, should we allow, shudder, p.r. people.

"Another group said: If we don't have them, we won't
have enough.

"Back then, I felt the more the merrier. I listened very
carefully to the arguments. I nominated Chuck Stone (for
president). It was interesting. Forty to sixty people were in
the room. Vernon Jarrett led the discussion. Chuck was sitting next to me. We were in the first row.

"There was a call for nominations. I nominated Chuck.
And that was it.

"Many of us didn't realize what an important group we
were creating."

Robinson stayed active with NABJ for nearly two years
and left because she entered public relations in 1976.

When Charlotte Robinson was interviewed she was vice
president of development for Moore Little Inc., an Atlanta-
based advertising and public relations firm.

Max Robinson (deceased)

Born May 1, 1939 in Virginia. His journalism career
spanned nearly 25 years. Robinson gained attention during
a 10-year stint as a reporter and anchorman at WTOP-TV
(CBS, and now known as WUSA-TV) in Washington, D.C.

At least a dozen NABJ founders vividly remember Robinson being a passionate advocate for establishing the organization. Did Robinson want to be NABJ's first president? The same dozen or so founders are split on that question. About half say he tried to drum up support behind the scenes. Others insist that he wanted to be a catalyst but was not interested in the office.

In 1978 he made history -- as the first African-American network anchor -- when he joined Peter Jennings and the late Frank Reynolds as a co-anchor on ABC "World News Tonight."

Robinson left ABC in 1983 after criticizing network newscasts as racist. He moved to Chicago in 1984 and became an anchor at WMAQ-TV. Again his tenure was marked by controversy. In 1988 he accused co-workers of attempting to sabotage his work.

At the start of Robinson's TV news career, a Virginia TV station would not allow him to show his face. Instead, a "news" sign appeared on the screen and only Robinson's voice was heard. He demanded to be seen as other anchors were. When Robinson protested, he was fired.

Robinson waged an almost daily battle to ensure that African-Americans were covered fairly.

He spoke his mind and paid a heavy price.

Robinson died Dec. 20, 1988 in Washington, D.C. from complications related to AIDS. He was 49.

Vince Sanders   (Interviewed in February 1991.)

Born in Orlando, Fla. He lived in Chicago from 1953 to 1973.

"Journalism chose me. I pursued an acting career and ended up in radio as a general practitioner. One of my mentors said I didn't have the personality for that music stuff. Why not get into news?

"I worked for NBC Radio in Chicago from 1970-73. I came to New York in 1973 to start National Black Network. It began with 35 affiliates and peaked at 175. There are currently 150 affiliates.

"Paul Brock invited me to the founding meeting. Even

though Paul was not a working journalist, he was at the forefront of organizing. Maybe that was to his advantage. A lot of people were uncomfortable with that.

"Paul was a sweetheart of a guy who does things without preparation and hopes it works out."

Sanders recalled the first fund-raising banquet shortly after NABJ was founded. Brock asked him for money to pay the bills. Sanders helped him.

"I had some anxious moments (at that founding meeting). I was a supervising journalist. I could not join in on some of the complaints people had because I was in sympathy with news directors and editors.

"The new organization was more geared to cub and beginning reporters. I was in a different mode.

"The Houston conference (1n 1976) was very unfortunate. It wasn't easy. There was a lot of infighting. I remained aloof."

When the interview was conducted Sanders was with WWRL-Radio in New York City.

Chuck Stone   (Interviewed November 1990 and June 17, 1991.)

Chuck Stone was born in 1924 in a segregated hospital in St. Louis. He grew up in Hartford, Conn. Stone went to Wesleyan University. He was the only black person in his class. Stone was the commencement speaker. His address was on America's broken promises to blacks.

In World War II, Stone was an Army Air Corps navigator. He was a CARE worker in India and the Gaza strip.

"Journalism chose me. It was fortuitous circumstances. Like the Broadway play 'A Funny Thing Happened to Me on the Way to the Forum,' a funny thing happened to me on the way to the train station in 1958.

"I had returned from India and Egypt, where I was working for CARE and was in New York getting ready to work for the Foreign Policy Association as an associate director. I was living with my sister.

"I was taking our mother to the train station on 125th Street and we ran into this old friend of mine, Al Duckett. This was very fortuitous. We stopped and talked. He had

been the editor of the *Hartford Chronicle* (the black newspaper in Stone's hometown).

"He asked me what was I going to do. I told him I was
going to work for the Foreign Policy Association. He said
'don't go work for those white people. Come work for me.'
He was editor of the *New York Age* at the time.

"I said 'I can't write.' He said 'yes you can. I used to read
your letters to the editor to *The Hartford Courant* and *Hartford Times*. You're a terrific writer. I can train you to be a
reporter. Come work for me and I'll let you cover Adam
Clayton Powell exclusively.' He knew I liked politics. I
said, "Let me think about it."

"My mother was horrified. She didn't want me to work
for a black, or segregated, newspaper.

"She always wanted us to be mainstream.

"Second, she didn't have high regard for journalists.

"So, when we got to the train station she said, 'Promise
me you won't do that.' I said 'I promise.'

"Then, I went back and got hired. That was August 1958.

"By October, I was writing a column. In February, Duckett resigned after a dispute with the publisher. The publisher jumped me over nine people and made me the editor.

"It was very fast, too fast.

"I didn't stay a reporter long enough to get the training
and discipline to be a good reporter. That is not a good career path."

Stone became editor of other black-owned newspapers,
The *Afro-American* in Washington, D.C. and *The Chicago
Defender*. At *The Defender*, Stone was fired for "author-
izing stories that made Mayor (Richard) Daley look bad."

He was press secretary for New York Congressman
Adam Clayton Powell Jr. Stone was author of several
books, including *Black Political Power in America* and
King Strut, a novel based on Powell's career.

When Stone was elected the first president of NABJ, he
was a columnist with the *Philadelphia Daily News*.

In July 1991 Stone left the *Philadelphia Daily News* to
become a distinguished professor of journalism at the University of North Carolina.

Jeannye Thornton　(Interviewed Nov. 30, 1990.)

She grew up in Chicago. "In high school a teacher thought I was a talented writer. (Thornton was editor of the school yearbook.)

"I wanted to be a doctor. My parents and grandparents were all professionals. I never knew a black journalist and nobody pushed that idea. The teacher says, 'Oh no, that's what you should be.' I thought she was trying to keep me down (the teacher was white).

"I was a pre-med student at Ohio State University.

"Journalism found me. I took a job at *The Chicago Tribune* (1970) as I was biding time to go to medical school.

"I stayed at *The Tribune*.

"A terrible problem in the late '60s and early '70s was justifying to other blacks why we were at white news organizations. It was a cross black journalists had to bear. Black newspapers were losing circulation. Black organizations wanted you to do their p.r."

In 1974, Thornton went to *U.S. News & World Report*.

She was the first black woman journalist hired by the magazine. She's been there ever since. Thornton is an associate editor. Thornton once received a marriage proposal from a letter writer when she appeared on the editor's page in 1975 for a story she reported on the anniversary of the *Brown vs. Board of Education* case.

Thornton was the first secretary of NABJ.

Norma Wade　(Interviewed April 23, 1991.)

Born May 15, 1944. "Journalism chose me in the fourth grade. I knew whatever I did it would have to do with writing or reading. A librarian? I never wavered.

"I grew up in Dallas. I was a sheltered little Texas female, very bookish, sheltered and unworldly. I traveled in my mind through books. I had strict parents. My father had two years of college. He was a postman. He was well thought of in the community. My mother was barely out of high school but she had mother-wit. She was a homemaker and hairdresser.

"I always excelled in English and Fine Arts. I was editor

of the school paper. It only produced one issue.

"I went to the University of Texas. I graduated with LBJ's daughter, Lynda Byrd, in 1966. LBJ was commencement speaker.

"I was in that first group that integrated. Campus housing was still segregated. Blacks stayed in the co-op houses, Colonial-style wood houses with sweeping verandahs. It (integration) was not called a test case, but a pilot program. Black women moved into the major white women's dorm. I stayed (in the co-op housing).

"During the summer I worked on the Dallas *Post-Tribune* (a black newspaper). After graduation, I wrote ad copy and edited a technical manual. I went back to the *Post-Tribune* as a reporter and assistant to the editor (early 1970s).

"When I graduated, *The Dallas Morning News* was not hiring blacks. They didn't say that. Julia Scott Reid was on the staff. She wrote a black issues column, "The Open Line." (Reid is 70-something. She had a stroke.)

"I was the first full-time staff reporter and the second black at the paper. I was hired in February 1974.

"They hired me because there were a number of murders in the black community, for example, at convenience stores (the word was that black kids in gangs were committing them). They needed someone who could get into the community. Buster Haas came to my house.

"'Would you like to do a free-lance assignment?'

"Yeah, I'll do it.'

"I got the mood of the community. They ran the story bannered across page one. I got an offer after that."

Wade has been at the paper since.

"It took a long time to integrate the staff. Burl Osborne came from *AP* in the early 1980s. The biggest changes started happening. The staff jumped from two blacks to 11.

"In three to four years it got up to 33 people."

How Wade remembered the NABJ founding: "I remember everyone being very enthusiastic and on a high at the reception afterwards. There was a sense of accomplishment. It was a boost. We would be fighting off our feelings of isolation.

"At the Houston conference, the board sat around a T-shaped table. It was a very spirited meeting. We would get into long, emotional debates, for example, who would be a member?

"We even wondered if we should accept photographers. We got caught up in those 'who disseminates the news' debates. P.R. people didn't.

"Vernon Jarrett made a strong case (for journalists only).

"There was no real animosity between broadcast and print journalists but there was a real competition. There was a feeling that broadcasting was real glamorous and print people felt intimidated. Emotions were strong and people were protective of their own interests.

"This went on for five to six years. Sometimes meetings got out of hand."

Francis Ward   (Interviewed Feb. 14 and July 26, 1991.)
He was born and reared in Atlanta.
"I chose to be a journalist.
"I wanted to be one way back in high school.
"My mother got me interested in it. She was a dressmaker (seamstress) and she went to Spelman (class of '23). She had a strong interest in reading and education.
"My father was a janitor at the Fort Benning army depot. He instilled in me a strong sense of duty. He influenced me to do the best job I could. He always admonished me. We used to clean stores together in Southwest Atlanta. He'd say, 'You always want to get a good rating' (which dad always got for his work as a janitor).
"My interest in journalism increased while at Booker T. Washington High School. I worked on the yearbook, wrote for the newspaper and was scorekeeper for the baseball team. The coach of the team talked a lot about how good it would be to be a sportswriter. Blacks then aspired to be doctors and preachers.
"I graduated high school in 1953. I went to Lincoln (Mo.) University because it had journalism. I stayed one semester. I did not have enough money and would not be able

to take journalism courses until my junior year.

"I transferred to Morehouse College. I lost a semester's work. I was in the same class with Maynard Jackson. I graduated in 1958.

"I was hired by the *Atlanta Daily World* in '58 as a janitor at $40 a week.

Six months later, I was promoted to proofreader and received a $4 raise, to $44. C.A. Scott fired a woman proofreader, accusing her of missing some ads that did not get into the paper (and costing the *Daily World* money). I did sportswriting on the side.

"In 1959, I went to Syracuse University and received a master's in journalism. In 1961, I was knocking around New York City, looking for work. There were seven daily newspapers in New York.

"The only blacks were Leyman Robinson at *The New York Times* and Ted Poston at the *New York Post*.

"I faced the iron law of journalism: With no experience I could not get hired. Reporters then started at the bottom as copy boys and worked their way up.

"This was tradition. I could not blame exclusion solely on racism."

Ward did social work. A break came in 1964 when he met Bob Johnson of *Jet* and was told that there might be an opening in Chicago. In January 1965, Ward began work as a reporter. He stayed until December 1967.

Ward's career moved this way:

• From January 1968 to June 1969 he was a reporter at the Chicago *Sun-Times*.

• From July 1969 to January 1978 he was a *Los Angeles Times* correspondent.

• From February 1978 to January 1980, Ward was a reporter and columnist for *The Miami Herald*.

• From 1980 to January 1984, he was with Howard University's TV station, WHMM-TV 32.

From 1984 to 1989 Ward was assistant press secretary for Chicago Mayor Harold Washington (and after Washington died, Eugene Sawyer). When Ward was interviewed, he was teaching journalism at Syracuse University.

How Ward remembered the founding meeting: "There was considerable discussion at our meeting over who could belong. What it came down to was the narrow definition (news gathering). I argued for that. That carried the day.

"Glen Ford (host, "America's Black Forum") said he didn't want it run by someone who did not work for a prestigious news organization. That was one of the things Chuck (Stone) had in his favor.

"One of the people who spoke on my behalf was Ellis Cose. Many people did not know me, but they may have been impressed by the *Los Angeles Times* affiliation."

John C. White (Interviewed in winter 1991.)
Born May, 5, 1942. "It was a good ride." This was White's reflection on 23 years in the news business.

"I chose it (journalism). I am a native of Baltimore.

"I always loved reading. I was not a good student, but I always read. Writing seems to follow reading.

"I wrote in the Air Force out of boredom. I came out of the Air Force in 1965 and started at Morgan State College.

"I was interested in becoming a 'serious' writer, another James Baldwin. My sophomore year I saw a news writing class in the catalogue. A requirement was to write for the school newspaper.

"It was instant love. I saw my name in the paper and I loved it. In 1967, I dropped out of school for a semester. In 1968, I received a Westinghouse internship to work at WJZ-TV. At the end of the summer I became the weekend news producer.

"I went to the *Afro-American* (Baltimore) for nine months and covered cops. Then I went to *The Evening Sun* (Baltimore).

"It (my career) was a lot of fun. I spent a lot of time on both sides of the journalism fence." White was a reporter at *The Chicago Tribune* and the *Philadelphia Daily News*.

In the late 1980s he was press secretary for Washington, D.C. Mayor Marion Barry. White returned to journalism, to WJLA-TV in Washington. When interviewed, he was recently laid off because of budget cuts.

Before NABJ's founding in December 1975, "I remember sort of chaos. Whenever we covered a black meeting there would be after-hour rap sessions about conditions in the media. Tom Johnson, Paul Delaney and Ed Blackwell were the vets. Nothing came out of it. Gary, Ind., 1972 was the first time I covered a national (black) story. There was a lot of word-of-mouth (from black reporters about starting an organization). It sounded like a good idea.

"I was one of three people who started the Association of Black Media Workers (ABMW, Baltimore)."

The others were DeWayne Wickham and Marie Cook of the *Afro-American*. Cook is related to the Murphy family, owners of the *Afro* newspapers.

"I was treasurer the first four years; DeWayne was president, Marie was secretary.

"The national thing was an outgrowth of what we did in Baltimore. I was working for *The Washington Star* and living in Baltimore.

"After everybody filed (their stories on the black political convention in December 1975) we got together."

DeWayne Wickham Interviewed Jan. 31, and July 26, 1991.

Born July 22, 1946. He grew up in Cherry Hill, the largest housing project in Baltimore. Wickham dropped out of high school and joined the U.S. Air Force. He was sent to Vietnam in the 1960s. "Not only was I a high school dropout, I was dumb enough to enlist at the height of the war."

Wickham returned home in 1968. He did odd jobs for two years. Then a veteran buddy encouraged him to enroll at Community College of Baltimore.

Wickham majored in business.

Wickham received good grades on his written essays. His English teacher told him he had the potential to be a writer. The University of Maryland was recruiting students. When the recruiter looked at Wickham's evaluations, he noticed the part about his writing talent.

"To the unsophisticated ear," said Wickham, "'writer' meant 'journalist.' "

Wickham enrolled at the University of Maryland as a

journalism major. "Journalism chose me."
Power was the element that attracted DeWayne Wickham to journalism.
"I liked the arrogance of power. I came to believe that journalism is one of the great power centers in this country. It had the power of persuasion and influence over people."
He read the writing of Ernest Hemingway and the iconoclastic Baltimorian, H.L. Mencken, to excess.
These writers molded Wickham's view of the press as power center.
He had two internships, at *The Evening Sun* in Baltimore and then a summer internship in 1973 at *The Richmond* (Va.) *Times-Dispatch.*
After graduating from the University of Maryland in spring 1974, he was hired as a Capitol Hill correspondent for *U.S. News & World Report.*
He was hired shortly after Jeannye Thornton became the first black journalist to write for the news magazine.
After six months, Wickham tried to leave. The pay was pretty good. But the down side for a young reporter like Wickham was that his work was anonymous; he and the other writers did not receive bylines.
USN&WR editors thought he was unhappy about the pay. Wickham received a $100 raise.
He stayed six months more before taking a job as a local reporter at *The Sun* in Baltimore. His new job was a demotion. But he wanted it because he would get his byline and the persuasive powers that he assumed came with it.
Furthermore, he would be working for his hometown newspaper.
Of the Baltimore newspapers, *The Sun,* the morning paper, featured a lot of Washington and international news and was considered more prestigious that *The Evening Sun,* which concentrated on local news.

Notes

page 4 -- Excerpt from Chapter 15, Kerner Commission report.

page 5 -- From the NABJ Directory, Hall of Fame segment

page 6 -- *The Powers That Be,* David Halberstam, Knopf.

page 7 -- In 1990, a television movie ("Heat Wave") was made about Richardson's feats during the Watts riots.

page 7 -- Survey, *Deadline for the Media: Today's Challenges to Press, TV and Radio,* James Aronson, The Bobbs-Merrill Co. Inc. 1972.

page 8 -- Carl B. Stokes was elected mayor in 1967.

page 9 -- Claude Lewis interviewed by D. Zimmerman, Oct. 18, 1967.

page 10 -- Ball & Chain Review, Vol. 1, No. 6, April 1970.

page 10 -- *Saturday Review,* Feb. 13, 1971.

page 11 -- *The New York Times,* March 8, 1972, page 25:11; March 9, page 19:1.

pages 11,12 -- Letter from Stone, Brock, et al.

page 12 -- NNPA is National Newspaper Publishers Association or Black Press of America.
DNC is Democratic National Committee.

page 13 -- A few more journalists, less than five, insist that they were founding members.

page 13 -- For years NABJ literature fudged an actual count. It said that it was founded "by approximately 50 members."

page 16 -- *The New York Times,* Feb. 7, 1972, page 28:5.

page 18 -- Mary McGrory column, *The Washington Star* (appeared in the *Camden Courier-Post* March 17, 1977). Wallace Terry called Maurice Williams "a black journalist from first to last" and (he) was the first to die in "the line of duty."

page 18 -- Founded in 1946, the Links promote civic, cultural and education activities.

page 23 -- CARE is Cooperative for American Relief Everywhere.

page 24 -- From "Road to justice paved with trust," by Larry Tye, *The Boston Globe,* Sept. 12, 1990.

page 26 -- Letter, "A first report," written by Chuck Stone, Dec. 23,
1975 to "Executive Board and Prospective Members."
It said "Sat. night Dec. 13, James Baldwin spoke to
NABJ's first dinner. He was warmly received and
conducted a press conference after his speech. We
managed to cover expenses."

page 47 -- "Their Finest Hour," from *Blood, Toil, Tears and Sweat* ,
The Speeches of Winston Churchill, Houghton Mifflin Co.

page 48 -- William Monroe Trotter founded the *Guardian* newspaper
in Boston in November 1901.

page 51 -- Panelist notes, "Covering the Black Community,"
Gayle Pollard, Baltimore conference.

page 60 -- From Lillian Williams' 1990 NABJ Lifetime
Achievement award nomination.

page 62 -- In 1972, ASNE conducted what was believed to be
the first census of minority journalists.

page 62 -- Frank E. Gannett Center Study, April 4, 1978, Jay T.
Harris.

page 62 -- ASNE Bulletin, October 1981, "Editors attitudes reveal
wide diversity on employing minorities," by Jay T. Harris
and Christine Harris.

page 63 -- *The World Almanac* says Roberts Harris was HUD
secretary from 1977-79, then secretary of the U.S.
Department of Health and Human Services (HHS),
formerly called HEW (Health, Education and Welfare.)

page 65 -- The official NABJ estimate from executive director Carl
Morris was 250 people. NABJ report, 1989.

page 65 -- Vernon Jarrett column, Chicago Tribune, Aug. 30, 1978.

page 66 -- The Wilmington 10 were nine black men and a white
woman charged in connection with the firebombing of a
white-owned grocery store in Wilmington, N.C. There
were worldwide protests and the imprisoned defendants
were called political prisoners. The defendants were
released, including the Rev. Ben Chavis (AP story,
December 1979).

page 66 -- President Mobutu ruled his central African country
brutally . He was repeatedly cited for human rights abuses.

page 67 -- UNA-USA editorial roster, from Linda Lockhart.

page 81 -- Vernon Jarrett column, *Chicago Tribune*, Oct. 3, 1980
page 81 -- *The New York Times* (re: John Anderson)
page 84 -- Aplin-Brownlee was hired in December 1968 but spent
the first month reporting for the *Cleveland Call & Post*. See page 8.
page 84 -- *Newsweek*, April 27, 1981 (re: Marion Barry.)
page 85 -- *AP* story (appeared in the *Courier-Post*) Janet Cooke
tells why she hyped credentials.
page 85 -- from the *Columbia Journalism Review*, July/August
1981, page 35.
page 86 -- re: "halfway house for liars" comment, *Newsweek*, 1982.
page 86 -- In summer 1992 Carl Rowan said through his assistant
Kristine Bock that he did not remember the 1980 NABJ award.
All of his awards at that time were being moved to Oberlin
College, his alma mater.
page 105 -- Atlanta child murders, 28 young African-Americans
were found dead. Wayne B. Williams was convicted.
page 105 -- In 1990 *The Tribune* won a Pulitzer Prize for
photojournalism. In fall 1991 the paper almost closed. In December
1992, Maynard sold the newspaper.
page 106 -- No official count of the election was available.
page 108 -- Bennett speech reprinted in *NABJ Journal*, winter 1982.
page 110 -- *Sepia* was to *Ebony* what *LOOK* was to *LIFE*.
page 117 -- *The National Leader* was a black weekly in Philadelphia
that published from 1982-84. Claude Lewis was the editor.
page 118 -- *Black Alumni Network* Newsletter, December 1987.
page 121 -- *Before The Mayflower*, Lerone Bennett Jr. Fifth edition.
page 136 – Aubespin's secretary was Marita Clark. December 1995
interview. . .Almost painless registration: For the first time,
registration and mailing lists were computerized, explained Shafeah
M'Balia in a summer 1984 *NABJ Journal* article.
page 137 – Fulwood is author of Waking from the Dream: My Life in
the Black Middle class. He is now a *Los Angeles Times* correspondent.
page – 138 Minister Farrakhan registered to vote when Jackson elected
to run for president. . . Coleman became an assistant managing editor at
The Washington Post. . . Jackson on the "Smart-ass white boys,"
Washington Post, Aug. 20, 1984
page 140 – Tucker's speech answered journalists who criticized Milton
Coleman at the convention. "Anyone who has to ask the question, 'Are
you black first or a journalist first?' is a bad, bad journalist," he said,
Washington Post, Aug. 20, 1984. Tucker, 52, died March 2, 1991.

page 144 – Fourie was envoy to the United States as of mid-1985.
page 146 – Minorities 9 percent of newspaper management in 1985: It grew to 12 percent the next year. In broadcast journalism, 13 percent minority representation reported by the Radio and TV News Directors in 1987 was down from 15 percent reported in 1978.
page 147 – Vanita was Wickham's production company. He was owner (established in 1982) and executive producer.
page 150 – A decade ago Gumbel was scorned by some blacks for being fluent in Russian. The 1993 award was a "coming home" of sorts... Ethel Payne, *NABJ Journal,* November 1994, *BAN,* December 1987, "Veterans of the press share wisdom with the young"; *And Still We Rise: Interviews with 50 Black Role Models,* Barbara Reynolds.
page 152 – Resisted apartheid again? It was another surge that received world attention. In the late '70s the was the Black Consciousness movement then the murder by police of its leader Stephen Biko.
page 153 – "Not a good idea to send blacks," Payne column in summer '83 *NABJ Journal* ... Payne said he did "mealymouth stories" about South Africa until authorities stopped watching him closely. He then dropped out of sight and blended in with Sowetans. Payne reported that authorities grossly underreported the death toll during rioting in 1976. Back in America Payne wrote an 11-part series that was recommended for a 1978 Pulitzer Prize by the award jury but was overturned by the advisory board. Payne calls himself a "Pulitzer Prize loser."
page 154 – Fourteen journalists in Africa, NABJ Journal summer '85.
page 155 – "Live Aid" drew 162,000 concert goers to London and Philadelphia shows. Broadcasts were heard or watched by 1.9 billion people worldwide, New York Times, July 13-16, 19-20, Nov. 12. . . Dallas, Statistical Abstract of the United States
page 157 – Foreign correspondent Al Friendly of *The Washington Post* won a Pulitzer Prize for coverage of the six-day 1967 Middle East war.
page 158 – Kenneth Walker's '81 South Africa trip; *Black American Witness,* Earl Caldwell; *BAN, NABJ Journal* accounts.
page 160 – Dawkins cast one of the four dissenting votes. . . upheaval in South Africa, "No news is bad news," Michel Mariott, *NABJ Journal,* summer 1986. "Colored" South African editor Tyrone August interviewed.*WEEKLY MAIL* photo illustrated trouble covering news.
page 163 – Percy Qoboza bio, *NABJ Journal,* February 1988. . . Zwelake Sisulu receives first Percy Qoboza award in jail. Nelson Mandela was vice president of ANC. After his imprisonment in the early 1960s Mandela was not seen in public until his release in 1990. Through the 1980s his words and image were banned in South Africa. Mandela became president of the country that imprisoned him.

page 164 – In the late 1980s, circa 1987, NABJ sports journalist members said that the organization was not doing enough to recognize the impact of black American athletes on sports and society. NABJ expanded its award categories to include sports, and a task force of sports writers and editors developed annual symposiums.

pages 169-70 – Eyes on the Prize, J. Hicks, *NABJ Journal*, page 14, Summer, '86 . . . Tyler film collection, *NABJ Journal*, Summer 1986

page 171 – Joseph Perkins, Young Black Journalists, Dan Holly, Black Alumni Network newsletter, January 1987.

page 172 – Perkins became a conservative pundit, first working for Vice President Dan Quayle and later as a commentator with the San Diego *Union-Tribune*. . . Robert L.Vann was founder and publisher of the *Pittsburgh Courier*. George S. Schuyler was editor and a widely read editorialist. . . special court was judge was elected.

page 173 – Buthelezi, head of Inkatha Freedom Party, KwaZulu chief.

page 173 – Schatzman appointment, BAN, September 1986. . . Schatzman notes that NABJ responds to Japan's racist statement about blacks and Hispanics. He highlights access NABJ now has to media associations, a past criticism. *NABJ Journal* Fall 1986.

page 175 – "NABJ, NAHJ Boards hold joint session," *NABJ Journal*, fall '86 . . . "Don't divide us," BAN Newsletter, November 1986.

page 176 – joint convention. The proposal to have it in 1992 was a sore point. Hispanics lobbied for it, African-Americans and Native Americans were cool to the idea. Asian Americans, feeling they were playing catchup, tried to buy time. The joint convention occurred in Atlanta in 1994 . It attracted more than 6,000 writers, editors, broadcasters, educators and industry executives.

page 180 – The underclass. Such criticism persists in the 1990s.

page 181 – Daily News 4 verdict. White media coverage said in essence "Newspaper lost." Black press coverage tone: "Journalists won." . . . *Daily News* 4 trial: there was one black woman among the four men and two women.) BAN May 1987, January 1988, NABJ Journal, Summer 1987. . . *Daily News* largest metropolitan daily? *The New York Times, Los Angeles Times* and *Wall Street Journal* were larger but their circulations were largely national and international).

page 183 – Miami convention, Harold Washington, *NABJ Journal*, Oct. 1987, *BAN* , September 1987. . . Myron Lowery sued WMC-TV (NBC) in Memphis in 1981. He was accused of selling tapes to news sources and pulled off the air. He sued for retaliation and won in 1983. Lowery quit WMC. He became a video communication specialist for Federal Express...Wickham elected, *NABJ Journal*, October 1987

page 184 – Winship. "Quiet Crisis" data from IJE contradicted

Winship. Most minorities stayed longer between moves.
page 186 – The investments were tied to the scholarship fund. Sources,
1987-88 annual report, BAN, April 1988.
page 187-188 – Texas Women's University, BAN, March, April 1988.
. . . Lucille Bluford, BAN, June 1988. . . page 187 – Kerner panel
recommendations, said Wickham, were published in a booklet that was
distributed to all NABJ members and selected industry leaders.
page 189 – One percent of supervisors, '68 Kerner Report.
Also, 1968 newsroom study (Trayes) of the country's 20 largest dailies
reported one black news executive out of 532. A year later Trayes' study
of 196 papers over 10,000 circulation reported five black news
managers or executives (0.4 percent).
page 190 – T. Reid and Hugh Wilson; NABJ Journal September, 1988.
. . Dan Holly reporting, BAN Newsletter, October 1988 . . . Tim Reid,
Ueberoth quote, NABJ Journal, Greg Freeman, September 1988 . . .
"Tribe becomes nation," Betty Winston Baye, BAN, October 1988
page 191 – Douglas vs. Douglass: The debate continues, NABJ
Journal, October 1988; "New look," BAN Newsletter, July 1989
page 192 – Futrell in a 1997 interview said the projected black teacher
decline unfortunately was consistent eight years after her speech.
page 194 – Before the Brawley case, there was the racial beating in
Howard Beach, N.Y. a white, Queens neighborhood. Mason, Mattox
and Sharpton rallied the community. Convictions were won in court.
pages 192-93 – joint meeting of four associations, BAN, November
1988. The complete statement was 500 words.
pages 193-94 – "Florida journalists protest Tribune firings, NABJ-
Journal," Rosemary Banks Harris reporting.
page 194 – Both lawyers and the minister rallied New York's black
community to demand justice in the Howard Beach, N.Y. racial attacks.
. . . Brawley case, NABJ Journal, November-December 1988.
page 196-97 – canopied table. Party of five at Detroit convention. By
the late '80s rooms were reserved for dozens of members in each region.
pages 196-98 – "Upping ante for NABJ office," Dan Holly, BAN
newsletter, August 1989 . . .Dan Holly, Black Alumni Network,
October 1989. . . CIA presence, the agency was listed among 81 job
fair participants as of June 30 in the July/August NABJ Journal....page
200 – CIA: The agency had a reputation in black communities for
participating in assassinations and the capture of revolutionary African
and Caribbean leaders in the 1960s and 1970s.
page 201 Manley died in March 1997 . . . Colin Powell spoke two
months before the wall partitioning East and West Germany was
pounded to rubble, signaling the collapse of the Soviet Bloc.

Bibliography

• *Africa,* Ralph Uwechue, publisher. No. 41, January 1975 to No. 149, January 1984 and No. 183, November 1986.
• *American Diary: A Personal History of the Black Press,* Enoch P. Waters, Path Press, Inc., Chicago, 1987.
• *Before the Mayflower: A History of Black America,* Lerone Bennett Jr., Johnson Publishing Co., Inc., Fifth Revised Edition, 1984.
• *Black Alumni Network* Newsletter, (Columbia University, Journalism), Mount Vernon, N.Y., Maple Shade, N.J., Philadelphia, 1982 to 1989.
• *Black American Witness,* Earl Caldwell, Lion House Publishing, Washington, D.C. 1995.
• *Blacks in Communications,* M.L. Stein, Julian Messner, 1970.
• *Blood, toil Tears and Sweat, The Speeches of Winston Churchill,* edited by David Cannadine, Houghton Mifflin Co. 1989.
• *The Book of America,* Neil Peirce and Jerry Hagstrom, W.W. Norton & Co., publisher, 1983.
• *Sunday Boston Globe* Magazine, Sept. 12, 1990.
• *Confessions of an S.O.B.,* Al Neuharth, Doubleday, 1989.
• *Death in the Afternoon,* Peter Benjaminson, Andrews, McMeel & Parker, publisher, 1984.
• *A Good Life,* Ben Bradlee, Simon &Schuster, 1995.
• *Knight: A Publisher in a Tumultuous Century,* Charles Whited, Dutton, publisher, 1988.
• *Long Walk to Freedom,* Nelson Mandela, Little, Brown, 1994.
• *My American Journey,* Colin Powell, Random House, 1995.
• *NABJ News,* 1981, and *NABJ Journal* 1982 to 1996.
• *Newsday: A Candid History of the Respectable Tabloid,* Robert F. Keeler, Morrow, 1990.
• *Nightline: History in the Making and the Making of Television,* Ted Koppel and Kyle Gibson, Times Books, 1996.
• *The Press,* Ellis Cose, Morrow, publisher, 1989
• *The Professional Journalist:* John Hohenberg, Holt, Rinehart and Winston, Inc. Third Edition, 1973
• *Volunteer Slavery,* Jill Nelson, Noble Press, 1993.
• *Waking From the Dream: My Life in the Black Middle Class,* Sam Fulwood III, Anchor Books, 1996.
• *Who's What and Where, a directory and reference book on America's minority journalists,* Ben Johnson and Mary Bullard-Johnson, 1988

People interviewed for this book:

Sam Adams, Donald Adderton, Vivian Aplin-Brownlee, Marilynn Bailey, A. Peter Bailey, Lionel Barrow, Betty Winston Baye, Ed Blackwell, Christine Bock (for Carl Rowan), Alice Bonner, Gerald Boyd, Paul Brock, Reginald Bryant, Crispin Campbell, Fletcher Clarke, Roger Clendening, Charlie Cobb, Leslie Crosson, George Curry, Marilyn Darling, Leon Dash, Joe Davidson, Allison Davis, Sandra Dawson (Long), Michael Days, Paul Delaney, Sheila Detrick-Brooks, William Dilday, Sandra Dillard Rosen, Angela Dodson, Joel Dreyfuss, Lewis Duiguid, Audrey Edwards, Sidmel Estes-Sumpter.

And, Diana Fallis, Albert E. Fitzpatrick, Sam Ford, Jeanne Fox-Alston, C. Gerald Fraser, David Gibson, Sandra Gilliam-Beale, Bob Greenlee, Martha Griffin, Derwood Franklin Hall, James Hamlin, Christine Harris, Jay T. Harris, Bob Hayes, Sheryl Hilliard, Karen Howze, Vernon Jarrett, Ben Johnson, Denise Johnson, Mal Johnson, Thomas A. Johnson, Tyree Johnson, Gerald Jordan, Toni Jones, Milton Jordan, Howard Chuku Lee, Claude Lewis, Jane Littleton, Linda Lockhart-Jones, Norman Lockman, Myron Lowery, Pluria Marshall, George McElroy, Jacqueline McLean, Jim McLean, Kevin Merida, Walter Middlebrook, Carlton Molette, Lionel Monagas, Acel Moore, Thomas Morgan, Carl Morris, Greg Morrison, Charles Moses, Jill Nelson, Joe Oglesby, Luix Overbea.

And, Les Payne, Curtis Peters, Rhetha Phillips, Alex Poinsett, Gayle Pollard, Claudia Polley, John Quinn, Richard Rambeau, Bob Reid, W. Curtis Riddle, Charlotte Robinson (Roy), Annette Samuel, Vince Sanders, Sarah Ann Shaw, Lena Sherrod, Elmer Smith, Chuck Stone, Reginald Stuart, William W. Sutton Jr., Ray Taliaferro, Keith Thomas, Ron Thomas, Garland Thompson, Jeannye Thornton, Monte Trammer, Bob Tutman, Raph Uwechue, Norma Wade, Paula Walker, Linda Waller, Francis Ward, Valerie Gray Ward, John White, Charlene Williams, Don Williamson, Roger Witherspoon, DeWayne Wickham, Alexis Yancey George.

Founders who appear on the book cover

Front cover, first row, from left: Ed Blackwell, Reginald Bryant, Maureen Bunyan, Leon Dash. Second row: Paul Delaney, William Dilday, Sandra Dillard, Joel Dreyfuss.

Back cover, first row, from left: Sam Ford, Bob Greenlee, Bob Hayes, Vernon Jarrett. Second row: Claude Lewis, Acel Moore, Pluria Marshall, Luix Overbea. Third row: Les Payne, Alex Poinsett, Claudia Polley, W. Curtis Riddle. Fourth row: Charlotte Robinson, Max Robinson, Vince Sanders, Chuck Stone. Fifth row: Jeannye Thornton, DeWayne Wickham (Thornton, U.S. News & World Report photo, 1979. Blackwell photo, 1979. Bryant, Moore photos, 1978.)

page 264

Acknowledgments

This book is possible because a lot of people believed in me and the subject. My heartfelt thanks to:

• Angela Terrell of *Gannett News Service*. She was principal editor of the manuscript. Also, Sharon Wilmore, Philip Wilhite, Patricia Donahue and Horace Shuman who read and critiqued the galleys.

• Rob King for reading early drafts of the manuscript. Rob designed the book cover and the August Press logo.

• Linda Waller, my "neighbor" 14 miles up the road in Lawnside, N.J., remembered dozens of anecdotes about NABJ people and gave me an endless supply of helpful advice and encouragement.

• Alice Bonner of the Freedom Forum was another source of advice and encouragement.

• Richard Prince of the Rochester *Times-Union*. With Terrell he helped locate founder Bob Hayes.

• Carol Chapman of WSOC-TV, Charlotte for offering leads in locating Derwood Hall. Also, Fletcher Clarke, Jane Littleton and Rhetha Phillips for helping locate founder Sandra Gilliam Beale.

• Gayle Pollard for providing a file that included programs from the 1976 NABJ Houston conference and the '77 Baltimore conference.

• Betty Winston Baye for reading the early drafts and for having me as a houseguest, twice in Cambridge, Mass. when I visited Boston to do initial reporting and in Louisville, Ky. Ditto for Jill Nelson in Washington, D.C. and David and Valerie Dent in New York City.

• Phyllis Bailey located Ed Blackwell for me. James Hamlin of KDKA-TV, Pittsburgh, helped me locate founder David Gibson.

Karen Thomas of *The Chicago Tribune* found clippings that had the date of the 1978 NABJ conference.

• Linda Lockhart Jones of the Twin Cities and Bob Reid of Los Angeles provided copious files that shed light on NABJ's early years.

• Mervin Aubespin, who kept hundreds of photographs of NABJ activities from 1981-83.

• Walter Middlebrook sent a roster of the 1980 conference attendees.

• Michael Days and Angela Dodson let me rummage through their attic in Trenton on a Saturday. I found many treasures, like a program from the 1979 conference.

• Chuck Stone, who granted a lengthy face-to-face interview after declining four times. Stone had the list of signatures of founding members, our "Declaration of Independence."

Index

Journalists in attendance
at Founding Meeting of
National Association of Black
Journalists — Dec. 12, 1975

1. Chuck Stone - Philadelphia Daily News
2. Bill Dildoy WLBT-TV Jackson, Miss
3. Leon Dash The Washington Post, Wash., D.C.
4. John C. White Washington Star, Wash., D.C.
5. DeWayne Wickham Baltimore Sun, Balto., Md.
6. Reginald Bryant Black Perspective on the News
7. Martha Griffin - National Public Radio
8. Sondra Dawson News-Journal Wilmington, Dele
9. Allison Day WBZTV Boston, Mass.
10. ... Thornton U.S. News & World Report - Wash.
11. THE Courier-Journal, Louisville, Ky.
12. S.F. Examiner
13. Les Payne Newsday, Garden City, N.Y.
14. Marilyn Darling WHYY-Channel 12 ..., Del.
15. Acel Moore Philadelphia Inq.
16. WKBO-TV Dayton, Ohio
17. Frances Ward - L.A. Times - Chgo bureau
18. Claude A Lewis - Phila Bulletin
19. Edward H. Blackwell - Milwaukee Journal - Milw, Wis
20. Bob Greenlee - New Haven Register, New Haven, Conn.
21. Howard Lee Africa Magazine - N.Y.

23. Norma A. Wade, Dallas Morning News
24. Lucia V. Overbea The Christian Science Monitor, Boston
25. Joe Davidson The Phila Bulletin ... BEST
26. Richard Lambson Project BAIT-Detroit
27. Charlotte Robinson - Detroit Free Press - Detroit
28. Max Robinson WTOP-TV D.C.
29. David Gibson Mutual Black Network DC
30. ... Chicago
31. Claude NBC New York
32. Joel Dreyfuss Washington Post
33. Maureen Bunyan WTOP-TV, Wash. D.C.
34. Charlie Cobb WHUR Radio, Wash., D.
35. Carole Bartel Core magazine n york
36. Toni Jones Detroit Free Press, Detroit
37. Sam Ford WCCO-TV Minn...
38. Gloria Marshall - 2027 Mass. Ave. N.W. 20036
39. Alex Poinsett - Ebony Magazine - Chgo
40. Crispin Campbell - WNET - New York
41. Bernard L. Shall - WSOC-TV - Charlotte, NC

Sandra Dillard - Denver Post - Colo.

WASHINGTON, D.C., 1975: List of the founders who established NABJ Dec. 12. At least 100 people attended the meeting. However, 44 men and women paid dues and signed on as founding members.

Wheeler Street News

Daily Newsletter   Vol. 1 No. 2   First Annual Conference   National Association of Black Journalists   Texas Southern University   October 2, 1976

NABJ criticizes Ford, Carter

By Morris V. Pyle

NABJ President Chuck Stone slashed the two 1976 Presidential candidates for "assiduously bypassing black voters."

At a press conference this morning in the Martin Luther King Center, Stone said President Gerald Ford and Jimmy Carter are not demonstrating the same political sensitivity to blacks that they have enthusiastically reserved for other ethnics.

Ford and Carter were invited to the first annual NABJ conference in Houston. However, according to Stone, both candidates' schedules did not permit acceptance of the invitations. However, Jimmy Carter attempted to arrange a meeting with black journalists today in Chevy Chase, Md. Many of the black ... Carter chose

instead to meet in Houston with the main NABJ.

Stone criticized Carter for trying for an "eleventh hour" meeting with a small group of black journalists in

Bumble Butz: tight, loose and warm

Agriculture Secretary Earl Butz obviously stuck his foot and possibly his career in his mouth recently when he took it upon himself to know exactly what "coloreds" want. But before we venture into what the secretary wants, let's delve into what we want. We would like to see the secretary tied to the cow catcher of a fast moving train, run through thorns, then shot with fish hooks. But so much for what we ...

Maryland and then for reducing the meeting time from 45 minutes to 15 minutes. This further indicates Carter's attitude toward the black journalist, Stone said.

Here's what Butz says, according to Associated Press, that "coloreds" want.

"I'll tell you why you can't attract coloreds. Because coloreds only want three things. You know what they want? I'll tell you what coloreds want, it's three things: first, a tight p...y; second, loose shoes; and third, a warm place to sh... that's all." Yes Butz, that's all, and ...

the end.

Wheeler Street News

Daily Newsletter   Vol. 1 No. 3   First Annual Conference   National Association of Black Journalists   Texas Southern University   Houston   October 3, 1976

NABJ ends today on sour note

This first annual conference of the National Association of Black Journalists ends in discord as several working media people stalked out of this morning's plenary session after being told they could not join the NABJ.

While the three-day conference succeeded in bringing together black journalists from across the nation, the benefits of the meeting seems to be outweighed by a negative attitude which resulted from an NABJ by-law prohibiting those journalists who are not employed by a media organization full-time.

As we all know, the media is not the highest paying profession and many journalists are forced to moonlight in order to obtain basic personal necessities.

While it is the law of the NABJ, the by-law excluding some media people is a mistake.

For example, here are two examples of the types of media people would be excluded from NABJ membership.

An editor of an old and respected black weekly newspaper who also works full-time elsewhere and pens a weekly column.

Another magazine editor is ineligible because a full-time job teaching complements the income from the newspaper.

The list could go on and would include hundreds of persons who are involved in the media full-time, but receive full-time compensation elsewhere.

Commentary

Message to Black Media People

by Diane Schiche

There is a definite need for the conscious awareness of journalists at Texas Southern University that the development of a professional atmosphere on campus is primary and should have the utmost importance.

If we are to produce a new generation to join the "old-hands" in the journalistic profession, it is a necessity that we seek an accurate definition of the word "professional" as it applies to our situation.

Black journalists are at a loss as to how they fit into the media picture. Or do we fit in? Should it be our goal as a group to attempt to identify with the established media to the extent that we totally divorce ourselves from all semblance of color. This color blindness could be detrimental to ourselves and to the future generation of Black people, who are hungry for accurate, honest and complete information on local, national and international levels.

Again, the excluding by-law is a mistake and we feel it would be detrimental to the survival and viability of NABJ, which for now is a damn good idea whose time is long overdue.

We sincerely urge that the clause be repealed.

The role or the function of the Black press is a topic that has long been discussed, written about and ...

And what we are ...

HOUSTON, 1976: Campus newspaper account of the first NABJ conference. It was held at Texas Southern University. At least 33 journalists from 13 states and the District of Columbia participated.

FEB. 16, 1978:
The NABJ board meets
with President Jimmy
Carter at the White House.
The boards of black-owned
newspaper publishers and
black-owned broadcasters
also participated.

LOUISVILLE, 1981: Ben Johnson, left, of *The Detroit Free Press*, campaigns for NABJ president. The fourth presidential election was the first officially contested race. Les Payne of *Newsday* was elected to a two-year term.

DETROIT, 1982:

Mervin Aubespin, *The Courier-Journal*, Louisville, Ky.,
chats with Randy Daniels, CBS correspondent
who established Jacaranda Productions, which trained
African broadcasters in the early 1980s.

NEW ORLEANS, 1983:

Ethel Payne, Washington
and foreign correspondent
of the *Chicago Defender*.
Traveling fellowships
to report from Africa
were named in her memory
in 1993.

BALTIMORE, 1985: From left, Presidents Les Payne (1981-83), Chuck Stone (1975-77) and Vernon Jarrett (1977-79) at the 10th convention.

BALTIMORE, 1985: Djbril Diallo, left, the Senegalese-born information officer with UNICEF, built a constituency for broader Africa coverage inside NABJ.

MIAMI, 1987:

Lorraine Branham,
The Philadelphia Inquirer,
tries the limbo during the
NABJ cruise from Miami
to the Bahamas.

ST. LOUIS, 1988: Tim and Daphne Maxwell Reid, W.E.B. DuBois speakers at the 13th convention.

ST. LOUIS, 1988: Local attorney Frankie Freeman watched Bobby Seale participate in a plenary session.